Evolution and
Developmental Psychology

THE DEVELOPING BODY AND MIND

Series Editor: Dr. George Butterworth, *Senior Lecturer in Developmental Psychology, University of Southampton.*

Designed for a broad readership in the English-speaking world, this major series represents the best of contemporary research and theory in the cognitive, social, abnormal and biological areas of development.

Evolution and Developmental Psychology

Editors

GEORGE BUTTERWORTH
Senior Lecturer in Psychology
University of Southampton

JULIE RUTKOWSKA
Lecturer in Psychology
University of Sussex

MICHAEL SCAIFE
Lecturer in Psychology
University of Sussex

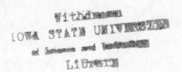

HARVESTER PRESS
1970 1985
FIFTEEN
FORWARD-LOOKING
YEARS

THE HARVESTER PRESS

First published in Great Britain in 1985 by
THE HARVESTER PRESS LIMITED
Publisher: John Spiers
16 Ship Street, Brighton, Sussex

© The Harvester Press Limited, 1985

British Library Cataloguing in Publication Data
Evolution and developmental psychology – (The Developing
Body and Mind; 4)
1. Developmental psychology
I. Butterworth, George, *1946*–
II. Rutkowska, Julie   III. Scaife, Michael
155′.01   BF713

ISBN 0-7108-0921-2

Photoset in Garamond 11/12 point by Witwell Ltd
Printed in Great Britain by
Whitstable Litho Ltd., Whitstable, Kent

THE HARVESTER PRESS PUBLISHING GROUP
The Harvester Press Publishing Group comprises Harvester Press
Limited (chiefly publishing literature, fiction, philosophy, psychology,
and science and trade books), Harvester Press Microform Publications
Limited (publishing in microform unpublished archives, scarce printed
sources, and indexes to these collections) and Wheatsheaf Books Limited
(a wholly independent company chiefly publishing in economics,
international politics, sociology and related social sciences), whose books
are distributed by The Harvester Press Limited and its agencies
throughout the world.

Contents

List of Figures

List of Tables

List of Contributors

Leo Apostel
Department of Philosophy, University of Ghent, Belgium.

Patrick Bateson
MRC Unit on the Development and Integration of Behaviour, University of Cambridge, England.

George Butterworth
Department of Psychology, University of Southampton, England.

John Churcher
Department of Psychology, University of Manchester, England.

Alan Costall
Department of Psychology, University of Southampton, England.

Kathleen Gibson,
University of Texas Dental Branch, Houston, Texas, USA.

Brian Goodwin,
Developmental Biology Group, The Open University, Milton Keynes, England.

Howard E. Gruber
Faculty of Psychology, University of Geneva, Switzerland.

Wolfe Mays
Department of Philosophy, Manchester Polytechnic, England.

Sue Taylor Parker
Department of Anthropology, Sonoma State University, California, USA.

Nancy Rader,
Department of Psychology, University of California, Los Angeles, USA.

Julie Rutkowska
Cognitive Studies Programme, University of Sussex, England.

Michael Scaife
Cognitive Studies Programme, University of Sussex, England.

Chris Sinha
Avery Hill College, London, England.

Preface

Developmental psychology has been profoundly influenced by evolutionary biology, both in its own history and in the explanations upon which it draws. Psychologists and biologists alike have been tempted to see parallels between the evolution of species and individual development, with the consequence that many concepts find interchangeable application between the disciplines. The aim of this book is to explore how evolutionary theory and development psychology may inform each other and yet respect the distinctive types of explanation which they represent.

This volume had its origins in a conference on 'Evolution, Development and the Acquisition of Knowledge' held in 1982, the year of the centenary of Darwin's death. The conference was sponsored jointly by the British Psychological Society and the British Society for Developmental Biology. The meeting proved to be a true voyage of discovery for many of the participants but an exciting one in seeing problems from a new angle.

The papers included here have been extended and revised since then, nonetheless much of the excitement of the interdisciplinary debate that took place remains. In this preface we have not attempted, as editors, to integrate all of the contributions into a single statement since the book itself shows clearly where there is common ground and where there is still a long way to go. In fact, there is no single synthesis which could be presented here, nor is there likely to be one for some time. Instead we will summarise some of the main concerns of the various authors as they relate to development and point out the theoretical issues to which they pertain.

The relationship between psychology and biology has always been a rather unequal one. On the whole it is fair to say that biologists have had little interest in the research or theorising of their colleagues in psychology. There have been areas of fruitful overlap, most notably in physiological investigations, but these have been atypical. Thus even the area of animal behaviour has historically tended to have two methodologies: the ethological (zoological) and the comparative (psychological). Where psychologists have tried to contribute to debates about evolutionary processes their work has been ignored (for example Piaget) or rejected (for example Baldwin, 1894, 1902). This situation can be readily understood for several reasons: one is the zeitgeist of reductionism that has held sway in the natural sciences for so many years—biologists look down (that is, up) to physics, not to psychology; another is simply the horrible over-simplications that psychologists go in for when discussing biological processes.

Nonetheless things are changing. There is much more interdisciplinary research and theorising going on. In a way this is a return to the era of Darwin who did not stop to question the need for observations on mentality as well as morphology in his own work. Today, as this book demonstrates, the impetus for collaboration comes from people in several areas who see the need for a richer and more general formalism for growth processes than is currently available within the confines of their own disciplines. In order to do this one inevitably confronts the question of the relationship between processes of change over different periods and within different domains. We have the evolutionary, the cultural, the ontogenetic and the microgenetic time scales for which we need some overall theoretical framework. The relationship between these has not always been made clear within single theories, although Vygotsky (*see* Scribner, 1984), Piaget (1971, 1978, 1980) and Werner (1948) made some fairly strong attempts to relate them. Even within biology the evolutionary and the embryological accounts were separate many years, whatever impression the continuing lay popularity of the recapitulationist view of embryogenesis may have given. The nature of the relationship between evolution and development is still very much an open question for both biology and psychology.

In this book we have arranged the chapters into five main sections, each of which is on a topic that is central to evolutionary and/or developmental thinking. The general format is to present a major chapter followed by a short commentary or brief chapter that elaborates the topics dealt with in that section from different viewpoints. Their main themes concern the relationship between the evolution of species and the development of individuals; the epistemology of developmental biology; the evolution of human intelligence and how it may be reconstructed from the fossil record; some issues for the future of an evolutionary approach to human ontogeny and the relations between biological and social levels of explanation. The authors included here come from a wide variety of backgrounds. What they share is a common concern with these issues. We shall now briefly try to summarise the links between the chapters.

In Chapter one Patrick Bateson discusses the relationship between phylogeny and ontogeny. He argues that the genetic consequences of evolutionary change can bear no direct relationship to the outcome of developmental processes. For example, a simplistic hypothesis in developmental psychology might be to suppose that those behaviours that are innate constitute the phylogenetic, inherited substrate for development while those that are learned are its ontogenetic constituents. However, development may influence the form of gene expression so that interaction between organism and environment can have different consequences at different times in the life span. It simply isn't possible to subdivide developmental mechanisms into genetic sources arising from a phylogenetic legacy versus learned, transitory effects to be acquired in ontogeny.

He suggests instead that we may use the metaphor of baking to understand the process of development. For example, although a cake may have recognisably distinct constituents in its raw state, the process of baking yields a qualitatively new object from which the parts cannot be reconstituted. By the same token, development cannot be understood as the simple additive relation of phylogenetic and ontogenetic effects. Developmental plasticity encourages variability in ontogeny and phylogeny, while canalisation or environmental buffering, may actually restrain processes of change both in evolution and in development.

In Chapter two Nancy Rader, in her commentary on Patrick Bateson's paper, carries the argument further. She makes use of Gould's (1977) theory of heterochrony to link evolutionary and developmental ideas. Gould argued that the evolution of modern man may have come about by a dissociation in the timing processes governing the development of body size and shape in our ancestors. The attainment of adult size has been relatively delayed while a juvenile shape is maintained into adulthood (the principle of neoteny). Rader argues that the concept of heterochrony may also be useful in psychology in enabling us to understand how individual differences may arise. Returning to Bateson's metaphor, she points out that not only the constitutents but also the timing of the baking process may yield quite a different product. Depending on whether leavened or unleavened bread is to result it is critical when the yeast is added. By analogy, the development of particular abilities, such as the differential verbal and spatial reasoning skills of males and females, may arise through differences in the timing of developmental processes.

These chapters illustrate well that the cautious use of evolutionary theory may profitably illuminate the process of development and that developmental ideas can contribute to theories of evolution. Alan Costall in Chapter three, however, points out that developmental psychology may have got off to a false start in the way that embryology was used as evidence for evolution in the late nineteenth century. Haeckel (1892) proposed that 'ontogeny recapitulates phylogeny' as evidence in favour of Darwin's theory of evolution by natural selection. In the absence of conclusive evidence from the fossil record, embryology with its observable progressive changes, became central in revealing the 'ancestral forms' of the organism. Development itself was of little significance except as a clue to ancestry; the lazy man's paleontology, as Costall puts it. He argues that a more adequate view of the relation between ontogeny and phylogeny in the late nineteenth century became available with recognition of the adaptive significance of development and its potentially active role in evolution. Development can no more be understood as the addition of experience to an unchanged organism, than evolution can be understood as the simple addition of more complex attributes onto a primitive organism. Both development and evolution gave rise to new organisms.

In Chapter four on embryology and evolution Brian Goodwin puts forward the latter point of view, that development can contribute to evolution. He is critical of atomistic approaches in contemporary developmental biology which stress the role of genes in regulating morphogenesis at the expense of explanations involving the whole developing organism, in its milieu. He argues that why organisms develop the forms they do cannot be reduced simply to the outcome of a 'genetic programme', which specifies which molecules will be made when, or where, in the embryo. Embryological development is better understood as the interaction among 'fields', of which the genes are only a part. Goodwin advocates that Piaget's genetic epistemology be applied in developmental biology, to yield a 'constructionist biology'—one in which the boundaries between phenotype and genotype are redrawn. He argues, for example, that heritable changes in morphology may be explained by the phenotypic assimilation of particular effects of the environment. Analogously, a genetic mutation may also alter the form of the developing embryo, again through a change in the total balance of forces. Rather controversially, in view of conventional thinking on the unidirectional transcription of DNA into RNA (and *not* the reverse); he argues that changes in the relationship between internal (genetic) and external (environmental) forces can work in both directions. An environmental perturbation may produce an abnormal morphology, which is then fixed in heredity by a gene mutation that copies the effect of the perturbation (a 'genocopy'). Reciprocally, a mutant gene may occur first and a 'phenocopy' will result later. The point is that perturbation of development whether by 'genetic' or 'environmental' effects, leads to a pattern of compensation of the developing form of the organism that is characteristic of the holistic laws governing its structural organisation.

Goodwin's is neither a Lamarckian nor a Neo-Darwinian position. The environment does not impose a heritable structure on the organism nor does evolution depend solely on the selection of an already adapted organism. His view is that evolution is more akin to a process of exploration of a finite set of possible phenotypes. Where his biological explanation overlaps with cognitive developmental psychology is in the capacity of organisms to internalise aspects of the environment. He sees the tendency towards representation, 'the internal model principle', both in 'biological' phenomena like the circadian rhythms and in 'psychological' processes such as the capacity for thought. Hence the need for a cognitive biology.

Michael Scaife points out in Chapter five that Goodwin has rendered psychologists a valuable service in his analysis of the problems faced by developmental biologists, for it is clear that biology itself has theoretical problems that remain to be resolved and this should alert other disciplines to the danger of uncritically adopting biological concepts. However Scaife suggests that Goodwin's account is limited in two main respects, namely that the organism he describes lacks substantiation in any particular case and that it cannot in principle bridge the gap between the biological realm and the fact that much human development occurs in relation to the social structure. Another difficulty is raised by John Churcher in Chapter six who points out that the 'internal model principle' may be acceptable as a spatial metaphor but it is not clear what its epistemological status is. It gets confused with distinctions between the 'known' and the 'unknown', the objective and the subjective, in psychology. (In fact, these issues are taken up in some detail by Chris Sinha in Chapter twelve.)

As has already been mentioned, the concept of recapitulation has been influential in evolutionary theory. In Chapter seven Sue Taylor-Parker adopts a recapitulationist stance in her approach to reconstructing the development of intelligence in the human species. She argues that Piaget's stages of intellectual development in modern children may provide a standard against which to gauge the relative complexity of intellectual processes required to invent the particular tools in the archaeological record. Her thesis is that the complexity of logic involved in invention may yield insights on the probable intellectual level that each precursor of man attained. For example, on her evidence she argues that *Homo habilis* (–1.9 to –1.35 million years) and *Homo erectus* (–1.5 to –0.5 million years) displayed the intellectual skills characteristic of modern children in Piaget's late preoperational and early concrete operational stages. Formal operational reasoning, she maintains, was a species specific characteristic acquired by *Homo sapiens* (–100,000 years). The archaeological evidence suggests that compound tools such as spear throwers or hafted tools were invented by early *Homo sapiens* and this leads her to conclude that other characteristics dependent upon formal operational reasoning, such as kinship systems and their associated social structures, would also have been in existence at that time.

Kathleen Gibson enlarges on this argument in Chapter eight, with detailed examples of the processes involved in the manufacture of flint tools and she agrees that an overall level of intelligence can be inferred from the archaeological record. However, she points out that there is plenty of evidence that human intellectual evolution also continued during the previous 100,000 years. In fact, only by the time of Cro-Magnon man (–35,000 years) did the brain achieve its modern size and shape. This was coincident with the flowering of culture and other artistic achievements and, on the basis of this evidence, Gibson favours the idea that formal operational reasoning is a relatively late-appearing human capacity, typical of more recent *Homo sapiens.*

Julie Rutkowska in Chapter nine is sceptical of Parker's use of Piagetian theory. She argues that contemporary developmental psychology shows us that abstract accounts of the structure of abilities need not coincide with the actual psychological processes involved in the performance of various tasks. She claims that such accounts reify logical processes in a misleading way. There is little empirical evidence that general purpose, content-free logical processes exist as a component of psychological mechanisms. For example, the structural level of analysis (which may nevertheless be valid as an abstract mode of categorising child and adult thought) distracts attention away from how the content of a problem dramatically influences performance, even at the level of formal or propositional reasoning. There is little reason to suppose that formal operational thought proceeds in the same way irrespective of its content. Thus, even if tools in the archaeological record did imply formal operational reasoning, this would not guarantee that other abstract systems, such as kinship terminologies, were also a feature of the lives of early *Homo sapiens.*

A second criticism concerns both Parker and Gibson's adherence to a strictly recapitulationist explanation of development. They view intellectual development in ontogeny and in phylogeny as arising from the 'terminal addition' of new stages or structures. In this additive recapitulationist framework, many aspects of development are difficult if not impossible to explain. For example, U-shaped developmental curves on many tasks suggest successive reorganisation of systems of representation by characteristically human developmental processes (Bever, 1982). Furthermore, such processes are implicated in the development of early human abilities which Parker considers to be prior acquisitions held in common with other, 'less intelligent' species. A modified recapitulationist theory has been put forward by Gould (1977), who suggests that human evolution occurred because the juvenile form of the ancestor was retained in the adult form of the descendents. Furthermore, different parts of the organism may have different developmental histories (mosaic development) and thus, not all juvenile features will be retained. Perhaps such an account may prove more relevant both to developmental psychology and to reconstructing the intellectual evolution of the species.

Since Piaget's death in 1980, there has been time for a reappraisal of his genetic epistemology and questions about its future have inevitably cropped up. How might Piaget's amalgam of philosophy of science and developmental psychology which he based on parallels with evolutionary theory develop in the future? In Chapter ten, Howard Gruber argues that Piaget's use of Waddington's (1969) model overemphasised regularity in development, to the neglect of variability. Gruber stresses the relevance of the notion of branching evolution, as opposed to the more linear conception of the *scala naturae*. Variation is fundamental in evolution; a modified genetic epistemology must rescue the variants that have been thrown out up to now. He argues that if different individuals have different skills, their variation is valuable not because, by a process of abstraction, one can discern in the variability one ideal type but because the different perspectives they bring to problems are actually conserved in the final outcome through the social cooperative solution of cognitive problems.

In his commentary in Chapter eleven, Leo Apostel reinforces Gruber's view. He makes it plain that the history of science is neither evolution, nor growth, nor embryogenesis. Instead, it should be remembered that science is the product of intentionally acting individuals. Arguments about development made by analogy with the history of science may not adequately explain how purposeful action is the product of a biological endowment. Furthermore, developing knowledge is often inconsistent, incomplete or fuzzy. Apostel argues that logic itself has now developed to the point that useful ideas about the properties of inconsistent systems may be incorporated into a future genetic epistemology. Piaget's theory led him to ignore sources of knowledge which do not fall into the scientific paradigm but which must nevertheless be explained. This again highlights the importance of accounting for variability in the process of acquiring knowledge.

Another theme that recurs through the book concerns the role of human social organisation and its influence on the development of mind. Chris Sinha in Chapter twelve contrasts psychological explanations arising from 'cognitive science' with those arising from 'ecological' schools of psychology. Broadly defined, the cognitive science paradigm comprises a synthesis of linguistics, philosophy, artificial intelligence, neuroscience and cognitive psychology. It focuses on a formal description of cognitive processes and on their instantiation in computer models that rely heavily on the concept of representation to explain the control of behaviour. He characterises this approach as 'Neo-Rationalist' since the mind is considered to select information on the basis of pre-existing mental models. The real environment is held at one remove, since it must always be filtered through the mental model to enter into the control of behaviour. 'Neo-Rationalism' and 'Neo-Darwinism' share a reluctance to admit organism and environment into a relationship of mutuality.

The ecological school, on the other hand, stresses that there is information available to control the behaviour of organisms, in the environment itself. Sensory input has real structure which is informative about the organism-environment relation. Sinha suggests that it may be possible to integrate the cognitivist and ecological perspectives in an approach which he calls 'epigenetic naturalism'. In particular, human cultural practices, artefacts, symbols, knowledge of the functional value of objects, in fact any of the myriad aspects of culturally accumulated human intentional action, can be thought of as representations of mind that have become instantiated in the material culture. The child develops by expanding its known habitat through exploration and this widening circle of adaptation, based on direct perception of the environment, includes and necessitates the support of the social structure as it has been meaningfully shaped by man.

In Chapter thirteen, Wolfe Mays considers the many ways in which Piaget's genetic epistemology is a socially constituted theory of cognitive development. He points out that an historical analysis of the structure of society is insufficient for a proper explanation of how the social structure influences thought, for at any particular moment, society exhibits characteristics that are not reducible to its historical antecedents. The psychologist requires a grasp of the synchronic as well as the diachronic aspects of the social structure. He is critical of the thesis that Piaget's epigenetic sequence of concrete and formal operational reasoning may simply reflect the particular forms of economic exchange that exist within different societies. It has been suggested that concrete operational thinking may reflect exchange based on the utility of objects, whereas formal operations may reflect a shift of emphasis to a system of exchange based on abstract values. This discussion is particularly interesting in the light of Sue Taylor-Parker's chapter, in which she views formal operational reasoning as a specific biological adaptation. The thesis which Mays is opposing would suggest that concrete and abstract forms of thought reflect the outcome of cultural, rather than biological evolution. Mays however argues that abstract thought is to be found in all cultures, its origins lie in the capacity for symbolic thought and not in the mechanisms of economic exchange.

In conclusion, this volume aims to make a contribution toward more informed attempts to relate evolutionary biology and developmental psychology. It is clear, however, that as yet a complete integration is distant. This is not only because the issues are difficult but also, as this volume testifies, it is only recently that a dialogue between researchers has begun to map out common ground.

George Butterworth, Julie Rutkowska and Michael Scaife
University of Southampton and University of Sussex

References

Baldwin, J.M. (1894), *Mental development in the child and the race*, New York, Macmillan.

Baldwin, J.M. (1902), *Development and evolution*, New York, Macmillan.

Darwin, C. (1859), *The origin of species*, London, John Murray.

Gould, S.J. (1977), *Ontogeny and Phylogeny*. Cambridge, Mass., Harvard University Press.

Haeckel, E.H. (1874) *The evolution of man*, English translation, London, Watts, 1906.

Bever, E.H. (1982), *Regressions in mental development: basic phenomena and theories*, London, New Jersey, Lawrence Erlbaum.

Waddington, J.C. (1969) The theory of evolution today. In A. Koestler and J.R. Smythies (eds.), *Beyond reductionism: New Perspectives in the Sciences*, London, Hutchinson.

Wozniak, R. (1982), 'Metaphysics and science, reason and reality: the intellectual origins of genetic epistemology', in J.M. Broughton and D.J. Freeman Moir (eds.), *The cognitive developmental psychology of James Mark Baldwin*, New Jersey, ABLEX.

Acknowledgements

This volume has its origins in a conference on 'Evolution, Development and the Acquisition of Knowledge' held in the year of the centenary of Darwin's death. It was sponsored jointly by the British Psychological Society and the British Society for Developmental Biology, and took place at the University of Sussex, in April 1982. This volume is not presented as a proceedings of that conference: the papers have been extended, revised and some material was not available. We are indebted to Robert Wozniak, who contributed an excellent intellectual biography of James Mark Baldwin (available in Wozniak, 1982) and to Andrew Whiten who offered a commentary. Other contributors included Annette Karmillof-Smith, Colin Patterson, Jaques Mehler and a very lively interdisciplinary audience. Wherever possible we have incorporated important points made by those individuals into the text.

We gratefully acknowledge permission from the Cambridge University Library to use Charles Darwin's illustration of the 'Tree of Life' taken from his notebook B, in the design of the dustjacket of this book.

PART I
PHYLOGENY AND ONTOGENY

1 Problems and Possibilities in Fusing Developmental and Evolutionary Thought

PATRICK BATESON

The barriers between evolutionary biology and developmental studies of behaviour are finally coming down. I, for one, welcome this detente because, as I have argued elsewhere (Bateson, 1982), the two approaches can actively nourish each other. After all, the outcome of evolutionary processes is expressed in an individual's development and natural selection has acted on the outcome of developmental processes. Nonetheless, enthusiastically encouraging a fusion between two separate styles of thought has its dangers which should not be ignored. The distinctions which Tinbergen (1963) drew between the four Why's of ethology included separating why an individual *develops* in the way it does from why its ancestors *evolved* in the way that they did. The logical point remains as true today as it did twenty years ago. Knowledge of how a particular car has been assembled does not tell us much about the history of automobile design; and the same is true for living organisms.

The muddling of different categories is probably easier than the perception of their differences. Certainly, studies of behaviour have been replete with examples of the confusion of evolutionary and developmental arguments. Much of the dispute generated by the sociobiology movement arose because it was thought that a conventional proposition about changes in gene frequency in the course of phylogeny implied genetic determination (as distinct from mere influence) in ontogeny. This particular confusion was probably given wide currency because the views about genetic determination of behaviour could so easily be accepted within an already existing and deeply ingrained notion of how developmental processes generate two kinds of behaviour, namely innate and learnt. I need hardly add that this view is controversial. Nevertheless, it is instructive to bring the underlying thought into the open just because the implicit assumptions are liable to generate difficulties when the subjects of ontogeny and phylogeny

3

are brought together. Therefore, I shall first consider this particular notion of how development works, along with its alternatives, and then move on to the interface between development and evolution.

In my own subject of ethology, whether or not it is permissible to talk about innate behaviour still generates argument. After Lehrman's (1953) critique of classical ethology, a great many people working in the subject abandoned the old terminology but continued to use circumlocutions which were effectively equivalent. Recently an increasing number of authors have grown impatient with what they regard as little more than intellectual dishonesty and have reverted to an explicit distinction between learnt and innate behaviour. I think that this was probably because the conceptual framework accompanying the old terminology was never abandoned. Anyway, before proceeding further it is as well to be clear about meanings, since the term innate is not used in the same way by everybody, and even the issue of definition raises some pertinent general points about behavioural development.

The Definition of Innateness

The term 'innate' most commonly means 'not learnt' and is used (by those who use it) for behaviour that develops without the individual experiencing the stimuli to which it will respond or without practice of the motor patterns that it will perform. In such usage a sharp distinction is made between the experience that has specific influences on behaviour and experience that has general effects. Obviously food and oxygen, along with a great many other external conditions, are required for normal development of all behaviour. The important role of these non-specific factors is admitted but not regarded as decisive in determining whether, let us say, a bird points its beak upwards or downwards while courting a potential mate. Therefore, the definition of innate behaviour is emphatically not behaviour that develops without experience in the broad sense. No such behaviour could exist. Innate behaviour, according to the most popular (and most questionable) definition, develops without the specific experience that could give the behaviour pattern its particular character.

In principle, it might be possible to identify innate behaviour by systematically excluding likely sources of environmental information. The isolation experiment, as it is called, can undoubtedly be of service in eliminating possible explanations. Excluding possibilities can never show precisely how the behaviour developed. Even so, the approach seems to have the merit of being positive and directed. Rather than bother about possible unknown sources of variation, the advice to the experimenter appears to be sensible: if you consider that something in the environment might be important, take it away and see whether the animal can do without it. However, the apparent straightforwardness of this approach is deceptive, and difficulties in interpretation can arise for a number of quite separate reasons.

In practice it is very hard to draw a sharp distinction between the experience on which the detailed characteristics of the finished behaviour might depend and experience which has more general effects on behaviour (Lehrman, 1970; Bateson, 1976a). Second it is often difficult to be certain when an animal will generalise the effects of one kind of experience to what superficially looks like a quite different context (Schneirla, 1966). Third, the animal may have different ways of developing a given behaviour pattern and the isolation condition might trigger an alternative, though perhaps more costly mode of development, bringing the animal's behaviour to the same point as would have happened if the animal had experienced the environmental conditions from which it was being isolated (Bateson, 1981a). Finally, an animal that is isolated from relevant experience in its environment may, nevertheless, do things to itself that enable it to perform an adaptive response later on. An example of self-stimulation comes from a long series of elegant studies by Gottlieb. Normally treated Peking ducklings are able to respond preferentially to the maternal call of their own species (Gottlieb, 1971). However, if they are devocalised in the egg so that they do not make sounds and thereby stimulate themselves, they do not show the same ability to recognise the calls of their own species (Gottlieb, 1976). The devocalised ducklings can behave normally if they are played a recording of the vocalisations made by other ducklings (Gottlieb, 1980). The experiments show clearly that feedback from an animal's activity can play an essential role in normal development.

The difficulties of finding clear criteria by which innateness can be recognised, have prompted attempts to redefine it. Lorenz (1965) suggested that the term should be used for phylogenetically adapted behaviour. The question of how behaviour is adapted to the environment is a separate issue (see Bateson, 1983a), but suffice to note here that such a change in usage does not reduce the problem of definition. Cassidy (1979) and Jacobs (1981) have argued that when the environment is varied in particular ways and yet produces no corresponding variability in behaviour, the activities in question should be termed innate. However, this redefinition suffers from the necessity to prove the universal negative as does the more common usage. A water-tight classification requires an impossibly large number of experiments. The problem is that, having satisfied oneself that variation in environmental conditions does not influence behaviour, somebody else can come along and show that a different set of conditions influences the behaviour, or that varying the same set of conditions at a different age has a big effect.

All the characterisations of innate behaviour mentioned so far ultimately rest on plausibility. The difficulty is that people have very different views about what constitutes adequate evidence to enable useful classifications to be made. When one person is well satisfied that a given pattern of behaviour is truly innate, another will feel that alternative explanations have been shut out prematurely. Therefore, as an aid to classification of behaviour, the term is usually more of a hindrance than a help.

Another uncontroversial usage of innate stems from the well-tried method of analysing sources of difference (see Hinde, 1968). If animals that are known to differ genetically are reared in identical environments, then any differences in their behaviour must ultimately have genetic origins and are sometimes spoken of as being innate. In such usage a source of a difference does not imply that there are no others. Nor does it mean that the source acts directly on the behaviour. For instance, a gene may predispose an animal possessing it to learn more (or less) than an animal not having it (for example, Dudai *et al*, 1976). This point draws attention to the punning and confusion that can arise when innate is used in the precise analytical sense of a genetic source of difference and also in a much looser way for classifying unlearnt behaviour. Many people immediately think of it in the latter sense, however careful an author has been to state that was not what was meant. For this reason, many of us studying behavioural development prefer not to use the term at all. Whatever view is taken about the label, it is more interesting to examine what assumptions are made about the nature of developmental processes. That is what I shall turn to next.

Different Models of Development

Behind the arguments over whether or not is is useful to divide behaviour up into innate and acquired components, lie two highly distinct views of how development takes place. I have attempted to represent two extreme positions in Figure 1.1 The first is most clearly recognised in the writings of Lorenz (1965), even though he had attempted to move away from defining innate behaviour as not learnt. He imagined a simple relationship would be found between the starting points of development and the end points. The second view shown in Figure 1.1. is derived from the thinking of Schneirla (1966) and Lehrman (1979). The current state of the developing animal influences which genes are expressed and also feeds back on to the external world and influences it. The animal is thought to be in a continual state of transaction with its environment, selecting and changing the conditions to which it is exposed.

The advantage of making the different views explicit is that it then becomes much easier to understand what predictions might flow from the two views. On the first view, the behaviour that was supposedly dependent on genetically coded information would not be modified by learning once it had been expressed. The accumulating evidence indicates that in its strongest form this prediction is false. It is possible to take a recently hatched laughing gull chick and show that it will peck at models of adults' bills. Advocates of the first view would almost certainly want to call the behaviour innate since the chick had previously been isolated from relevant experience. Nevertheless, as the chick profits from its experience after hatching, the accuracy of its pecking improves, and the kinds of bill-like objects it will peck at become increasingly restricted (Hailman, 1967).

The first view of development shown in Figure 1.1 also leads to the expectation that adult behaviour can be analysed into learnt

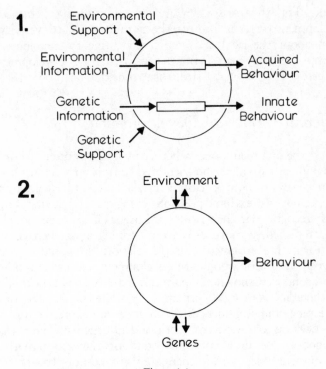

Figure 1.1

Two views of the ways in which genetic and environmental factors might influence behaviour during development. In studies of animal behaviour, the first view would be associated with Lorenz (1965), and the second view has grown out of the ideas of Schneirla (1966) and Lehrman (1970).

and unlearnt components. Eibl-Eibesfeldt (1970) has argued strongly for the notion of instinct-learning intercalation. Among other examples, he cited his own study of squirrels opening nuts in which a complex sequence can be analysed into components, some of which are learnt and some of which are thought to develop without specific opportunities for practice. This kind of analysis may be profitable sometimes, but in many cases its value seems to be exceedingly dubious (Bateson, 1976a; Jacobs, 1981). Consider the normal adult songs of three species of American bird shown in Figure 1.2, and the songs of birds that have been socially isolated at

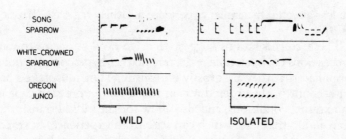

Figure 1.2

Songs of adult males of three species of birds which have been reared naturally or in social isolation (from Marler, 1976).

an early stage. In the normal birds which have had their song modified by learning, we can see no obvious component resembling that of the isolated or deafened birds (*see* Marler, 1976). The notion of separable elements of learnt and unlearnt behaviour is actively misleading in these cases—as it probably is in most examples of adult behaviour.

It is not easy to rescue much from the idea that behaviour can be invariably divided up into that which is innate and that which is acquired by learning. However, a more reasonable alternative remains, namely, that behaviour varies from examples that are unaffected by learning (though dependent on experience with more general effects) through to examples that are greatly affected by learning. Indeed, Alcock (1979) attempted a four-part classification which ran from Closed Instincts through Open Instincts and Restricted Learning, to Flexible Learning. This approach may seem sensible but the problems of definition remain as formidable as ever. For that reason alone such classifications are unlikely to command widespread agreement.

The second view of development shown in Fig. 1.1 does not escape criticism. A model should simplify and point to particular problems that are amenable to analysis. This one primarily seems to tells us that life is complicated. Furthermore, in one respect it can be positively misleading since it implies that the continuous interaction between the animal and its environment modifies behaviour throughout life. Many examples of behaviour are greatly influenced by experience at one stage of development but are less affected by similar experience at other stages (see Bateson, 1979).

These considerations suggest that we need to move towards conceptions of development that are neither hypercomplex nor so simplified that they are grossly unrealistic. They must take a proper account of the ordered way in which gene expression depends on external conditions, and also allow for the radical transformations in internal state which can arise from experience. In searching for ways of organising our thoughts about behavioural development, it is helpful to employ the metaphor of baking a cake (Bateson, 1976a). The flour, the eggs, the butter, and all the rest react together to form a product that is different from the sum of the parts. The actions of adding ingredients, preparing the mixture and baking, all contribute to the final effect. Despite the recognisable raisins (if it were that kind of cake) no-one could be expected to identify each of the ingredients and each of the actions involved in cooking as separate components in a slice of cake.

The upshot of this type of argument, which is commanding an increasing amount of support in many areas of biology (for example, Oster and Alberch, 1982: Wright, 1980) is that the genetic consequences of evolutionary change bear no straightforward relationship to the outcome of developmental processes. It is essential that we be clear about this before we embark on an attempt to forge links between studies of phylogeny and ontogeny.

New Approaches to Evolution

I shall mention the developmental approaches to studies of evolution only briefly because I have dealt with them elsewhere (Bateson, 1982, in press) and because they are not really the concern of developmental psychologists.

One obvious implication of developmental plasticity is that the phenotype changes adaptively with the nature of the environment. A less obvious implication is that ontogenetic adaptation to some environments may be costly for animals endowed with particular kinds of genotype. They can do it, but others can do it more efficiently. Furthermore, when pushed by an environment that changes steadily in one direction, most members of a species may eventually use up their capacity for adaptive ontogenetic change (G. Bateson, 1963). The sudden appearance on the East African plains of very fast cheetah may not mean that antelope are doomed. The majority of antelope may be able to produce an extra burst of speed and so elude even super cheetah. However, the strains and energy costs of doing so could provide an additional evolutionary selection pressure favouring antelope that can run very fast at lower cost than others. In such cases the environmental change producing a prompt response by individuals also exposes a population to a new selection pressure. The short-term plasticity gives the selection pressure time to work. This is one of the few ways in which the so-called Baldwin effect could work, if, as was implied by Baldwin (1896), the adaptive short-term response was necessary for the subsequent phylogenetic change.

The Baldwin hypothesis is often presented as though it is identical with Waddington's notion of genetic assimilation. However, the classic evidence produced by Waddington (1953) implies something rather different from what Baldwin had in mind. Waddington's evidence suggests that a change in environmental conditions altered the dominance relations of alleles at a given genetic locus. The effect could have been that heterozygotes normally expressed as one phenotype were expressed as a different phenotype when external conditions were changed. When the new phenotype was selected, then the normally recessive alleles were increased in frequency and eventually the unusual phenotype was expressed even in the absence of the unusual environmental conditions (see Bateson, 1982, p. 145, and Maynard Smith, 1975, p. 307).

While plasticity generates variability in the phenotype, other processes inhibit or gobble up variation. This inertia or elasticity relates to all the buffering mechanisms that are variously labelled developmental homeostasis, homeorhesis, canalisation and catch-up. It is particularly obvious in growth curves. Growing animals that have been starved or have fallen ill, fall behind other members of their own species of the same age, in size and weight. However, if the discrepancy does not exceed a certain critical value, they rapidly catch up as soon as they obtain adequate supplies of food or recover from their illness (see Bateson, 1976b). Such elasticity in developmental processes has some important implications for evolutionary thinking as Mayr (1963, p. 230) clearly perceived. If the homeostatic mechanisms can cope with deviations from the norm initiated from inside as well as from without, genetic mutations may well have no phenotypic effect. In the short term at least, the mutations will be neutralised. This would restrain certain kinds of evolutionary change.

One important aspect of developmental homeostasis and developmental inertia is that every possible configuration between radically different states need not be stable, and so a relatively minor force can dramatically alter appearance from one extreme to another. Such systems are a bit like a light switch that has two stable positions. Steady pressure on the switch results at first in no change, but as the switch passes the mid-point, the light suddenly comes on. Oster and Alberch (1982) argued that developing systems are sometimes like that and refer to the effects as 'developmental bifurcations'. These ideas obviously have relevance to the discussion about discontinuities in development, but they also have interesting implications for evolution. Imagine two populations in which two different kinds of mutation have

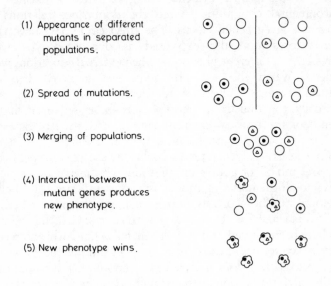

(1) Appearance of different mutants in separated populations.

(2) Spread of mutations.

(3) Merging of populations.

(4) Interaction between mutant genes produces new phenotype.

(5) New phenotype wins.

Figure 1.3

A possible way in which two merging populations, both containing different mutants, could give rise to a new phenotype that then displaces the old one.

occurred (see Figure 1.3). Because of elasticity or stasis in the developmental machinery, neither of these mutations do very much for the phenotype. However, let us suppose that they have some marginal selective advantage so that they spread. (They could spread in other ways as well as Dover (1982) suggested.) Now consider the possibility that as a result of migration the two populations mix. Interbreeding occurs and when the two mutant genes occur in the same organism, their combined effect flips the phenotype into a new configuration. Now, the new phenotype and the old phenotype come into competition and the new phenotype wins. In a generation or two it may have replaced the old one. The new phenotypes would not suffer the fate of isolated mutants because there would be others of a similar kind with which to mate. Indeed, the new phenotypes might be thrown together because they were not chosen or accepted as mates by normal-looking members of the population. In brief, the involvement of developmental buffering might provide the first step of the take-off condition for occasional discontinuities in evolution (cf Gould and Eldredge, 1977).

Functional Approaches to Development

I believe that functional and evolutionary arguments can help us to focus on evidence which simply would be ignored in the all too common absence of satisfactory causal theories of development. I will give two examples where I feel that research conducted at our laboratory at Madingley has been helped by considering functional explanations. The first is from studies of imprinting, and the second from parent-offpsring conflict in mammals.

When Lorenz (1935) first put the process of imprinting in birds on the map he set it in a functional context. He argued that the process is concerned with learning the characteristics of the species. Although Lorenz saw imprinting as a single process, a distinction was increasingly made between filial imprinting which has a short-term influence on social preferences early in life, and sexual imprinting which influences mate choice. By degrees evidence accumulated that sexual imprinting takes place later in development than filial imprinting (for example, Schutz, 1965; Gallagher, 1977; Vidal, 1980). In addition, it has become increasingly apparent over the years that neither process need play an essential role in species recognition, because a bird that can be imprinted can also show a predisposition to respond to members of its own species, even when it has had no direct experience with any of them except itself (Schutz, 1965; Immelmann, 1969; Gottlieb, 1971). A possible explanation is, then, that both filial and sexual imprinting have evolved to enable birds to recognise their close kin, but that the necessity for kin recognition is different in young and adult animals (Bateson, 1979).

The young bird needs to discriminate between the parent that cares for it and other members of its species because parents discriminate between their own offspring and other young in the same species, and may actually attack young that are not their own. Adult behaviour of this kind is well known in many mammals and birds (for example, Burtt, 1977). In most cases the parent that cares exclusively for its own young will be more likely to rear them to independence than a parent that accepts and cares for all the stray young that come up to it. The suggestion is, then, that filial imprinting is required for individual recognition of parents and is a secondary consequence of the selective pressures on parents to discriminate between their own and other young. In each generation individuals may differ in the stage of development when their filial responsiveness to parent-like objects first increases. Those that do it too early obtain inappropriate or insufficient information about their parents. They might, for instance, have inadequate opportunities to explore all facets of their parent and so fail to recognise it quickly enough later on when quick recognition is important. Those that do it too late respond in a friendly way to hostile members of their own species and consequently suffer. In these different ways the optimal timing for the increase in intrinsic responsiveness could have evolved. It would be critically affected by how rapidly the parents learn to discriminate between their own young and other young.

The evolutionary pressures that gave rise to sexual imprinting are likely to have been quite different. The suggestion is that sexual imprinting enables an animal to learn the characteristics of its close kin and subsequently it can choose a mate that appears slightly different (but not too different) from its parents and siblings. The advantage of behaving in this way arises because of the evolutionary pressures to avoid inbreeding on the one hand,

and excessive outbreeding on the other (Mather, 1943). Just what constitutes excessive outbreeding is a matter of debate at the moment (Maynard Smith, 1978; Bateson, 1983). But assuming that some balance has to be struck between inbreeding and outbreeding the solution is for each individual, using the sexual imprinting process, to learn the characteristics of its parents and siblings and, when adult, to choose a mate that looks a bit different from its immediate kin. The underlying assumption is, of course, that there is a correlation between the relatedness and similarity of external appearance—and assumption which is backed by some evidence (for example, Bateson, Lotwick and Scott, 1980).

If these speculations about the functions of filial and sexual imprinting are correct, some sense can be made of why sexual imprinting occurs later in development than filial imprinting. In order for a bird to maximise its chances of recognising close kin when choosing a mate, it should delay learning about them until its siblings are old enough for their juvenile characteristics to provide a strong indication of their adult appearance.

My second example of how a functional and evolutionary approach has helped studies of development, comes from weaning in mammals. It is not unfair to describe the old view of the mother–offspring relationship as one of exquisite co-adaptation (for example, Bowlby, 1969). The mother ministers to the needs of the young and the young obediently respond to the dictates of the mother. Admittedly, people noticed that around weaning a mother might snap at her young, but the mother's behaviour was commonly explained in terms of a trivial response to the painful effects of her offspring's sharp new teeth. At a much more rigorous and quantitative level, Robert Hinde and his colleagues described the growing process of rejection by the mother of her offspring that occurs in rhesus monkeys (reviewed in Hinde, 1977). They showed elegantly that the young monkey's role in maintaining contact with its mother increases steadily over this period. I think it is fair to say that the full significance of this work was only appreciated as the evolutionary thinking of Trivers (1974) became well known. Trivers pointed out that in a sexually reproducing species, the offspring is not genetically identical to its mother and so the interests in the two individuals in terms of maximising their reproductive success are not identical either.

The point about parent–offspring conflict can perhaps be

brought into sharp focus if one considers a simplified case of a mammal that only has two litters (see Bateson, 1981b). When should a mother wean the first litter? Producing milk is extremely costly for the mother; indeed, Blaxter (1971) has estimated that the energy costs of producing milk for 1.5 days is equivalent to the total energy costs of pregnancy. So, if the mother feeds the first litter on milk for too long, she will put herself in such a poor condition that the second litter will suffer and will be less likely to survive (see Fig. 1.4). This means that as far as the mother's interest in maximising her reproductive success is concerned, the optimum time for weaning the first litter is at an earlier stage than would be ideal for those offspring. The discrepancy in interest is particularly likely to lie over the weaning period. The point about this evolutionary argument is that it puts the parent–offspring conflict in a completely different light. Instead of sweeping the subject under the carpet as a phenomenon of relatively little interest, attention is focussed on it as something that may have profound and long-term consequences to both parent and offspring.

It will be apparent from Figure 1.4 that the knock-on effects of

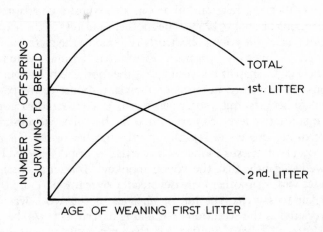

Figure 1.4

The hypothetical numbers of offspring surviving to breed in the first and second litters plotted against the time of weaning of the first litter. The optimal weaning for the mother is not ideal for the offspring in the first litter (from Bateson 1981b)

one litter on the next are likely to be highly dependent on environmental conditions. At times when food is plentiful, the drain of providing milk is much less severe than at times when the mother is partly starved. Consequently, in times of plenty she will be much less run down when she starts the second litter and weaning the first litter somewhat later may actually be advantageous to her. The significance of this is that we should expect weaning time to be variable and, therefore, the young animals should be able to cope with the possibility that a radical change in their diet (and their environment) may occur at any time over a wide age range. The young mammal must be flexible and it also must be responsive since the time of weaning may dictate the best developmental route it should take.

With these thoughts in mind, we have done some experimental studies on the early weaning of the domestic cat and found that differences between early-weaned and control litters are evident weeks after the early weaning procedure, which can be as mild as blocking the mother's lactation for only one day (Bateson and Young, 1981: Bateson, Martin and Young, 1981: Martin, 1982). The most striking and surprising aspect of these results was that the early weaned kittens played significantly *more* in particular ways than the controls. We do not yet understand fully the functional significance of these results, but have speculated that the early weaned animals may be on a developmental route adapted to an impoverished environment in which opportunities for play later in development will be greatly reduced relative to the animal's living in plentiful environments. The pattern of this research has shown how an argument derived from evolutionary theory and from considerations of biological function, has started to open up a new area of research. It points forward to the analysis of individual differences reflecting, not just statistical noise or pathological effects of abnormal conditions, but appropriate responses to the particular environmental conditions in which the individual developed.

Conclusion

In this chapter I have sought to emphasise both the dangers and the attractions of bringing developmental and evolutionary approaches to the study of behaviour together. The principle danger is that logically distinct questions can become muddled and, in the general loss of conceptual rigour, naive and almost preformationist notions of development can be given much more encouragement than they ever deserved. It is essential that such crudities should not obscure the growing awareness that developmental systems are multiply influenced from outside the individual and from within. This realisation is a necessary precondition for understanding how developmental processes actually work.

With a clear perception of the differences between developmental and evolutionary approaches to behaviour, we can usefully allow them to help each other. I am sure that how much help is obtained will depend a great deal on the training and habits of the research worker. Biologists, like myself, are steeped in evolutionary theory and are only too willing to invent pretty, functional stories to explain any example of behaviour that we come across, we feel at ease moving backward and forward from one level of discourse to another. Others with a training in psychology or in the social sciences, often find this style alien and even repellent. Admittedly, the biologists do not always know when they have changed their mode of thought, and so they can easily generate muddle not only in their own minds but in the minds of others. However, I have tried to argue in the second part of this chapter that the rewards of bringing different types of thought together can be real in the sense that they open up new lines of research. Also coherence is brought to what would otherwise look like totally unrelated particles of knowledge.

Acknowledgements

I am grateful to Robert Hinde for discussion of an earlier draft of this chapter.

References

Alcock, J. (1979), *Animal Behavior: An evolutionary approach*, 2nd ed, Sunderland, Mass., Sinauer.

Baldwin, J.M. (1896), 'A new factor in evolution', *American Naturalist*, 30, pp. 444–51, 536–53.

Bateson, G. (1963), 'The role of somatic change in evolution', *Evolution*, 17, pp. 529–39.

Bateson, P.P.G. (1976a), 'Specificity and the origins of behavior', in J. Rosenblatt, R.A. Hinde, C. Beer (eds.), *Advances in the Study of Behavior*, Vol 6. New York, Academic Press, pp. 1–20.

Bateson, P.P.G. (1976b), 'Rules and reciprocity in behavioural development', in P.P.G. Bateson and R.A. Hinde (eds.), *Growing Points in Ethology*, Cambridge, Cambridge University Press, pp. 401–21.

Bateson, P. P.G. (1979), 'How do sensitive periods arise and what are they for?', *Animal Behaviour*, 27, pp. 470–86.

Bateson, P. P.G. (1981a), 'Ontogeny of behaviour', *British Medical Bulletin*, 37, pp. 159–64.

Bateson, P. P.G. (1981b), 'Discontinuities in development and changes in the organization of play in cats', in K. Immelmann, G.W. Barlow, L. Petrinovich and M. Main (eds.), *Behavioral Development*, Cambridge, Cambridge University Press, pp. 281–95.

Bateson, P. P.G. (1982), 'Behavioural development and evolutionary processes', in King's College Sociobiology Group (eds.), *Current Problems in Sociobiology*, Cambridge, Cambridge University Press, pp. 133–51.

Bateson, P. P.G. (1983a), 'Genes, environment and the development of behaviour', in T.R. Halliday and P.J.B. Slater (eds.), *Animal Behaviour*, Vol. 3: *Genetics and Development*, Oxford, Blackwell, pp. 52–81.

Bateson, P. P.G. (1983b), 'Optimal outbreeding', in P. Bateson (ed.), *Mate Choice*, Cambridge, Cambridge University Press, pp.257–77.

Bateson, P. P.G. (in press), 'Sudden changes in ontogeny and phylogeny', in G. Greenberg and E. Tobach (eds.), *T.C. Schneirla conference on Levels of Integration and Evolution of Behavior*, Hillsdale, NJ, Erlbaum.

Bateson, P. P.G. and M. Young, (1981), 'Separation from the mother and the development of play in cats', *Animal Behaviour*, 29, pp. 173–80.

Bateson, P. P.G., W. Lotwick and K.K. Scott, (1980), 'Similarities between the faces of parents and offspring in Bewick's swan and the differences between mates', *Journal of Zoology, London*, 191, pp. 61–74.

Bateson, P. P.G., P. Martin and M. Young, (1981), 'Effects of interrupting cat mothers' lactation with bromocriptine on the subsequent play of their kittens', *Physiology and Behavior*, 27, pp. 841–5.

Blaxter, K.L. (1971), 'The comparative biology of lactation', in I.R. Falconer (ed.), *Lactation*, London, Butterworths, pp. 51–69.

Bowlby, J. (1969), *Attachment and Loss*, Vol. 1: *Attachment*, London, Hogarth Press.

Burtt, E.H. (1977), 'Some factors in the timing of parent-chick recognition in swallows', *Animal Behaviour*, 25, pp. 231–9.

Cassidy, J. (1979), 'Half a century on the concepts of innateness and instinct: survey, synthesis and philosophical implications'. *Zeitschrift für Tierpsychologie* 50, pp. 364–86.

Dover, G. (1982), 'Molecular drive: a cohesive mode of species evolution', *Nature*, 299, pp. 111–17.

Dudai, Y., Y.-N. Jan, D. Byers, W.G. Quinn, and S. Benzer, (1976), '*Dunce*, a mutant of *Drosophila* deficient in learning', *Proceedings of the National*

Academy of Science U.S.A., 73, pp. 1684–8.

Eibl-Eibesfeldt, I. (1970), *Ethology: the biology of behavior*, New York, Holt, Rinehart and Winston.

Gallagher, J.E. (1977), 'Sexual imprinting: a sensitive period in Japanese quail (*Coturnix coturnix japonica*)', *Journal of Comparative and Physiological Psychology*, 91, pp. 72–8.

Gottlieb, G. (1971), *Development of Species Identification in Birds*, Chicago, University of Chicago Press.

Cottlieb, G. (1976), 'Early development of species-specific auditory perception in birds', in G. Gottlieb (ed.), *Neural and behavioral specificity*, Vo. 3: *Studies on the development of behavior and the nervous system*, New York, Academic Press, pp. 237–80.

Gottlieb, G. (1980), 'Development of species identification in ducklings: VI, Specific embryonic experience required to maintain species typical perception in Peking ducklings', *Journal of Comparative and Physiological Psychology*, 94, pp. 579–87.

Gould, S.J. and N. Eldredge (1977), 'Punctuated equilibria: the tempo and mode of evolution reconsidered', *Paleobiology*, 3, pp. 115–51.

Hailman, J.P. (1967), 'The ontogeny of an instinct', *Behaviour*, Suppl. 15. Leiden, Brill.

Hinde, R.A. (1968), 'Dichotomies in the study of development', in J.M. Thoday and A.S. Parkes (eds.), *Genetic and Environmental Influences on Behaviour*, Edinburgh, Oliver and Boyd.

Hinde, R.A. (1977), 'Mother-infant separation and the nature of inter-individual relationships: experiments with rhesus monkeys', *Proceedings of the Royal Society, London B.*, 196, pp. 29–50.

Immelmann, K. (1969), 'Über den Einfluss frühkindlicher Erfahrunfgen auf die geschlechtliche Objektfixieruing bei Estrildiden', *Zeitschrift für Tierpsychologie*, 26, pp. 677–91.

Jacobs, J. (1981), 'How heritable is innate behaviour?', *Zeitschrift für Tierpsychologie*, 55. pp. 1–18.

Lehrman, D.S. (1953), 'A critique of Konrad Lorenz's theory of instinctive behaviour', *Quarterly Review of Biology*, 28, pp. 337–63.

Lehrman, D.S. (1970), 'Semantic and conceptual issues in the nature-nurture problem', in L.R. Aronson, E. Tobach, D.S. Lehrman and D.S. Rosenblatt (eds.), *Development and Evolution of Behavior*, San Francisco, Freeman, pp. 17–52.

Lorenz, K. (1935), 'Der Kumpan in der Umvelt des Vögels', *Journal of Ornithology*, 83, pp. 137–213; 289–413.

Lorenz, K. (1965), *Evolution and Modification of behavior*, Chicago, Ill., University of Chicago press.

Marler, P. (1976), 'Sensory templates in species-specific behaviour', in J.C. Fentress (ed.), *Simpler Networks and Behavior*, Sunderland, Mass., Sinauer Associates.

Martin, P. (1982), *Weaning and Behavioural Development in the Cat*, Unpublished Ph.D. dissertation, University of Cambridge.

Mather, K. (1943), 'Polygenic inheritance and natural selection', *Biological Reviews*, 18, 32–64.

Maynard Smith, J. (1975), *The Theory of Evolution*, London, Penguin.

Maynard Smith, J. (1978), *The Evolution of Sex*, Cambridge, Cambridge University Press.

Mayr, E. (1963), *Animal Species and Evolution*, Cambridge, Mass., Harvard University Press.

Oster, G. and P. Alberch (1982), 'Evolution and bifurcation of developmental programs', *Evolution*, 36, pp. 444–59.

Schneirla, T.C. (1966), 'Behavioral development and comparative psychology', *Quarterly Review of Biology*, 41, pp. 283–302.

Schutz, F. (1965), 'Sexuelle Prägung bei Anatiden', *Zeitschrift für Tierpsychologie*, 22, pp. 50–103.

Tinbergen, N. (1963), 'On aims and methods of ethology', *Zeitschrift für Tierpsychologie*, 20, pp. 410–33.

Trivers, R.L. (1974), 'Parent-offspring conflict', *American Zoologist*, 14, pp. 249–64.

Vidal, J.-M. (1980), 'The relations between filial and sexual imprinting in the domestic fowl: effects of age and social experience' *Animal Behaviour*, 28, pp. 880–91.

Waddington, C.H. (1953), 'Genetic assimilation of an acquired character', *Evolution*, 7, pp. 118–26.

Wright, S. (1980), 'Genic and organismic selection', *Evolution*, 34, pp. 825–43.

2 Change and Variation: On the Importance of Heterochrony for Development (Commentary on Bateson)

NANCY RADER

In his paper, Patrick Bateson presents us with his reflections on how a consideration of evolution can enlighten the study of development. In the first part of his paper, he addresses the learned versus innate controversy. Bateson argues against classifying *a behaviour* as innate, stressing the complex interplay of organism and environment that determines any observed behaviour. Later in the paper, he demonstrates, through a discussion of his own animal research, how evolutionary thinking has enabled him to make sense of his data. Through an evolutionary approach, results may be understood in terms of functional significance; individual differences may be seen as important adaptive responses to particular environmental conditions rather than as statistical error.

Bateson argues convincingly that developmentalists would do well to consider ethology and the relationship between genes and behaviour more carefully. And, he rightly admonishes those who would attempt to draw conclusions based on analogies between ontogeny and phylogeny. However, I believe that a discussion of the relationship between evolution and development needs to consider recent advances in evolutionary theory that suggest a link much more fundamental than analogy. If the kernel of the evolutionary theorising of Eldredge and Gould (1972) is accepted, then processes of development are themselves mechanisms of evolution, and the variation natural selection acts on, is in the relative timing of developmental processes. If this is the case, then developmentalists need to consider the relative timing of events in development to understand possible sources of individual differences.

The essence of Eldredge and Gould's theory, which has been described in detail by Gould (for example 1977), is that heterochrony in development is the mechanism that produces speciation. Heterochrony, for their purpose, is defined as the displacement of a feature along a developmental time line relative to the time that this same feature appeared in an ancestral form. Such a theory of evolution by heterochrony, and subsequent natural selection, requires that features of an organism are dissociable in their developmental histories and that the pattern of development is controlled largely by genes.

To claim that features are dissociable in development is to say that an organism is a mosaic of characteristics, each of whose appearance in development is separately controlled by a gene or set of genes that is independently modifiable. Such a notion is not to be found in the *zeitgeist* of developmental psychology today. The prevalent assumption appears to be that maturation unfolds along a single time course; maturation may be slowed down or speeded up, but always as a process that affects the organism in toto. This unitary view is expressed by such concepts as 'the slow maturer' or 'developmental lag'. Yet, the evidence for the dissociability of features in development is strong when one considers pattern differences across species. Gould (1977) presents a number of examples, typically making use of size and shape as characteristics, as might be expected given his training as a paleontologist.

Given that features are dissociable in terms of their developmental histories, a change in the pattern of temporal characteristics across features becomes a possible basis for speciation. The major tenet of Gould's theory is that relatively accelerated or retarded rates of growth lead to saltatory changes sufficient for speciation to occur. Thus, a potentially simple change in a regulatory gene can produce a change in form that provides an advantage for selection to act on. Within such a theory of evolution by heterochrony, the appearance of a wholly new trait plays a relatively minor role. Displacement of features in development, rather than the introduction of new features, is the key to evolutionary change.

Bateson makes use of a metaphor with cake as the topic to persuade his reader that there is no straightforward relationship between the genetic consequences of evolutionary change and the *outcome* of developmental processes. Another baking metaphor may be used to emphasise the difference between attempts to link outcome and genetic change and those linking timing and genetic change. If one is making leavened bread, the recipe's timing becomes very important, in addition to the ingredients, in producing a particular form for a purchaser to select. When making leavened bread, the yeast is added after the mixture has cooled to a temperature of about 110 degrees F. If the yeast is added either too early—before cooling—or too late—when the mixture is too cool—a very different sort of bread develops. As a result of a change in timing, beyond a certain range, a 'catastrophic' change in the form of the bread occurs. It is now flat or unleavened. Note that no new elements have been added or removed; it is the displacement in time of one element that is responsible for the change in form. The purchaser who selects the leavened bread would not be selecting a recipe with a different ingredient, but it would be a different recipe nevertheless. Without dwelling on the metaphor too long, one may also note that the environment, in terms of room temperature, will affect the point at which the yeast must be added for the loaf to be leavened

Gould (1977) has introduced the use of what he calls 'clock models' to illustrate differential change in independent vectors, moving at their own rates through development. The clocks are simply tools that help us to visualise the change in the timing pattern of several variables. In constructing clocks that describe changes in evolution, the ancestral form is used to create the scales of the clock. A horizontal scale forming the base of the clock is used to indicate the age of the organism. Semi-circles radiating from the midpoint of the base are used for each characteristic considered. The scales on the clock are designed such that they are aligned with respect to development. The midpoint of the clock reflects the values for a chosen stage of development. Figure 2.1 below is taken from an example in Gould's book *Ontogeny and Phylogeny* (1977), and illustrates hypothesised changes in the evolution of *Homo sapiens*. Figure 2.1a shows the construction of the clock based on an hypothesised ancestral form. The developmental stage that has been chosen is the adult stage. The first radial scale plots shape and the second radial scale plots size, where shape is defined as the ratio of facial to cranial length, and size is defined as body weight. The midpoint of the clock points to the size and shape values found in the adult stage of the ancestral form. Figure 2.1b illustrates the hypothesised change to modern man. The horizontal bar at the base shows that the adult stage is reached later than in the ancestral form. The hand pointing to the

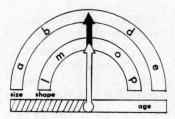 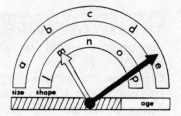

Figure 2.1

Clock model showing hypothetical evolution of *Homo sapiens* from an ancestral form (1-a) to modern man (1-b) in terms of shape and size.

shape scale shows that the adult shape is similar to a juvenile shape in the ancestral form. The hand pointing to the size scale shows that a greater size is reached in the adult form of modern man. Thus, a reading of the clock tells us that as the process of reaching the adult stage was retarded, size increased and a juvenile shape was maintained.

Gould's theory of evolution by heterochrony argues that genetically controlled rates of development for various aspects of an organism, taken relatively, are critical in understanding evolution. Given heterochrony as a mechanism of evolution, the spectre of the hopeful monster disappears. A small change in the regulatory aspects of the genetic base permits continued functioning of an integrated whole, while allowing for significant change. It is not that the underlying change needs to be 'slow and continuous' to avoid the spectre of a hopeful monster, as much as that the change must maintain a functioning organism that is able to mate with members of the population.

Having looked at the role development plays in Gould's evolutionary theory, let us now turn to the implications Gould's theory has for developmental psychologists interested in the acquisition of knowledge. I would like to put forward the notion that the temporal displacements proposed by Gould as central to evolutionary change are also critical to an understanding of individual differences. From a Darwinian viewpoint, processes underlying evolutionary change should be reflected in phenotypic variation within a species. If selection is going to favour certain phenotypes, those phenotypes must be present in the population. Thus, if Gould's theory is correct, the relative timing of events in development would be an important source of individual differences. Furthermore, and critical to the issue at hand, such changes in the patterning of development with evolution should lead not only to differences in size and shape, but also to changes in behaviour. To the extent that cognitions underlying behaviour are affected by a developing nervous system, *patterns* of growth across multiple aspects of the nervous system should have implications for cognition. If this is the case, a consideration of temporal displacements in development, *relative to a species norm*, should help us understand individual differences and, perhaps, such aberrations in cognition as are found in specific learning disabilities, retardation, or autism.

A model of development that incorporates temporal displacement, relative to a norm, as a contributor to individual differences is presented in Figure 2.2 below. In the model, the genotype functions to determine developmental time tables that lead to a particular balance or organisation at the neurophysiological level. These time tables can also be influenced by environmental conditions, such as nutrition, infection, or sensory deprivation. The neurophysiological organisation that emerges, in turn, gives rise to what I have called 'cognitive talents'. The term 'cognitive talents' refers to the ease with which certain kinds of sensory information can be processed or operations carried out. Such underlying talent would interact with environmental input,

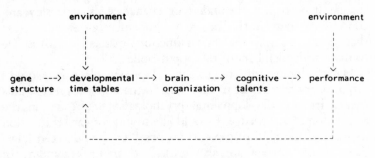

Figure 2.2

Model of development incorporating temporal displacements as a variable leading to individual differences in cognitive talents.

instruction, and stimulation in determining achievement level. For example, some individuals start out with an 'ear for music', that is, a talent for processing and manipulating those aspects of sound related to music. Such an individual could achieve a high level of musical achievement quickly and with little effort, given some musical exposure and training. An individual with a different neurophysiological structure might require much more training and sustained effort to reach the same achievement level. Still other individuals would never achieve the same level of performance, regardless of the amount of training. The interaction of environment with cognitive talent would similarly influence such skills as reading or formal reasoning.

Neurophysiological research over the past few decades has focused on delineating areas of the brain in terms of their functional relationship to cognitive, sensory, and motor activities. Recent research in developmental neurophysiology has begun to specify the timing of functional maturity for specific regions and pathways of the brain (for example, see Goldman, 1975; Maurer and Lewis, 1979). However, there has been very little research directed at investigating the relationship between individual differences in temporal aspects of development and cognitive performance. One exception is the research undertaken by Deborah Waber (Waber, 1976, 1977, 1979; Waber, Bauermeister, Cohen, Ferber, & Wolff 1981) of Children's Hospital in Boston. Her research findings have led her to propose that delayed sexual maturity leads to greater hemispheric differentiation, with the consequence of achieving greater spatial skills, at the expense of sequencing skills. To illustrate the proposed effect of the temporal displacement of sexual maturation on cognition, a clock model is presented in Figure 2.3. In this case, the scales of the clock are determined by population norms. The horizontal scale forming the base of the clock is used to indicate age, with the midpoint representing the average age at which puberty is reached. The inner radial scale presents values for spatial skills, while the outer radial scale contains values for sequencing skills. The midpoints are the population norms. Figure 2.3a represents the norm, with the hands of the clock pointing to the midpoint of the two radial scales, and the average age for onset of puberty located at the midpoint of the horizontal scale. Figure 2.3b illustrates the proposed shift with delayed sexual maturation. The age bar shows

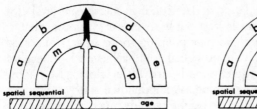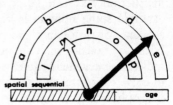

Figure 2.3

Clock model showing proposed shift from norms for spatial and sequential skills
with delayed sexual maturation.

that puberty occurs later in development, and the hands of the
clock point to the resulting effect on the achievement level for
spatial and sequencing skills.

In closing, I would like to summarise the argument I have
presented here. By postulating heterochrony as a key mechanism
in speciation, Gould's theory of evolution points to the
importance of temporal displacements from the species norm in
the development of individual differences. To the extent that
temporal displacements are as important in affecting structure and
function in the nervous systems as they are in affecting the shape
and size of bones, they become an important variable to be
considered by developmental psychologists interested in a
biological approach to individual differences in cognition. Gould's
theory motivates a paradigmatic shift to an analysis of individual
differences in terms of temporal patterns of maturation in the
nervous system. Perhaps a search for temporal displacements will
lead to a better understanding of exceptional cognitive
achievement as well as cognitive disabilities.

Notes

1. The concept of the 'hopeful monster' (Goldschmidt, 1940) acknowledges
   that gross changes in an organism are a risky evolutionary strategy.
   Evolution requires transformation and adaptation of the organism and a
   gross change, for example through mutation, may result incongenial

surroundings being difficult to find. *See* R. Goldsmith (1940), *The material basis of evolution*, New Haven, Yale University Press, 390–3.

References

Eldredge, N. and S.J. Gould (1972), 'Punctuated equilibria: an alternative to phyletic gradualism', in T.J.M. Schopf (ed.), *Models in Paleobiology*, San Francisco, Freeman, Cooper.

Goldman, P.S. (1975), 'Age, sex, and experience as related to the neural basis of cognitive development', in N.A. Buchwald and M.A.B. Brazier (eds.), *Brain Mechanisms in Mental Retardation*, NY, Academic Press.

Gould, S.J. (1977), *Ontogeny and Phylogeny*, Cambridge, Mass., Harvard U. Press.

Maurer, D., and T.L. Lewis (1979), 'A physiological explanation of infants' early visual development', *Canadian Journal of Psychology*, *33*(4), pp. 232–52.

Waber, D.P. (1976), 'Sex differences in cognition: a function of maturation rate?' *Science*, *192*, pp. 572–4.

Waber, D.P. (1977), 'Sex differences in mental abilities, hemispheric lateralization, and rate of physical growth at adolescence'. *Developmental Psychology*, *13*, pp. 29–38.

Waber, D.P. (1979), 'Cognitive abilities and sex-related variations in the maturation of cerebral cortical functions', in M.A. Wittig and A.C. Petersen (eds.), *Sex-related Differences in Cognitive Functioning: Developmental issues*, NY, Academic Press.

Waber, D.P., M. Bauermeister, C. Cohen, R. Ferber and P.H. Wolff (1981), *Developmental Psychobiology*, *14*, pp. 513–22.

3 Specious Origins? Darwinism and Developmental Theory

ALAN COSTALL

Introduction

In 1896 a reviewer of James Sully's *Studies of Childhood* (1896) raised the interesting question of why such studies had not begun 'as long ago as there were children and thoughtful men to study them' (Bryan, 1896, p.432). A number of plausible, and by no means incompatible, answers could be offered, ranging from the growing influence of German Idealism with its emphasis upon genetic explanation, to the changing role of the child in society. Here I want to re-examine what, according to the textbooks at least, is supposed to be the most obvious answer: Darwinian theory set developmental psychology in motion (for example, Flugel, 1951, chap. 5; Russell, 1978, p. 40). Now Darwinism certainly did play an important part in the origin of developmental studies, but I will question the idea that this was because developmental psychology could at last base itself upon a sound foundation of established evolutionary theory. In fact Darwinism was itself forced to lean rather heavily upon developmental evidence for support and as a result of this dependent relation Darwinism initially imposed upon psychology a peculiar concept of development quite contrary to that required for a truly *developmental* theory. Darwinism undoubtedly set things moving but in quite the wrong direction.

The point of going over all this old history is that although developmental psychology has largely broken away from its initial unfortunate relation with Darwinism—a relation based on a commitment to the doctrine of recapitulation—the alternative can hardly be autonomy but rather a much happier relationship.

Darwinism: the Problem of Evidence

It is hardly news that Darwinian theory is currently suffering something of a crisis of confidence. But it would be a mistake to think that Darwinism at least enjoyed an untroubled past. The enduring issue of continuity *versus* discontinuity in evolution last came to a head with the rediscovery of Mendel's laws at the turn of the century (*see* Provine, 1971), but it was also central to the initial reception of Darwin's *On The Origin of Species* (1859).

Although Darwin was perfectly happy to allow that natural selection was not perhaps the exclusive mechanism of evolution, he obstinately clung to what Thomas Huxley, for one, saw as 'an unnecessary difficulty in adopting *Natura non facit saltum* so unreservedly' (F. Darwin, 1887a, p.232). Indeed the major impact of Darwinian theory upon philosophy and psychology seems to have concerned the principle of continuity rather than the question of *how* modification came about (Kellogg, 1907, p.21). When Darwin himself came to consider the fundamental implications of his ideas to psychology, it was the *gradual* acquirement of mental powers and capacities that he identified (Darwin, 1859, p. 488).

Unfortunately the Darwinists were hard put to provide any compelling evidence for such continuity in evolution. Indeed it followed from Darwinian theory that such evidence should be difficult to obtain. As Darwin put it (Darwin, 1859, p.292), it was as if Nature had 'guarded against' the frequent discovery of her fine transitional or linking forms!

The fossil record, for instance, might reveal evolutionary change, but not continuous change. In response, Darwin calmly explained that the earth's crust was no well-filled museum, but a poor collection made at hazard and at infrequent intervals. If the geological record failed to reveal any finely graduated organic chain, well then the record must be at fault (Darwin, 1859, p.280).

Again, the obvious similarities among existing species were certainly compatible with an evolutionary principle, but could not be expected to confirm continuity; as Darwin explained, as early as 1837, 'the tree of life should perhaps be called the coral of life, base of branches dead so that *passages cannot be seen*' (cited in F. Darwin, 1887a, p.6).

The theory of natural selection is of course based on the analogy with selective breeding, yet even the case for gradual change in selective breeding itself required special pleading. As Secord (1981) has recently emphasised, Darwin was not primarily impressed by the changes that occur from deliberate selection, which in any case drew upon striking, novel variations; he was concerned with the very slow and subtle changes which he supposed to occur through 'unconscious selection'. Once again the problem of evidence arose, though this time in relation to the historical record of such change, as kept by the breeders themselves. As Darwin put it

As soon as the points of value of the new sub-breed are once fully acknowledged, the principle, as I have called it, of unconscious selection will always tend ... slowly to add to the characteristic features of the breed, whatever they may be. But the chance will be infinitely small of any record having been preserved of such slow, varying, and insensible changes (Darwin, 1859, p.40).

The Theory of Recapitulation

The sparsity of positive evidence did not go unnoticed. In a critical article in the *North British Review*, 1867, Fleeming Jenkin described the 'true Darwinian believer' as an adversary commanding a huge domain of fancy:

He can invent trains of ancestors of whose existence there is no evidence; he can marshal hosts of equally imaginary foes; he can call up continents, floods, and peculiar atmospheres; he can dry up oceans, split islands, and parcel out eternity at will (cited in F. Darwin, 1887b, p.108).

Although Darwin was relatively undisturbed by such criticism, his followers were eager to provide some convincing demonstration of gradual change in the organic realm. The natural example was, of course, that of individual development. In his book *The Descent of Man*, first published in 1871, Darwin argued that the possibility of gradual evolution of man's mental and moral faculties 'ought not to be denied, for we daily see these faculties developing in every infant' (Darwin, 1901, p.194). John Tyndall's address to the British Association at Belfast in 1874 brought the question of evolutionary continuity to wider public attention, and a *Punch* cartoon at the time shows a very substantial Victorian gentleman appalled by the suggestion of such minimal beginnings (Figure 3.1).

The appeal to developmental evidence became a dominant feature of the writings of the early Darwinists:

In the case of every individual human being, the human mind presents to actual observation a process of gradual development, extending from infancy to manhood. For it is thus shown to be a matter of observable fact

Figure 3.1

Portly Old Swell (on reading Professor Tyndall's Speech) 'DEAR ME! IS IT POSS'BLE! MOST 'XTR'ORDINARY! — (*throws down the Review*) — THAT I SHOULD HAVE BEEN ORIGINALLY A "PRIMORDIAL ATOMIC GLOBULE"!!'

that, whatever may have been the origin or the history of human intelligence in the past, as it now exists ... it proves itself to be no exception to the general law of evolution: it unquestionably does admit of gradual growth from a zero level, and without such a gradual growth we have no evidence of its becoming (Romanes, p. 391).

As it stands, the argument from ontogeny simply insists upon the *possibility* of continuity in evolution. In order for developmental evidence to constitute *proof* of actual continuity an additional principle, not entailed by Darwin's theory itself, was invoked. This was the theory of recapitulation, and it is important to be clear that the theory of recapitulation is indeed a *theory*. It is not simply the descriptive claim that parallels can be found between ontogeny and phylogeny, but a particular explanation of *why* such parallels should occur. Specifically, it proposes that ontogeny provides very direct evidence of phylogeny since phylogeny is the *cause* of ontogeny.[1] The theory draws upon the concepts of terminal addition and acceleration; the idea is that evolutionary changes can only occur at the end point of the developmental sequence and that such changes become 'packed down' in subsequent generations as new modifications arise.

What could be obtained at the cost of this additional assumption was truly remarkable. Ontogeny could be taken to provide a continuous record of evolution 'just as the contents of rocks and their sequence teach us the past history of the earth itself (Lubbock, 1895, p.108)'. Here, as Conklin wryly observed, 'was a method which promised to reveal more important secrets of the past than would the unearthing of all the buried monuments of antiquity (Conklin 1934, p. 70)'. What is more, a combination of embryology and developmental psychology could 'reveal not only the animal ancestry of Man, and the line of his descent, but also the method of origin of his mental, social, and ethical faculties', (Conklin, 1934, p. 70).[2]

The Reaction

The theory of recapitulation has been subject to repeated criticism over the years (for example, Sedgwick, 1909; Garstang, 1922; deBeer, 1940). As one critic observed, if the theory were universally valid, then the adult common ancestor of man and apes must have been a pretty odd sort of animal subsisting exclusively upon its mother's milk, and, at an earlier stage of its evolution, attached to its parent by an umbilical cord (W.K. Gregory, quoted in deBeer, 1951, p. 9). Most commonly, critics have pointed to the fact of neoteny (that is, the retention of formerly juvenile characters by adult descendants) as a falsification of the recapitulation doctrine as a general law.

It is important to note that the recapitulation doctrine was not a deduction from the Darwinian theory of evolution at all, even though it was certainly compatible with Darwin's discredited theory of inheritance. It was invoked as an additional but highly convenient principle which promised to solve Darwinism's problem of evidence at a stroke. It alone could help provide some kind of convincing and vivid evidence of gradual evolution.

Darwin certainly appreciated its potential value to his cause, though he mainly drew upon the more widely accepted idea that embryological development can represent the juvenile rather than adult forms of the ancestors. What was perfectly clear to Darwin was that if the embryo can be considered as some kind of picture of its ancestry, it is a picture which must become obscured by natural selection itself (Darwin, 1859, p. 440). The organism cannot remain in business as a living museum but must cope with present conditions (Romanes, 1896, p. 103).

Many characteristics of the developing organism must represent adaptations to current conditions of life, and could not therefore have been present in the adult (or even embryological) form of its ancestors. Darwinian adaptation would obscure the evidence the Darwinians so sorely needed. For this reason, Haeckel (1866) made a distinction between coenogenetic and palingenetic characteristics, between specific adaptations to existing conditions, and those characteristics reflecting its ancestry. But once this distinction is acknowledged, the idea of developmental research as a lazy man's palaeontology is undermined. As Gegenbaur complained:

If we are compelled to admit that coenogenetic characters are intermingled with palingenetic, then we cannot regard ontogeny as a pure source of evidence regarding phyletic relationships. Ontogeny according becomes a field in which an active imagination may have full scope for its dangerous play (Gegenbaur 1889, quoted in Conklin, 1934, p.71).

The point here is not that a limited commitment to the recapitulation theory is illogical as such, but that in its qualified form it was of little help in solving the Darwinists' problem of evidence, since it could no longer sanction the idea of developmental research as an easy method of uncovering the past. As a result, the early developmental psychology, motivated (if not inspired) by evolutionary considerations, was eventually displaced. The mental test movement and, following Thorndike's lead, good, honest experimental toil, seemed to provide a more convincing basis for a psychology eager to impress its scientific peers (Sants, 1980, pp. 22–8). A similar reaction occurred within embryology and morphology, once again in the form of an exclusive concern with contemporary causes, the successful identification of such causes being (wrongly) taken as evidence against the relevance of phylogeny.

If this initial evolutionary basis for developmental psychology was rejected, what exactly had it entailed? As in the case of embryology, it led to an obsession with the developing organism solely as a key to ancestry (Oppenheimer, 1968, p. 321). The essential argument was that the course of ontogeny was nothing but an embarrassing legacy, a vestigial period *of no adaptive significance to the developing organism.* As in comparative psychology, where the eagerness to demonstrate evolutionary continuity often led investigators to ignore the complexities entailed by comparison within the Darwinian scheme, and to revive the old idea of *scala naturae* (Hodos and Campbell, 1969), developmental psychology could serve as a direct source of vivid evidence for evolutionary continuity only as long as it neglected the full implications of Darwinian theory itself.

Alternative Formulations

Within developmental psychology, the predominant reaction to recapitulationism was the rejection of any appeal to evolutionary considerations. A more constructive reaction did occur, however, in attempts to define a more adequate relation between evolution and development. In these alternative formulations, development not only came to be viewed as an active process of becoming, rather than an incidental, atavistic phase, but it was also afforded a central, directive role in evolution itself. This shift in perspective is evident in the following passage from Claparede's *Experimental Pedagogy and the Psychology if the Child*, published in 1911:

It seems to us quite natural that there should be children, and that children should not come into the world 'grown-up'. But in reality there is no logical necessity for this. One can quite well imagine beings springing into the world fully armed, like Minerva, for the combat.... The question is whether childhood is simply a contingent circumstance, secondary and accidental as it were, a necessary evil—as, for example, senility—or whether it has a particular function of its own. In other words, is the child a child *because* he has had no experience, or is he a child *in order that* he may gain experience? (Claparede, 1911, pp. 101-2)

Claparede's answer was that if this period of youth has thus triumphed, it must be because it has 'a certain utility either for the individual or the race' (p.101). But in adopting a functionalist approach to development, Claparede himself saw no contradiction between the theory of recapitulation and the idea of development as an adaptation (Claparede, 1911, pp. 187-8). Archaic structures, he suggested, might not simply reappear from 'force of habit', as it were, but have a positive role, providing a kind of temporary scaffolding in the process of development.

The zoologist Garstang (1922) and later deBeer (1940) were very emphatic, however, in their rejection of the recapitulation idea. First of all, they argued, it was wrong to think of phylogeny, as Haeckel certainly did, as a string of adult ancestral forms of the kind set out in museum cases. To quote Garstang:

The real Phylogeny of Metazoa has never been a direct succession of adult forms, but a succession of ontogenies or life cycles.... Phylogeny [in Haeckel's sense] is the product, the 'record'—not the precedent cause—of successive ontogenies.... Ontogeny does not recapitulate Phylogeny: it creates it (Garstang, 1922, p.82).

Furthermore, within the Mendelian scheme, there is no reason to suppose that a character which evolved after another must maintain that sequence in ontogeny; its rate of development can change through the timing of action of the relevant genes (deBeer,

1951 p. 20).Indeed, as has frequently been argued (*see* Gould, 1977; Bonner 1982), changes in developmental rates might well explain much of evolutionary change.

Considerably earlier, Baldwin had recognised the possibility that development might play a directive role in evolution (Baldwin, 1896, 1902; *see also* Gottlieb, 1979). According to his principle of organic selection, accommodations which occur in development could provide a screen for the evolution of similar congenital adaptations by natural selection: thus acquired characteristics could, as it were, become inherited on a purely Darwinian basis.

Within recent psychology, Piaget was exceptional among developmental theorists in insisting upon the need to examine the possible relations between ontogeny and phylogeny. Although he often gave the impression of invoking the old recapitulation doctrine (for example, Piaget, 1972), his real concern was to identify constraints common to both development and evolution (*see* Gould, 1977, pp. 144–7). In one of his last books *Behaviour and Evolution* (Piaget, 1979), he attempted to define a more intimate relation between the two, drawing upon Baldwin's ideas. Piaget insisted that the evolutionary process could not involve fixation of the new phenotype, but rather its *replacement* by a genetically controlled phenotype. Here, it seems to me, Piaget fell into the rather common error of supposing that the *capacity* to adjust to changing circumstances is itself independent of genetic control (cf. Waddington, 1975, p.30).

Ecological psychology deserves a final comment since it is extremely self-conscious about its proper grounding in evolutionary theory, even if its proponents at times seem keen to talk certain developmental theorists out of a job. The crucial point of the ecological approach is (or should be) that the organism and its environment cannot be considered as independent, as though they existed prior to entering into any kind of co-ordination. A recent text *Direct Perception* by Michaels and Carello (1981) presents some insightful comments concerning development. The authors propose that the role of experience and the role of evolution should be viewed in the same way: 'both lead to a new animal better able to cope with its environment' (Michaels and Carello, 1981, p. 77). They argue that we should no more think of development as the addition of experience to an otherwise unchanged organism than we think of evolution as involving some primordial organism upon which more complex attributes are overlaid. Rather both evolution and experience lead to a *new* organism.

Now, this suggestion is fine as far as it goes, but it fails to explore the full implication of the *dual* relation which is supposed to exist between organism and environment. If a particular organism implies a particular environment, then it is equally the case that a particular environment implies its appropriate organism (Foerster, 1966, p.44).

Although ecological psychology has yet to explore the full implications of the fact that the niche of an organism does not pre-exist but is negotiated (Costall, 1981), the idea is quite familiar within evolutionary theory that it is the context or ecosystem that evolves. The environment evolves with the animal: turf, for example, was the evolving response of vegetation to the evolution of the horse (Bateson, 1973, p.128). The important *developmental* conclusion which needs to be drawn is that not only does the environment in this sense *evolve* with the organism but it must also be considered to *develop* with it as well.[3] Yet this conclusion—to a chapter that has already dwelt upon so much old history—is itself neither original nor new. It is stated perfectly clearly in John Dewey's lectures on psychological and philosophical ethics given in 1898:

The increasing control over the environment [by the organism] is not as if the environment were something there fixed and the organism responded at this point and that, adapting itself by fitting itself in, in a plaster-like way. The psychological or historical fallacy [occurs when] we conceive the environment, which is really the outcome of the process of development, which has gone on developing along with the organism, as if it was something which had been there from the start, and the whole problem has been for the organism to accommodate itself to that set of given surroundings (Dewey, 1976, p. 284).

Notes

1. Haeckel's major scientific writings are not available in English translation, and commentators have often resorted to his more popular presentations. See Bölsche (1906, pp. 188–239) for a sympathetic account of his contribution, and its intellectual and historical context.

2. See Gould (1977) and Sulloway (1979) for excellent discussions of the
    pervasive influence of the recapitulation theory in the history of psychology.
3. Compare the following:

Most stimuli acquire control because of their place in contingencies of
reinforcement. As the contingencies become more complex, they shape and
maintain more complex behavior. It is the environment that develops, not a
mental or cognitive possession (Skinner, 1977, p.2).

Since [the] environment has been transformed in conjunction with the
formation of the phenotype, there is nothing surprising about the fact that
the new mutations selected by the modified internal environment 'mimic'
this phenotype (Piaget, 1979, p.19).

References

Baldwin, J.M. (1896), 'A new factor in evolution', *American Naturalist, 30*, pp.
    441–51, pp.536–54.
Baldwin, J.M. (1902), *Development and Evolution*, New York, Macmillan.
Bateson, G. (1973), *Ecology of Mind*, London, Paladin.
Bolsche, W. (1906), *Haeckel: His Life and Work*, London T. Fisher & Unwin.
Bonner, J.T. (ed.) (1982), *Evolution and Development*, New York,
    Springer-Verlag.
Bryan, W.L. (1896), 'Review of James Sully's *Studies of Childhood*', *Psychological
    Review, 3*, pp. 432–33.
Claparede, E. (1911), 'Experimental pedagogy and the psychology of the child'
    (trans. M. Louch and H. Holman), London, Edward Arnold.
Conklin, E.S. (1934), 'Embryology and evolution', in F. Mason (ed.), *Creation by
    Evolution*, London, Duckwork, pp. 62–80.
Costall, A.P. (1981), 'On how so much information controls so much behaviour',
    in G. Butterworth (ed.), *Infancy and Epistemology*, Brighton, Harvester Press,
    pp. 30–51.
Darwin, C. (1859), *Origin of Species*, (1st ed.), London, John Murray.
Darwin, C. (1901), *Descent of Man* (new ed.), London, John Murray.
Darwin, F. (ed.) (1887a), *Life and Letters of Charles Darwin*, Vol. 2., London, John
    Murray.
Darwin, F. (ed.), (1887b), *Life and letters of Charles Darwin*, Vol 3, London, John
    Murray.
deBeer, G.R. (1940), *Embryos and Ancestors*, Oxford, Oxford University Press.
deBeer, G.R. (1951), *Embryos and Ancestors*, (2nd ed.), Oxford, Oxford
    University Press.
Dewey, J. (1976), *Lectures on Psychological and Political Ethics: 1898* (ed.
    D.F. Koch), New York, Hafner Press.
Flugel, J.C., (1951), *A Hundred Years of Psychology* (2nd ed.), London, Duckworth,
Foerster, H. von (1966), 'From stimulus to symbol: the economy of biological

computation', in G. Kepes (ed.), *Sign, Image and Symbol*, London, Studio Vista, pp. 42–61.

Garstang, E. (1922), 'The theory of recapitulation: a critical re-statement of the biogenetic law', *Journal of the Linnean Society, Zoology, 35*, pp. 81–101.

Gould, S.J. (1977), *Ontogeny and Phylogeny*, Cambridge, Mass, Belknap Press of Harvard University Press.

Gottlieb, G. (1979), 'Comparative psychology and ethology', in E. Hearst (ed.), *The First Century of Experimental Psychology*, Hillsdale, NJ, Lawrence Erlbaum, pp. 147–73.

Hodos, W. and C.B.G. Campbell (1969), 'Scala Naturae: why there is no theory in comparative psychology', *Psychological Review, 76*, pp. 337–50.

Kellog, V.L. (1907), *Darwinism Today*, London, George Bell.

Lubbock, J.L. (1895), 'On the origin and metamorphoses of insects'. London, Macmillan.

Michaels, C. and C. Carello (1981) *Direct Perception*, Englewood Cliffs, Prentice-Hall.

Oppenheimer, J.M. (1967), *Essays in the History of Embryology and Biology*, Cambridge, Mass, MIT Press.

Piaget, J. (1972), *The principles of Genetic Epistemology*, London, Routledge & Kegan Paul.

Piaget, J. (1979), *Behaviour and Evolution*, London, Routledge & Kegan Paul.

Provine, W.B. (1971), *The Origins of Theoretical Population Genetics*, Chicago, University of Chicago Press.

Romanes, G.J. (1888) *Mental evolution in man*. London, Kegan Paul, Trench and Co.

Romanes, G.J. (1896), *Darwin and After Darwin*, Vol 1: *The Darwinian theory* (2nd ed.), Chicago, Open Court.

Russell, J. (1978), *The Acquisition of Knowledge*, London, Macmillan.

Sants, J. (1980), 'The child in psychology', in J. Sants (ed.), *Developmental Psychology and Society*, London, Macmillan, pp. 15–45.

Secord, J.A. (1981), 'Nature's fancy: Charles Darwin and the breeding of pigeons'. *ISIS*, 72(262), 163–85.

Sedgwick, A. (1909), 'The influence of Darwin on the study of animal embryology', in A.C. Seward (ed.), *Darwin and Modern Science*, Cambridge, Cambridge University Press, pp. 171–84.

Skinner, B.F. (1977), 'Why I am not a cognitive psychologist', *Behaviourism, 5(2)*, 1–10.

Sulloway, F.J. (1979), *Freud, biologist of the mind*, London, Burnett Books.

Waddington, C.H. (1975), *The Evolution of an Evolutionist*, Edinburgh, Edinburgh University Press.

PART II

GENETIC EPISTEMOLOGY AND BIOLOGY

4   Constructional Biology

BRIAN C. GOODWIN

The Disappearance of the Organism in Neo-Darwinism

Piaget's remarks about evolution being 'the results, as the simplistic doctrine in fashion would have it, of numerous chance events sorted out by later selections' (Piaget, 1971) are reminiscent of Driesch's (1914) comment that 'Darwinism explained how by throwing stones one could build houses of a typical style'. Both of these eminent and influential scientist-philosophers were reacting to the conceptual impoverishment which biology suffered in the second half of the nineteenth century as a result of the adoption of a purely historical and contingent view of biological process, of history without structure. What is rather remarkable is that this limited and limiting viewpoint has persisted for so long in biology, resulting in the virtual disappearance of the organism as a structural entity, when other closely related subjects such as linguistics and anthropology have undergone transformation to more balanced sciences in which a perfectly legitimate empiricism, which stresses diversity of appearances and contingencies, is combined with rationalist theories of language and of mind. Piaget and Driesch both deplored the absence of a rationalist theory of the organism from biology, and they argued strenuously in favour of a non-reductionist (in the material sense) or a structuralist approach to the problem of biological form and its generative origins, although they each arrived at rather different conceptual schemes to achieve this.

The reason why biology has remained so long without a theory of the organism is not, I believe, because of Darwin's theory of natural selection, although this was the focus of attack by Driesch and Piaget. On its own, ths functionalist view of stability and change in the morphology and behaviour of plants and animals is in no sense incompatible with a belief in organisms as entities which obey distinctive principles of order and hence which undergo constrained transformation, despite Darwin's antipathy to such a rationalist conception. Darwinism may consistently be seen as a theory which can account for the origin of diversity of form and behaviour in the biological realm; but it does not, and cannot, account for the systematic regularity which is observed in the evolutionary record in the form of invariant structures defining the typical forms to which Driesch referred. Regularity and diversity can, however, be understood as two aspects of a single process, theme and variation, transformations which preserves invariance, and one might have anticipated in biology as in other subjects, a balanced development in which function and form are adequately accounted for in terms of history and structure, empiricist and rationalist constructs combining to give a comprehensive account of biological process.

What seems to have delayed this development is the theory which saved Darwinism from self-contradiction by providing a categorically non-Lamarckist theory of inheritance, while at the same time presenting what appeared (and to many, still appears) to be a satisfactory causal account of both embryogenesis and evolution. This truly brilliant conceptual scheme, developed by August Weismann in the 1880s, introduced into biology a radically dualist conception of the organism in terms of a generative and immortal germ plasm and a transient, mortal somatoplasm which was effectively the adult organism. In Weismann's description, the germ plasm is a 'highly complex structure' which has 'the power of developing into a complex organism' (Weismann, 1885). This material,which he surmised to be located in the cell nucleus, was also the vehicle of inheritance so that 'The essence of heredity is the transmission of a nuclear substance of specific structure' (Weismann, 1885) This germ plasm was assumed to be made up of a number of particulate units each of which stood in a specific causal relation to a particular part of the organism. There is thus, in this scheme, a direct causal connection between hereditary units and all aspects of adult morphology and behaviour.

With the (re)discovery of Mendel's laws, the identification of chromosomes and their behaviour during meiosis, and the development of the gene concept, Wiesmann's germ plasm must have seemed one of the most prophetic constructs ever to have been developed in biology. It is scarcely surprising, then, that the twentieth-century biological imagination has been hypnotised by a view of organic process which focusses on the development of diversity in terms of a set of atomic causal elements undergoing random variation within the organism, and historical, contingent forces outside the organism which select appropriate variants. The discoveries of molecular biology during the past two decades seem to have vindicated this view thoroughly, so that Weismann's germ plasm with its 'power of developing into a complex organism' is now described in terms of a 'genetic programme' which determines when and where different molecules are produced in cells within the developing organism.

Clearly the organism as an entity structured by distinctive principles of order and organisation had disappeared, and the biological realm becomes one of irreducible complexity in which each individual is a law unto itself, shaped by the historical events which have designed its 'genetic programme' and the environmental forces which have acted upon it during its development. This is a biology dominated by the evolutionary paradigm (Webster and Goodwin, 1982). It has been dramatically successful in accounting for the appearance of diversity, both the variety of species generated in evolution and the variety of molecules produced during development. But can evolution be reduced to variation and selection, and can development be reduced to molecular differentiation? I shall now argue that neither is true. This will then lead to a different view of evolution, which is in basic agreement with what I understand to be Piaget's constructional or constructionist biology, though with a shift of emphasis. The resulting approach to biological problems has close parallels to those which are generally described as cognitivist in psychology, revealing their relationship to the general research programme of genetic epistemology.

Phenocopy and Genocopy

We have seen that Weismann described a clear and unambiguous causal relationship between his particular units of inheritance and the details of adult form: each character in the adult is determined in a direct manner by a specific hereditary determinant. Weismann suggested that, during the course of embryonic development, the total set of determinants in the fertilised egg is partitioned to different cells, each cell receiving those determinants which specify its final differentiated state within the adult body. According to such a scheme, if at any stage of development a cell is isolated from the others in an embryo, then it can behave only in accordance with the limited set of determinants it has in it; that is, the cell will show what is known as 'mosaic' behaviour, developing into that bit of the embryo which it was destined to become by its causal determinants.

Driesch's experiment with the sea urchin, in which the first two cells (blastomeres) were separated and each developed into a complete pluteus larva (the free-swimming stage of the sea urchin), destroyed Wiesmann's theory and reminded biologists that causal relationships in developing organisms are more subtle than a simple partitioning of (Humean) bundles of atomic hereditary causes. However, such is the attraction of atomism that one can see the whole of the twentieth-century biology as a persistent attempt to rescue Weismann's simple and elegant scheme from unwanted complications. The mystification that has resulted from this is impressive. A great variety of linguistic and metaphorical devices has been used to save the atomistic picture of organisms, the current fashion being to conceal the area of difficulty by using the metaphor of a computer programme. Thus it is claimed that the genes of an organism contain a set of instructions or algorithms which not only specify the primary sequence of proteins, but also, by virtue of the specific patterns of interactions that occur between these proteins, define the whole of the developmental process including morphogenesis.

Monod (1972) describes this genetic determinism in the following way: 'And to the extent that all the structures and performances of organisms result from the structures and activities of the proteins composing them, one must regard the total organism as the ultimate epigenetic expression of the genetic message itself.' One might be tempted to regard such atomism as a result of Monod's prefessional training, since he was initially a chemist. However, developmental biologists say the same thing: 'A theory of development would effectively enable one to compute the adult organism from the genetic information in the egg' (Wolpert and Lewis, 1975). The reasoning behind these statements is unfortunately as flawed as the claim that cookery books bake cakes, for reasons which we shall now examine.

The phenomenon of the phenocopy is a useful point at which to start our analysis. It was discovered in the 1930s that the morphological abnormalities correlated with the presence of certain genetic mutations in the fruit fly *Drosophila*, could be mimicked or copied by exposing developing embryos, at particular stages in their development, to an environmental stimulus (Goldschmidt, 1935). These stimuli include exposure to elevated temperatures, ether, X-rays, nicotine, boric acic, and so on, a number of which are clearly non-specific. However, the morphological abnormalities produced are not either random or non-specific; they fall into the same categories of characteristic perturbation as genetic mutations which affect organismic form. Thus environmental perturbations whose 'information content' is low, and hence which have low specificity, have the same causal status as genetic perturbations. If one uses the metaphor of a programme directing development, one finds that the phenocopy phenomenon is not explicable. This is because, if a specific mistake is made in a programme such as consistently replacing one symbol by another, which may be regarded as the analogue of a mutation, then the likelihood of this being duplicated by a mistake resulting from a malfunction caused by, say, transient overheating of the computer, is vanishingly small. The two categories of perturbation are radically different in this case, unlike the situation in the developing organism. We are thus led to the conclusion that genes are not specific causes of morphology in Weismann's sense of carrying sufficient information to specify form, since their role can be duplicated by non-specific perturbations. Rather, both genes and environmental stimuli are acting upon a self-organising morphogenetic process, classically referred to as a morphogenetic field, and it is the (limited) set of possible responses of this field which is responsible for the phenocopy phenomena. Thus genes (or rather, gene products) can act as 'evocators' of specific responses in the field, which we may technically describe as a process of stabilising one of the possible solutions of the field equations which then determines the morphology, and environmental perturbations do the same.

This language can provide an exact description of morphogenesis and how it is influenced by internal (for example, genetic) and external influences. The developing organism is to be understood as a field (or a set of primary, secondary, and tertiary fields with defined spatial boundaries within the embryo) whose solutions define the potential set of morphologies which it can realise. Morphogenesis consists of a well-defined sequence of field solutions, some of which are stabilised by specific gene products, but many of which arise from processes intrinsic to the field which establish a sequence of 'boundary values' for successive solutions in a self-organising manner (for example, an ordered set of bifurcations arising from particular non-linearities characteristic of the process). An example of the latter is the well-defined geometrical sequence of cell division planes which is observed in holoblastic cleavage, the earliest stage of morphogenesis in many species or organism. A formal field of description of the process has been given (Goodwin and Trainor, 1980), and a more complete theory in terms of visco-elastic field equations, incorporating some of the molecular detail underlying the process, is being studied. A visco-elastic field model of the next stage of morphogenesis, known as gastrulation, has been developed by Oster *et al.* (1980).

Other examples of field descriptions of morphogenesis can be found in the work of Gierer and Meinhardt (1972) and of Flench, Bryant and Bryant (1976). The latter is exceptional in providing a set of generative rules for limb regeneration in urodeles (tailed amphibia) and insects which doesn't mention genes, molecules, or cells; that is, there are non-trivial properties of morphogenetic fields which are independent of molecular and cellular composition, and are also invariant over large taxonomic classes such as Arthropods and Vertebrates. Finding out their relationships and expressing them in terms of field equations and generative rules is a difficult and demanding research programme. But what is quite clear is that a detailed knowledge of the 'genetic programme', which specifies which molecules are made when and where in the developing embryo, will not provide a solution to the question why organisms take the forms they do any more than the knowledge that a liquid is made of H_2O provides a solution to why it flows with spiral motion down a drain; or that knowledge of the composition of a cake and the sequence of mixing operations is sufficient to make it. A great deal of specific knowledge is taken for granted.

The causal equivalence of internal (including genetic) and

external stimuli on morphogenesis, each acting as stabilisers or selectors of specific field solutions, means that the relationship works equally in either direction. Thus, it is possible to observe an environmental perturbation producing an abnormal morphology first, and then to discover a mutant gene which mimics or copies this perturbation; or to observe the mutant first and discover a phenocopying agent later. The former relationship can then be called a 'genocopy' of the environmentally induced abnormal morphology. Piaget's view of the phenocopy phenomenon seems to have been largely dictated by what he saw as the cognitive parallel.

Children presented with a particular environment (for example, a given volume of water plus vessels of different capacity, objects of the same shape but different size) are capable, at certain stages of their psychological development, of 'internalising' aspects of the external environment so that they can make cognitive 'copies' of external event-patterns; that is, they can generate predictive models, correctly anticipating the results of certain operations (for example, pouring water from a vessel of one shape to another of equal capacity but different shape). The learning process, according to Piaget, starts overtly with 'tentative trials' wherein the child explores the consequences of particular actions on the environment and then involves the gradual consolidation of a coordinated, structured, and appropriate behaviour pattern from which the internal model is developed by a process of abstraction involving the progressive dissociation of form (universal) from content (particulars). The role of the environment in this process is seen by Piaget as primary: 'If it were not for the multiple problems raised by the environment or the outside world, both organism and subject would remain conservatively oriented and incapable of new invention' (Piaget, 1980, p.79). This, I believe, is the key to his whole approach to the relationship between biology and cognition, and it is also the source of what I see as some of the difficulties in which he gets involved. He regards learning as problem-solving, the environment as 'something to be overcome', the evolutionary process as the 'conquest of the environment'. It is from this that his quasi-Lamarckism derives, for he wishes to see organisms doing more than simply being filtered by adaptive necessity (natural selection); he considers that they conquer their environments by a positive response to the challenge with which they are confronted. Thus he spends much of his time describing possible mechanisms whereby adaptive states induced in organisms by the environment give rise to genetic changes which stabilise these states so that the phenotypic 'norm of reaction' of the new genotype copies the state which had previously been reached only in response to a particular environmental stimulus. Piaget is at pains to emphasise that in his scheme the environmental stimuli in no sense instruct or inform the organism of the appropriate genetic change to make in order to achieve the adapted state in the absence of external influence. What the organism experiences, he claims, is a state of internal 'disequilibrium' resulting from the stress of developmental (in the embryological sense) and physiological adaption to an environment with which the organism is not genetically equilibrated. The examples which Piaget (1980) uses come from his own work on variations in the pitch of the spiral helix in the shells of various snail species in response to varying environments and differing genotypes, and on the change in the size, leaf shape, and chlorophyll content of Mediterranean species of the plant *Sedum*, again as a result of both genetic and environmental changes. His studies involve some genetic analysis, but certainly not enough to establish a convincing empirical case for his interpretation of the means whereby genetic adaptation arises. Therefore we must remain within the domain of plausible speculation about the mechanisms which are operating.

There seems now no doubt that Lamarckist-type heredity mechanisms occur in organisms. A well-established instance of the inheritance of acquired phenotypic characters is provided by studies on the unicellular ciliate protozoan *Paramecium* reported by Sonneborn (1970). For the case of multicellular higher organisms, there is now the work of Gorczynski and Steele (1980) on the inheritance of acquired immunological states in mice. Piaget, however, does not wish to go this far. He claims only that stress or disequilibrium results in an increase in the frequency of spontaneous genetic mutations or recombination, from which appropriate ones can be selected by the usual neo-Darwinian mechanisms. This is certainly not an implausible suggestion, but I know of no direct evidence for such a process of 'channelled genetic variation'. Piaget sees this as 'directly comparable with what is thought of on the level of conduct, as groping by trial and error. Both share in the element of chance, but also in a general orientation directed by the need to re-establish equilibrium.' And it is of course by analogy with the cognitive process that he is led to the postulate in the biological case. The question that arises is whether he actually needs such a mechanism to establish his major objective, the parallel between cognition and evolution. I shall now argue that, with an articulated structuralist conception of the organism and of evolution, the parallel may be clearly drawn independently of arguments concerning details of mechanism, which are largely irrelevant to the case.

Cognition and Evolution

The cognitive process described by Piaget as a groping by trial and error for 'successful' operations under the stimulus of a specific environment is surely only one of the ways in which children generate useful, coordinated behaviour patterns from which the formal elements are later abstracted to give internal logical structures of thought. Another process which must be involved is the spontaneous internal reorganisation of elements from the store of memory and habit to generate new patterns of behaviour which demand a new environment, and this will then be either discovered, or created if the appropriate environment can be realised. There is no doubt that such reorganisations of established conceptual elements occur in a great deal of mathematical and scientific thought; and assuming the continuity between this and the earlier, less abstract cognitive processes of child development which Piaget constantly stresses, we must assume that not only are children stimulated to produce appropriate operative schemes by specific environments, but that they also spontaneously create new schemes of behaviour for which appropriate environments are then realised if possible. In the first instance there is a 'copying of an exogenous formation by an endogenous one', which Piaget calls phenocopying in the broad sense, in the second, there is the discovery or creation of an exogenous formation which 'copies' an endogenous one, a process which Piaget does not consider.

If we now translate these into biological terms, then we see that appropriate (genetically adapted) organisms can be generated by either a response to a new environmental challenge, a hereditary state arising by some means and resulting in an appropriate organismic form for that environment; or spontaneous reorganisations within the hereditary constraints can occur, procucing organisms with new morphologies and behaviour patterns which must then either discover or create appropriate environments. According to our earlier analysis, the equivalence between external and internal contingencies acting upon organisms as self-organising structures means that there is no theoretical difficulty in understanding how an external stimulus, producing an adaptive modification of biological form, can be replaced by an internal, heritable constraint, a process which Waddington called genetic assimilation; and clearly, spontaneous variations of inherited constraints can produce organisms of modified form which may then discover or create appropriate environments, as Waddington (1957) and others have emphasised. This second process includes the neo-Darwinist mechanisms of spontaneous mutation and genetic recombination as sources of internal variation in some of the inherited constraints or particulars (those deriving from the genes), but the generation of new organismic forms from this internal change is now understood in structuralist terms as a process which follows invariant laws of biological form (for example, field equations of particular type), so that only specific types of order or morphology can emerge, others being excluded. Natural selection then acts with more or less intensity on these forms, playing no generative role whatsoever and simply acting as an *a posteriori* filter on the autonomously generated organisms. Because neo-Darwinism does not have a theory of organisms as self-organising entities, simply assuming that they can be described by the set of sufficient atomic causes which are located in their genomes (wrongly, as argued above and elsewhere—Webster and Goodwin, 1982), organisms become irreducibly complex systems whose properties derive entirely from the contingencies or particulars defined by their genomes (plus, of course, the principles of physics and chemistry which are assumed in molecular biology). The biological realm is therefore, within the current theory, rationally unintelligible: organisms are the sediments of contingencies which have passed the survival test. Hence Piaget's caustic remarks about evolution being 'the result, as the simplistic doctrine in fashion would have it, of numerous chance events sorted out by later selections'.

However, abandoning this simplistic neo-Darwinist doctrine and adopting a structuralist view of organisms need not entail abandoning chance events or natural selection as aspects of the evolutionary process. What it does require is inserting the organism, the generator of biological order in accordance with universal generative laws of form, between chance or contingency, whether external or internal, and selection as the stability test of the generated form. In the context of a structuralist biology, this testing is extremely trivial from the point of view of understanding what organisms are; that is, it contributes very little to rendering the biological realm intelligible, since it only tells us that stable forms persist, a statement with no specifically biological content. Piaget's error, I believe, was his view that to correct the more preposterous claim of neo-Darwinism that it provides an explanation for the origin of reproducing organisms of specific form (species), it is necessary to reject the mechanisms proposed within the theory as a source of organismic variation.

My view is that structuralist biology is catholic as regards the nature and origin of the perturbations acting upon organisms, so that details of mechanism are not important in initiating the case for a parallel between evolution and cognition. What *is* fundamental is to establish that one is dealing, in both the cognitive and the biological realms, with an exploration by self-organising entities or structures (subjects and organisms) of the range of possibilities open to them, among which are those forms or patterns appropriate to actual or realisable circumstances. The perturbations which drive this exploratory process may come from within or without, but what always emerges is order or pattern characteristic of the structure, arising from the invariant relationships which define its laws of organisation and transformation. I have articulated this argument in the biological domain, but I simply assume an equivalent position to be valid for cognitive processes. At the basic level of a structuralist analysis then, there is a clear basis for genetic epistemology which does not depend upon the rather restrictive assumptions imposed by Piaget in his conception of cognition and evolution as essentially problem-solving processes initiated by environmental challenges which are to be conquered or overcome. Rather, these processes are characterised by the property of transforming randomness and contingency, whatever its source and nature, into appropriate order, whether cognitive or biological.

Structuralist Biology and 'Progressive' Evolution

Structuralist biology attempts to render the biological realm intelligible by giving an account of how organisms are possible in a manner similar to the way in which Newtonian mechanics gives an account of how celestial motion is possible. Each actual organism is seen as an instance of the possible, a specific manifestation from a potential set defined by the invariants which characterise the entity 'organism'.

A field description of organisms is an example of a structuralist analysis which seeks to describe organismic morphology and its transformations in terms of the solutions of particular field equations which define the potential set of developing forms in a particular developmental process such as, for example, embryonic cleavage (Goodwin and Trainor, 1980). As far as morphology is concerned, organisms are then seen as transformations of one another within the group defined by changes in initial and boundary conditions of the field solutions describing their form, which delimits the set of possible generative processes available to organisms as structures of a particular type. From this perspective, the major problem of biology is to articulate and develop a theory of biological organisation in these terms, attempting to define the transformation rules which underlie embryonic development and the relationship between different species as generative transformations of one another (that is, transformations via developmental trajectories). Behaviour also needs to be understood in these terms, extending to the rules of transformation which underlie developmental cognitive processes.

Despite the occurrence of time as a parameter in these sequential transformations, the emphasis of such a study is more on the logic of organised transformational relations, with time as a derivative dimension. Such principles elucidated within the study of biological form would provide a rational taxonomy of organisms, like a periodic table of the elements, showing the relationships between different forms and the transformational process required to go from one to another, the biological equivalent of transmutation of the elements. In an evolutionary cosmology such as the Big Bang theory, the actual order of appearance of the elements is something one may speculate about in relation to various contingencies such as the rate of cooling of the nascent radiant cosmos, local temperature fluctuations, density of mass-energy, and so on, but it is not a question which physicists regard as primary to an understanding of the nature of the physical domain. Similarly, a structuralist biology does not regard the actual evolutionary sequence, the order of manifestation of biological forms, as of primary biological concern. Those evolutionary trees which have dominated so much of biological thought and discussion in consequence of Darwin's geneological preoccupations, now constructed at the level of protein and DNA sequences, are largely irrelevant to an understanding of organisms as transformational structures. This is because the evolutionary record merely presents us with a sample of those forms which are possible and have survived long enough for evidence of their existence to have become apparent to us. Historical reconstruction cannot solve any problems about the nature of the entities with which biology is faced and the organisational principles which are embodied in organisms. However, the comparative study of organismic morphology and development is of the greatest importance in this task, for it is here that the empirical regularities emerge which provide the evidence that the biological realm is one of systematic order, as the pre-Darwinian rational morphologists had established (see Russell, 1916). Darwin's failure to understand their arguments led to the greatest error of Darwinism and neo-Darwinism, which is to describe biological process at the organismic level in terms of pure contingencies, organisms being seen as the manifestations not of rational order together with contingencies, but solely in terms of contingent evolutionary histories. Having attempted to correct this error by articulating the line of argument which Piaget himself used, and having made somewhat clearer why the structure of organisms makes possible a process in which internal contingencies replace external patterns of influence, it is now necessary to see if the argument can be extended to include Piaget's proposition that there is in fact a temporal asymmetry in evolution which involves the progressive internalisation of environmental patterns.

Although Piaget correctly dismissed neo-Darwinism as

'simplistic' in relation to problems of biological form and organisation, he was in agreement with some global deductions which many neo-Darwinists have drawn from the evolutionary evidence. This is that there is a general direction of organismic change, a transformational asymmetry, which makes it legitimate to talk about evolution as 'progressive', or at least directional. This is described by Piaget (1980) as 'an increasing control of the environment by the organism and a gradual accompanying growth in the independence of the organism from environmental influence'. We have seen that this process of 'phenocopying in the broad sense', wherein an exogenous formation is replaced by an endogenous one, is the general principle which Piaget considers to be at work both in evolution and in cognitive development, both of which he describes in terms of a concept of equilibration which necessarily involves an internalisation of the environment. We have also seen that within a structuralist view of organisms such an internalisation is compatible with a theory of organisms as self-organising, transforming wholes, under the principle of the equivalence of categories of external and internal contingencies. But this is not to be thought of as the environment imposing a heritable structure on the organism, which is the Lamarckist view; nor is it simply the selection of 'adapted' phenotypes from an infinitely variable set of possibilities, a set without internal constraints or order, which is the neo-Darwinist view. Rather, it implies an asymmetry in the transformations which define the process of exploration of the rationally delimited set of possibilities available to organisms as structures. Such a principle goes beyond a purely structuralist description of evolution as an undirected creative adventure wherein the range of realisable possibilities of organismic forms is probed and tested. It involves a 'law' akin in its asymmetry properties to the second law of thermodynamics, which defines a general direction of spontaneous change for physical processes compatible with, but supplementary to, the organisational principles describing the structure of 'matter' such as those embodied in the periodic table of the elements, the quantum mechanical principles of atomic state transformations.

The Internal Model Principle

The principle that organisms internalise exogeneous formations is, as we have seen, an additional proposal which must be studied independently, being superordinate over a rationalist treatment of the generative principles of biological form and transformation, which is largely synchronic in its emphasis. A formalisation of this concept within the context of abstract automaton and regulator theory has been provided by Wonham (1976) in a very interesting paper which treats the linear case rigorously and suggests an extension to the non-linear domain of regulation and control. He defines an 'Internal Model Principle' in the following manner: 'A regulator for which both internal stability and output regulation are structurally stable properties must utilize feedback of the regulated variable and incorporate in the feedback loop a suitably reduplicated model of the dynamic structure of the exogenous signals which the regulator is required to process.' As far as the purely regulative aspects of organisms are concerned, it is thus sufficient to interpret Piaget's concept of biological equilibration to mean 'the development of structurally stable regulation within the organism in response to changes in environmental variables' to provide a more formalised description of a principle of evolutionary asymmetry (assuming the plausibility of an extension of the internal model principle to the non-linear domain, as Wonham suggests). So long as organisms undergo a process of heritable parametric variation, due to either internal or external perturbation, then the criterion of structural stability of dynamic behaviour within the organism and in its interaction with the environment will drive organisms to states of order involving regulatory feedback loops which make organisms independent of the environment by virtue of possessing internal copies of external patterns of variation. This implies a highly dynamic mode of physiological adaption which is perhaps most obviously revealed in the remarkable range of physiological rhythms possessed by organisms, with periodicities matching those of the environment. The best known of these are the tidal (about 12 hr) feeding rhythms of littoral marine organisms, the ubiquitous circadian (about 24 hr) rhythms, and the lunar (28 day) and annual (one-year) rhythms. It is not at all obvious from a purely homeostatic perspective why, for example, homeotherms (organisms which control their body temperature) show a circadian rhythm of body temperature. But in relation to an internal model principle this is what one could expect of terrestrial forms exposed to a daily external temperature cycle. Marine forms which did not experience such an environmental temperature periodicity never become homeothermic although they have developed circadian cycles which respond to, compensate for, and anticipate (that is, are 'adapted to') the daily light-dark cycle to which they are exposed.

Because 'system' and 'environment' are defined relative to one another, and organisms may be seen, in control terms, as hierarchies of such relationships (Goodwin, 1976; Allwright and Wonham, 1980), a great deal of the complexity of physiological dynamics can be comprehended within the principle. Thus rhythmic activity in, say the mitotic activity of the epidermis, which does not seem to be related directly to any external environmental periodicity, may be understood as the internalisation by this tissue of the periodic environment to which it is exposed (that is, the blood). However, rhythmic activity is only one of the environmental patterns which may be internalised, since by the principle any defined pattern (including a stochastic one) must be internalised if structural stability is to be satisfied.

Although the emphasis of the above discussion is on physiological control, the internal model principle should be capable of extension to the morphological domain. Thus for an aquatic organism, the process of internalising its environment means not only developing circadian physiological rhythms, but also adopting a morphology which 'internalises' hydrodynamic properties of the aqueous environment such as stream flow and incompressibility. These are reflected in the shape of protozoa and their mechanisms of movement by means of cilia and flagella, in the body patterns of fishes and the propulsive movements of their fins, and so on. However, it must be remembered that from a structuralist perspective, all such 'adapted' aspects or organisms must be consistent with universal constraints on biological form, which are primary to the very being of organisms as living entities. Thus although some degree of adaptation to the external environment is clearly a requirement for all species of organism which persist, the internal model principle shifts the emphasis from mere survival to a notion of harmonisation or dialectical stability between organisms and their environments, and between different levels of order within organisms.

The transformational asymmetry which is provided by an internal model principle is a weak constraint in relation to the actual pathways of change which may be followed by evolving organisms, for there is nothing in the principle prescribing which environmental variation is to be internalised first, which second, and so on. Furthermore, there is no necessary relationship between the internalisation of exogenous patterns and the development of complexity in organisms. This is because organisms which have reduplicated certain environmental patterns may then move into environments where these variations are absent, and lose them again (since an appropriate internalisation of no change or constancy is to have an unregulated internal variable which is constant because it is never perturbed). This is what appears to have happened to some parasites which lost various physiological functions on taking up residence in the interior of other organisms which perform the regulatory activities for them; or the loss of sight in cave-dwelling crayfish. On the other hand, we have already seen that terrestrial forms which become homeothermic and then returned to the relatively constant temperature of the oceans, such as whales and porpoises, have not subsequently lost their capacity for temperature regulation and one can see good reasons for this connected with internal 'system-environment' relations. These considerations show that the implications of an internal model principle need extensive working out before any clear consequences can be deduced regarding detailed patterns of evolutionary change.

Because there is no time unit associated with the asymmetry of the internal model principle, nothing can be deduced about rate of organismic transformation, only about direction. Thus it is perfectly possible for particular forms such as the horseshoe crab or the plant, *Equisetum*, to persist for very long periods of time, although of course persistence requires independent explanation. Again, small- and large-scale transformations of form in the evolutionary sequence can both occur, since parametric variation within structured entities can bring about small or large alterations of form depending on whether or not the parameter is near a critical point for the morphology or the dynamic. Thus micro- and macro-evolutionary change are equally plausible. Some degree of adaption of the resulting forms to the external environment continues to be a necessary condition for survival, but as more and more of the environment becomes internalised, this criterion becomes progressively less important in relation to the requirement of structural stability of dynamic and morphological relationships within organisms.

I have said practically nothing about the application of these ideas to the domain of behaviour, and more generally to cognition. Wonham (1976) has himself indicated the relevance of his principle to this area. My final objective is to draw together some ideas which approach the problems addressed by genetic epistemology from a slightly different veiwpoint, while preserving the overall objective of uniting the biological and the cognitive realms within a single conceptual framework while at the same time avoiding any simplistic reduction of the one to the other.

Cognitive Biology

Knowledge acquisition as the development of internal models or representations of aspects of the external world was used as the basic concept underlying an approach to developmental and evolutionary processes which I called 'cognitive biology' (Goodwin, 1976, 1977, 1978). I was led to this by the arguments of both Piaget and Chomsky, as well as by the conviction that there is a rational continuity of order between nature and mind despite a discontinuity in relation to degrees of freedom and constraint. One of the reasons for choosing the term 'cognitive biology' was deliberately to reduce the emphasis which tends to be placed upon knowledge, rationality, creativity, and intelligence as the prerogatives of the human realm and to extend these to biological processes in a much more general sense. At the same time, it is important not to lose sight of what I believe is the true discontinuity between the biological and the human levels, which relates to symbolism and morality; that is, to freedom and responsibility (or, more appropriately, response-ability). The continuity which I stressed was based upon the view that organisms and minds make use of descriptions or models of their environments in order to reach more stable states of relationship with them, and that the development of such models is a creative process. Within the context of a more clearly developed structuralist view of organisms as elaborated here and elsewhere (Webster and Goodwin, 1982), and with the notion of transformational asymmetry provided by the internal model principle, the case for a 'cognitive view of biological process' (Goodwin, 1978) is, I feel, considerably strengthened (see also Boden, 1979, 1980).

One of the objectives of this cognitive viewpoint in biology relates directly to the problem of human freedom and responsibility. The search for common principles of wholeness, order, and transformation in the biological and the cognitive realms has the goal not of reducing one level of order to another and so gaining some intellectual or technological control over it, but of discovering the rational elements of a common creative enterprise between nature and culture and a direction of transformation which could suggest what it might mean to become aligned with a process involving the emergence of greater and greater freedom to engage in appropriate response. The view of organisms and their evolution developed in this paper derives from both empirical evidence and a belief in the intelligibility of the biological realm, and describes biological process as one in which aspects of the 'plan of creation', of reality, are revealed in the structure and transformations of organisms, just as they are revealed in the motion of the planets. This contrasts with the neo-Darwinian view that organisms reveal only historical contingencies and historical continuity, not rational principles of order and transformation, a view which is consistent only with existentialist notions of freedom in which anything can happen and there is absolute creative liberty. One can only feel gratitude to Monod (1972) for demonstrating so clearly in his book *Chance and Necessity* that the existentialist metaphysic is the appropriate philosophical context for neo-Darwinist biology where, at the level of organisms, anything can happen and just does, with the proviso that only the survivors survive. Organisms and their evolution are then fundamentally unintelligible, conforming only to principles of opportunism. Alignment with such a view of biology and culture, as encouraged by Social Darwinism in all its forms including contemporary sociobiology, leads to a social order in which survival depends upon fitness to compete successfully, the educational process having the task of selecting the 'fittest' and equipping them with the requisite tools for survival in a competitive environment. The human condition is then basically unintelligible (meaningless) and without direction or purpose.

The alternative view of biological and cognitive reality developed in this essay is that the creative transformations of evolution and development (biological and cognitive) are constrained by law and proceed in accordance with generative rules; and that there is an asymmetry which defines the general direction of biological and cognitive processes in terms of the concept of progresssive internalisation of environmental patterns of variation. In the cognitive realm, this involves the development of symbolic representations and structures, which have an important degree of freedom over the internal models operative in organisms insofar as symbolic descriptions bring the realm of the potential or the virtual into a kind of manifestation which is independent of biological form or behaviour, although they can influence these. It is the dramatic increase in creative potential which distinguishes the activities of mind from those of organic nature. However, this freedom is still constrained by law, in a structuralist conception; and Piaget's suggestion is that it is also constrained by the asymmetry of internalising the environment. This environment includes other cultures. Internalising other cultures is possible only if one is liberated from one's own sufficiently to perceive their validity and creative potential, to see them as transformational equivalents of one's own cultural heritage. Thus to be aligned with the scientific vision of a rationally ordered, creatively transforming biological and cultural continuity is to stress transformational equivalence and unity,while recognising difference and dissimilarity, universals as well as particulars, law and intelligibility as well as contingency and accident. And the internalisation process requires the continuous transformation of cognitive structures in the generation of a responsive intelligence which acts appropriately because it aligns itself with the creative order of reality.

References

Allwright, D.J. and W.M. Wonham (1980), 'Time scales in stably nested hierarchical control systems'. *Large Scale Systems, 1*, pp. 229–44.

Boden, M.A. (1979), *Piaget*, Fontana Modern Masters.

Boden, M.A. (1981), 'The case for a cognitive biology', in *'Minds and Mechanisms', Philosophical, Psychological and Computational Models*, Brighton, Harvester Press.

Driesch, H. (1914), *The History and Theory of Vitalism*, London, Macmillan.

French, V., P.J. Bryant and S.V. Bryant (1976), 'Pattern regulation in epimorphic fields, *Science, 193*, pp. 969–81.

Gierer, A. and H. Meinhardt (1972), 'A theory of biological pattern formation', *Kybernetik, 12*, pp. 30–9.

Goldschmidt, R.B. (1935), 'Gen und Ausseneigenschaft (Unter-suchengen an Drosophila I, II)', *Zeits. indukt. Abst. u. Vererb.*, 69, pp. 38–131.

Goldschmidt, R.B. (1935), *Theoretical Genetics*, Berkeley and LA, U. Calif. Press.

Goodwin, B.C. (1976), *Analytical Physiology of Cells and Developing Organisms*, London, Academic Press.

Goodwin, B.C. (1977), 'Cognitive biology', *Comm. and Cog.*, 10, pp. 87–91.

Goodwin, B.C. (1978), 'A cognitive view of biological process', *J. Soc. Biol. Struct.*, *1*, pp. 117–25.

Goodwin, B.C. (1981a), 'A structuralist view of biological origins', in *The Study of Time*, Vol. IV, NY, Springer-Verlag.

Goodwin, B.C. (1981b), 'Developing organisms as self-organising fields', in F.E. Yates (ed.), *Self-Organising Systems: The Emergence of Order*, Oxford, Pergamon.

Goodwin, B.C. and L.E.H. Trainor (1980), 'A field description of the cleavage process in embryogenesis', *J. Theoret. Biol.*, 85, pp. 757–70.

Gorczynski, R.M. and E.J. Steele (1980), 'Inheritance of acquired immunological tolerance to foreign histo-compatibility antigens in mice', *Proc. Nat. Acad. Sci.*, 77, pp. 2871–75.

Landauer, D. (1958), 'On phenocopies, their developmental physiology and genetic meaning', *Am. Nat.*, 92, pp. 201–13.

Monod, J. (1972), *Chance and Necessity*, London, Collins.

Oster, G., G. Odell and P. Alberch (1980), 'Mechanics, morphogenesis, and evolution', *Lectures on Mathematics in the Life Sciences*, 13, pp. 165–255.

Piaget, J. (1971), *Structuralism*, London, Routledge & Kegan Paul.

Piaget, J. (1980), *Adaptation and Intelligence: Organic Selection and Phenocopy*, University of Chicago Press.

Russell, E. (1916), *Form and Function*, London, Murray.

Sonneborn, T.M. (1970), 'Gene action in development', *Proc. Roy. Soc. Lond. B.*, 176, pp. 347–66.

Waddington, C.H. (1957), *The Strategy of the Genes*, London, Allen & Unwin.

Webster, G.C. and B.C. Goodwin (1982), 'The Origin of Species: A structuralist approach, *J. Soc. Biol. Struct.*, 5, pp. 15–47.

Weismann, A. (1885), reprinted in J.A. Moore (ed.) (1972) *Readings in Heredity and Development*, NY, Oxford University Press.

Wolpert, L. (1971), 'Positional information and pattern formation', *Curr. Top. Dev. Biol.*, 6, pp. 183–224.

Wolpert, L. and J. Lewis (1975), 'Towards a theory of development', *Fed. Proc.*, 34, pp. 14–20.

Wonham, W.M. (1976), 'Towards an abstract model principle', IEEE Trans. SMC-6, pp. 735–40.

5 The Implications of a Structural Biology for Developmental Psychology (Commentary on Goodwin)

MICHAEL SCAIFE

Looking back over the history of much of developmental psychology, certainly the English-Language part of it, one can detect a fairly uncritical borrowing of concepts from mainstream biology. For much of the time psychologists seem to have construed such borrowing as unproblematic appearing to believe that the terms employed within biological theory, such as adaptation, selection and variation, were to be taken as transparent and pliable, easily extended to any ontogenetic problem. I start from the assumption that, while it is an open question as to how we might see psychological processes as latent in biological ones, there are principles of development that are specific to human ontogenesis. Thus I feel the need for the utmost care in the way we formulate assertions of continuity between psychological and 'more basic' biological processes. We must avoid, for instance, the sort of reductionism where ontogenetic change is 'explained' by the (naive) postulation of adaptations that anticipate future events. This, of course, pushes the developmental question back into biology. Implicitly, at least, it assumes that biological theory is a unified entity capable of providing answers to psychogenetic problems. Are such assumptions justified?

Biological theory offers two models of change, differing in time scale and in terms of the kind of explanation offered. These are the phylogenetic and the embryogenetic accounts. Indeed, as Cassirer (1950) pointed out, there is a long history within biology itself of the difficulties of reconciling these two approaches. Recent developments, like modern versions of the 'epigenetic' viewpoint, which appear explicitly to comprehend both time scales offer some hope in this direction but even so it appears that there is little agreement on what the precise form of an integrated model should be. For psychologists one difficulty this creates lies in the lack of a readily identifiable conceptual entity, within biological theory, which might be seen as underpinning the 'subject' in psychology. If we look at evolutionary theory we find that the genes, the species and the organism all serve as basic units in one account or another. At the risk of coining a rather clumsy term we can say that we find it hard to locate a 'phylogenetic subject' from which lessons can readily be drawn for ontogenesis.

The difficulty that psychology has, or should have, in using biological concepts is given fresh emphasis by Brian Goodwin's work since, at the very least, it points to deep problems in the area of biological theory itself. His programme is based upon a criticism of the prevailing spirit of genetic reductionism, the primacy of the genome as the 'explanation' for biological processes, allied to the rejection of contingency as the sole factor in the historical derivation of forms. He puts forward a synchronic characterisation of the coherent organism, to be described in terms of 'transformations' and 'fields'. He also outlines a diachronic tendency towards increased stability by the construction of (internal) representations of possible external circumstances, the Internal Model Principle. Goodwin argues for or asserts three important equivalences: (1) the equivalence of developmental processes in all organisms (the theory of the general organism); (2) the equivalence of cognitive and biological processes; and (3) the equivalence of internal and external sources of perturbation in leading to change. How far does Goodwin's approach facilitate the going between biology and psychology? More specifically, how far does his account, as he claims, offer support for Piaget's genetic viewpoint?

Many of the problems that arise in evaluating this work stem, at least in part, from the relative novelty of a theory of the general organism, that is, all organisms, where the endeavour is the characterisation of globally possible generative processes. Thus there are problems in seeing the nature of the relationship between the conceptual entities 'organism' and 'species', both terms that Goodwin employs. The organism is typified as a 'self-organising, transforming field'. As I understand it, the specific form that is manifested depends upon local factors, for example gene products, such as proteins, constraining the solutions to, something like, a field equation. But what would it mean for an organism to be 'tranformed' into something with a different set of possibilities? What, specifically, has been altered and, even more important, what has been conserved? Different forms are linked by a 'developmental trajectory', an idea that is familiar enough from Waddington's work, but in the present case one wonders as to the method of inheritance and stabilisation of such transformations as do occur. The useful aspect of the idea of species, even if regarded as a set of local populations, is that of a commonly held potential for development in certain ways. What then do members of a species have in common with each other? Is it a defined level of complexity in terms of their organisation, perhaps in terms of their degree of internalisation of the environment? Or should we seek an answer in the degree of specificity of the set of field equations or, rather, envisage a common set of constraints on possible field solutions?

Goodwin sees the organism as 'the embodiment of fields'. This leads one to ask about the specificity of fields—what size 'unit' of morphogenesis is governed by a field in its own right? We have, for example, 'limb fields' but not 'digit fields' in vertebrate limb development. Are there theoretical, as opposed to empirical, reasons for this? How modular is field organisation? Are there families of fields perhaps, related in some manner that one could link to different levels of order? These questions are relevant to understanding how interdependent the fields are and thus to getting some idea of what model(s) of organisation are potentially applicable in describing the developing organism.

One beauty of Goodwin's approach is that he can, in theory, point to the way in which a small number of changes in the field leads to quite large morphogenetic changes. The range of variation in the vertebrate limb is a particularly good example of this. This has implications for our view of taxonomy and the lessons to be drawn from the taxonomic enterprise itself. In rejecting phylogenetic trees as largely irrelevant Goodwin argues instead for a 'rational taxonomy' of organisms, which he has likened to the periodic table of the elements. Perhaps due to ignorance, I find this analogy a little confusing since it seems that this table is of a 'transformational process', to use Goodwin's term, that not only represents a space of possible, stable 'systems' (that is elements) but also can be taken to show how system properties are altered by the additive accumulation of identical parts. Particular elements are not connected by developmental trajectories in any immediately relevant sense.

The use of the analogy hints at a further question. This is how

Goodwin intends there to be something radically different about the organismic as opposed to the physical world? For Piaget the idea of 'organisation', the defining function of life, served to divide the two. One presumes that Goodwin's use of 'self-organising' serves the same purpose but he parts company with Piaget on the nature of this process, specifically on the roles of the environment and the organism as forces for change. Goodwin takes Piaget to task for seeing this relationship as solely one where the organism, in being 'threatened' by the environment, constructs evermore elaborate internal representations of the world. Goodwin agrees that this does occur, that endogenous copies result from exogenous factors, but wishes to assert equally the possibility of spontaneous, endogenous restructuring prior to appropriate external events. He thus seems to add a further possibility to Piaget's account of how new forms arise. The particular form of Goodwin's argument here is worth a look for he goes from the fact of spontaneous restructuring within a cognitive system, that is, reorganisation of schemes of behaviour, to the biological case. This rather unusual direction of reasoning asserts, rather than argues for, the equivalence of cognitive and biological processes, albeit at a general level.

Goodwin's argument of a strict formal equivalence between internal and external sources of perturbation is to the exclusion of a concern with details of mechanism, a question left for empirical enquiry. Can Goodwin's position support Piaget's? For both authors the idea of increasingly complex internalisation of the environment is found. There is however a distinct difference in the sense in which the continuity between the biological and cognitive is handled. Piaget's (1980) programme was to insist upon the search for 'deep parallels' between the acquisition of knowledge from the senses, analogous to the phenocopy in biology, and the processes of formation of logico-mathematical knowledge. In so doing he noted that a fundamental difference between organic, evolutionary change and cognitive change is that the former cannot become stabilised without adjustment to the environment. Goodwin's scheme does not seem to recognise this distinction explicitly. This is unsurprising since, for Piaget, the impetus for development is due to the organism's status as an 'open' system, thus liable to disturbance which it seeks to minimise by closure. (We are not concerned here with the important issue of whether

Piaget's system is open only to non-specific perturbations, as he indicates in his account of the phenocopy phenomenon, or to information of a specific kind as well, for example, Wilden (1972)). Goodwin's insistence upon the importance of spontaneous, endogenous restructuring leaves open the question of whether he, too, regards 'closure' as a useful concept in development.

Whether or not one accepts Piaget's theory, it can at least be said that it provides a strong rationale for the development, phylogenetic and ontogenetic, of relatively autonomous cognitive processes. Within Goodwin's version a sense of 'necessity' in development, akin to Piaget's, is absent. What we have instead is a synchronic necessity, similar to that of Cuvier's formulation of the 'laws' of biological structure. The Internal Model Principle, the diachronic principle in Goodwin's account, allows some formalisation of the idea of internalisation. It gives us only a weak directionality to development and, as Goodwin remarks, is not prescriptive in terms of the precise historical sequence of forms that will occur. This argument is not inconsistent with the sychronic part of his theory but, nonetheless, seems to point to problems with the way constraints on the space of possibilities can be specified. Thus he gives the example of animals 'adopting a morphology which internalises hydrodynamic properties of the aqueous environment such as stream flow and incompressibility'. This example, which seems almost paradigmatic for a neo-Darwinist in demonstrating how environments 'shape' organisms, gets the following comment. Goodwin remarks that we should remember that from a structuralist viewpoint, 'all such "adapted" aspects of organisms must be consistent with the universal constraints on biological form which are primary to the very being of organisms as living entities'. However there is nothing in this discussion nor does there seem likely to be any way of knowing what such constraints are except perhaps by inference from the comparative morphology of realised forms. It is important to remember here that the issue is not to say that, for instance, the density of water constrains movement in certain ways but rather to be able, in principle, to give an account of the limitations on forms that will necessarily result. How is the realm of the possible going to be delimited in a manner that is theoretically more systematic than that so scathingly criticised in the case of the neo-Darwinist approach?

A major problem for developmental psychologists, however, is that both Goodwin's and Piaget's organism is an abstracted entity, represented within the theory by formal structures whose relationship to actual, 'real-world' processes and structures is equivocal. To make the familiar point: the kinds of constraints that operate in the construction of the formal model—such as satisfying the needs to constitute a 'group'—may not have any correlates in the world of the organism. The recent tendency in the work of Inhelder and Piaget for example, (1979), now talking of 'procedures', as well as structures, shows the recognition of the need to extend the analysis to the individual, realised case. In one respect Goodwin's insistence on the role of particulars, defining individual solutions from a range of possibilities, seems to allow for hope of a detailed analysis but this seems distant as yet since his primary task is rather the opposite.

But, over and above the question of the remoteness or otherwise of the organism, there is the accusation that such accounts of psychogenesis inappropriately extrapolate the language of biology to a domain where it does not apply: the socialised world of the child. In the case of Piaget the argument is well-enough known to avoid repetition here. Goodwin's programme is too much in its infancy to allow more than a remark that it is sure to encounter this kind of criticism. However in recent years there have been other attempts to employ ideas from embryogenesis in accounts of the infant's social abilities. Of these the work of Trevarthen and his colleagues stands out although it can only be mentioned briefly in the present context. What one finds are sophisticated descriptions of the complexities of prenatal neurogenesis, discussed in terms of a 'plan' for brain development. Infancy is seen as 'a stage', in the same plan for brain development and social competence; as arising by the same mechanisms as control neurogenesis. The essence of this position is to 'build into' the infant, and into the parent, a highly complex set of mechanisms that actually constitute the abilities defining human social life. Thus, to give but one example, we have the postulation that 'the infant possesses an innate capacity for intersubjective behaviour' (Trevarthen, Hubley and Murray, 1981, p.250). The point here is that concepts like 'intersubjectivity', 'person' and 'communication' which psychology ought to be attempting to explain are referred back to biology. Yet biology, even sophisticated embryology, has nothing to say about such things, they belong to a separate realm of explanation. Human embryology is not a special kind of embryology, except in a very limited sense. Human psychogenesis, on the other hand, is quite unique. As Leontiev remarked in this context: 'inherited, innate mechanisms and processes are only the necessary inner (subjective) conditions making their (psychological functions) emergence possible; they do not, however, determine either their composition or their specific quality' (1981, p.296).

In one sense there is of course a continuity of pre-and post-natal growth. But there is also a profound discontinuity. As Bullinger (1981) points out the newborn enters a milieu of novel physical, biological and social properties. We can illustrate this with an example from Leontiev, that of the baby feeding with a spoon. Leontiev argues that the baby's mastering of such a 'specifically human action' proceeds from handling the spoon as 'any other ... natural object', to where, via adult intervention, the movements of the baby's hand 'are radically re-organised ... subordinated to the objective logic of using a spoon' (1981, p.306). The point should be obvious: this 'logic' does not reside in, nor is explained by, neurological programs.

Whatever position one takes on these issues, one can be certain that the arguments for a structuralist biology are important for psychologists. At the very least the theoretical problems posed by Goodwin's work for 'orthodox' biology should be sufficient grounds for avoiding simplistic borrowing of neo-Darwinian mechanisms as explanations for psychogenesis.

References

Bullinger, A. (1981), 'Cognitive elaboration of sensori-motor behaviour', in G. Butterworth (ed.), *Infancy and Epistemology*. Hassocks, Sussex: Harvester Press.

Cassirer, E. (1950) *The Problem of Knowledge*, New Haven: Yale University Press.

Inhelder, B. and J. Piaget (1979), 'Procedures et structures', *Archives de Psychologie*, 47, p.181.

Leontiev, A. (1981), *Problems of the Development of Mind*, Moscow, Progress Publishers.

Piaget, J. (1980), *Adaptation and Intelligence*, University of Chicago Press.
Trevarthen, C., L. Murray and P. Hubley (1981), 'Psychology of infants', in J.A.
    Davis and J. Dobbing (eds.) *Scientific Foundations of Paediatrics*, 2nd edn.
Wilden, A. (1972), *System and Structure*, London, Tavistock.

6 Biology and Cognition: Goodwin and Piaget (Commentary on Goodwin)

JOHN CHURCHER

Dr. Goodwin's project is towards a structuralist, cognitive biology. It would be structuralist in that it would show the double constraint: how actual organisms are instances of possible ones; and how possible organisms are a subset of conceivable ones, a subset constrained by 'laws of form'. It would be cognitive at least in that the relations between biology and cognition would be made clear, but more strongly also (for Goodwin) in that both biology and cognition would be instances of a more abstract domain, of which cognition (rather than biology?) is at once the paradigm. It would be a biology, nevertheless, because it would take living organisms as its specific object.

I want first briefly to examine Goodwin's proposal with respect to the following questions. How does it explain the relations between different domains or levels, such as biology and cognition? How well does it cope with historical time? With the directedness or asymmetry of evolution or ontogenesis? Can it allow a materialist approach to a theory of representation? And does it offer any prospects for understanding the relations between the biological and the social?

We can easily agree that there are *parallels* between biology and cognition, at least as served up by most theories: the subject/object relation parallels the organism/environment relation; self-regulation and negative feedback control appear in some sense in both; and so on. But is this all? Piaget, by making a clear distinction between continuity of function and diversity of structures or levels, asserts a definite priority, both logical and genetic, of biology in relation to cognition, analogous perhaps to Althusser's 'determination in the last instance' in political economy (Piaget, 1953; 1971; Althusser, 1970). Piaget's 'circle of the sciences' does not invalidate this point, since the circle has more than two stations, and biology depends reciprocally on psychology in a different and indirect way. Differences of *level* of functioning

75

are crucial for Piaget, and when this is misunderstood his theory is distorted. He carefully observes, for example, that the infant who shows lack of visuomanual coordination at the sensorimotor level already shows such coordination at the level he calls morphologico-reflex (1957); similarly, the biological phenocopy is one phenomenon, its cognitive equivalent is another (1980).

For Goodwin the continuity is *not* only functional; instead, there is a rational continuity of *order* between nature and mind (which is stronger). But there seems to be no structuralist principle for *contrasting* the cognitive capabilities of an architect, a bee, and the *lac operon* system.

The question of levels is closely related to the theoretical problem of time, and whether development is directed, indeed what is meant by 'development'. 'Organisms are transformations of one another', says Goodwin. A good thing about this slogan is that it reasserts the mutual dependence of concepts of structure and concepts of transformation. Much of developmental psychology assumes that first you must understand the state of a system at time *t1*, then its state at time *t2*, and only afterwards try to theorise the transition between the two states, time being assumed as the independent container dimension within which it all happens. One might argue that the reverse is equally good; that transformations are therefore 'primitive' and states are 'derivative'. But neither view is adequate, for as Piaget insists: there can be no structure without genesis, and no genesis without structure (1980a). How to take this principle seriously is a challenge any developmental theory must face.

If organisms are transformations of one another, they also possess the property of stability, or (more accurately) self-stabilisation. Transformations between organisms must therefore be realised as transformations from one relatively stable system to another, via a region of relative instability. *How* does this happen?

Piaget offers an account in terms of phenocopying, which for him is the reconstruction in the genome of a form first arrived at in the phenotype (1980). This is not due to a Lamarckian 'direct action' of the environment, but to an active search by the genes during epigenesis. The space searched is in effect the space of alternative forms, but the genes are blind to forms as such and only distinguish them as more or less stable, or in Piaget's term 'equilibrated'.

At this point, Goodwin wants both to sidestep Piaget and to go beyond him. There is, he agrees, a principle of internalisation at work, but he doubts whether it can be the one that Piaget offers, because in epigenesis there should be no asymmetry between endogenous and exogenous, which are equivalent because they perturb a self-organising system in a similar manner and hence result in the same form. Instead, progressive internalisation is accounted for separately and much more abstractly, in Goodwin's theory, by Wonham's 'Internal Model Principle' (IMP), which makes the generation of internal models a condition of all successfully self-stabilising structures (Wonham, 1976).

This is where I find a lot of problems with Goodwin's argument. First, as far as I'm aware, the IMP has been generalised only to smooth non-linear systems, whereas it may be precisely the non-smooth non-linearities (for example, catastrophes) with which it needs to cope.

Second, although Goodwin presents them as complementary, I feel there is a tension between the IMP and the principle of equivalence between exogenous and endogenous perturbations. The one describes a system in which the feedback specifies a model, a copy of something; the other implies that the feedback, as in Piaget's theory, specifies merely the degree of disequilibrium.

Third, I suspect that my unease stems (if not from misunderstanding) from a deeper problem with the whole notion of 'internal' and 'external'. It is one of the commonest metaphors in psychology, and multiply ambiguous. The spatial (topological) metaphor gets confused with an epistemological one, and 'internal' means 'unknown' or 'invisible', and 'external' means 'known' or 'visible'. Again something can be internal in the sense that it has become internalised (Vygotsky, 1978; Piaget, 1949); or in the sense that it has not yet become externalised, being 'latent' or 'virtual' as Goodwin (problematically) calls the infinity of yet unrealised forms.

The contradictions of the spatial metaphor are nicely revealed in the indispensable phrase 'internal environment', whereby the organism or the subject is doubly internal, sandwiched between two 'environments', one 'external' the other 'internal'. And, of course, what is internal to one thing can be external to another, which is important in thinking about (for example) Piaget's account of coordination by reciprocal assimilation. (In Wonham's terms the 'exosystem' may itself be a 'plant').

It would be easy at this point, but unhelpful, to make pious noises about the general inadequacy of our habitual epistemology, its assumption of a constitutive subject, and so on. More useful, I believe, is to try to work towards a materialist theory of representation, as Chris Sinha (Chapter 12, below) is trying to do, in which to say that knowledge copies reality is to say that reality copies—that is, represents—reality; that representation is not primarily a process of 'internalisation'; not least because it does not take place only inside the head, or 'inside' anything. And for the same reason, representation cannot be regarded as primarily 'externalisation' either; that is, it is not just a process of 'expression' (Althusser and Balibar, 1970).

Now at one level Goodwin is taking a clear stand against any notions of organisms as expressive totalities, as mere expressions of their genotypes. But perhaps by regarding the domain of possible organisms as 'latent' or 'virtual', as somehow pre-existing as forms waiting to be discovered by the 'creative adventure' of evolution, he is adopting a theory of one grand expressive totality. And this illustrates a second tension I detect in Goodwin's paper, between *discovery* or revelation, and *construction*, as sources of novelty. Piaget insists a thousand times, if he says it once, that new forms are genuinely *constructed*; and if they then have a necessary character, this is not because they are innate *a priori* but rather because necessity is a property of certain kinds of constructions, namely, operational ones. (Piaget's discussion of 'pseudoempirical abstraction', 1980b, chap. 7, is relevant here.)

If we then ask what it means to talk about a genuine construction' (how you would recognise one if you came across it), we can approach the last question in relation to which I would like to evaluate Goodwin's project—what prospects does it offer the development of what Denise Riley has called 'socialised biology'? In her 1978 article, Riley remarks that attempts within developmental psychology to theorise 'socialisation', involve the jamming together of radically incompatible ontologies. We are not the results of adding together biological and social factors in any sense of the phrase 'adding together'. Rather, biology for us is always 'lived-out' in various specific forms, as individual men, women, who are healthy, sick, young, old and so on, which are all categories of experience and culture, as well as biology. I think both Piaget and Goodwin are aware of struggling with at least part of this problem, because they both recognise the peculiar status of the body as both object and subject of experience. And the process of representing your body by, as it were, rationally reconstructing it 'in your head' is certainly part of growing up, or of surviving an average day. But there is much more to it than that, and we should not be seduced by the charm of any pure rationalism, structuralist or otherwise. Intelligibility and rationality are not the same thing, as Freud (1900) and our own lives should by now have convinced us. Since we are not merely organisms, nor merely persons, but children, women, men and so on, we need to ask: what has a structuralist cognitive biology to offer that will help us understand, for example, age or sexual difference and the several ways we 'live out' our lives and our human sexual dimorphism through endless representations of them?

References

Althusser, L. and E. Balibar (1970), *Reading Capital*, London, New Left Books.

Freud, S. (1900), *The Interpretation of Dreams*, London, Hogarth, 1953.

Piaget, J. (1949), 'Le problème neurologique de l'interiorisation des actions en operations reversibles', *Arch. Psychol. Geneve*, 32(128), pp. 241–58.

Piaget, J. (1953), *The Origin of Intelligence in the Child*, London, Routledge & Kegan Paul.

Piaget, J. (1957), *Logique et Equilibre*, Paris, Presses Universitaires de France.

Piaget, J. (1971), *Biology and Knowledge*, Edinburgh University Press.

Piaget, J. (1980), *Six Psychological Studies*, Brighton, Harvester Press.

Piaget, J. (1980b), *Adaptation and Intelligence: Organic Selection and Phenocopy*, Chicago, University of Chicago Press.

Riley, N. (1978), 'Developmental psychology, biology and marxism', *Ideology and Consciousness* 4, pp. 73–92.

Vygotsky, L.S. (1978), *Mind in Society*, Cambridge, Mass. and London, Harvard University Press.

Wonham, W.M. (1976), 'Towards an abstract internal model principle', *IEEE Transactions*, SMC-6(11), pp. 735–40.

PART III

THE PHYLOGENY OF CONCEPTUAL DEVELOPMENT

7 Higher Intelligence as Adaptation for Social and Technological Strategies in Early *Homo Sapiens*

SUE TAYLOR PARKER

The majority of people agree that *Homo sapiens* is the most intelligent species, and that intelligence has been an important element in the evolutionary success of our lineage. In this paper, I will try to explain just how intelligent we are, that is, how various behaviours can be ranked as more or less intelligent, and how we came to be so intelligent.

Any attempt to trace the evolution of intelligence in our ancestors must begin with a description of different degrees of intelligence and their characteristic manifestations. Such an explication should allow us to distinguish the levels of intelligence involved for example in using a stick to rake in an object, or a stone to open a hard-shelled fruit, making an Oldowan stone tool, aiming a missile at a target, inventing a launcher for a missile, making an abstract rule, inventing a measurement system.[1] Many arguments concerning the adaptive significance of primate and hominid intelligence have omitted this critical step, relying instead on an intuitive sense of which activities imply more or less intelligence.

Intuitive criteria are not only unreliable but unnecessary because Piagetian stages of intellectual development in human children provide a standard for diagnosing the relative complexity of various activities and achievements in human and nonhuman primates (Jolly 1972; Parker 1977; Chevalier-Skolnikoff, 1977), and for reconstructing the relative complexity implied by the design of particular tools in the archaeological record (Wynn 1979; Parker and Gibson, 1979).

Application of the Piagetian framework in studies of the behaviour and development of monkeys and apes has revealed that prosimians, old world monkeys, great apes and humans constitute a series of grade levels of intellectual abilities corresponding to the sequence of stages of intellectual development in human infants and children: our closest relatives, the great apes, display the

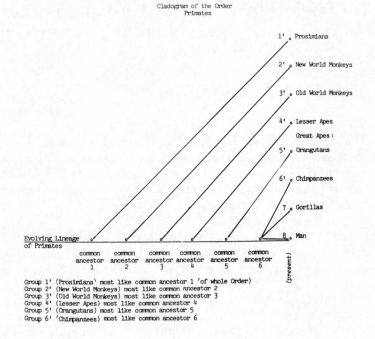

Cladogram of the Order
Primates

Group 1' (Prosimians) most like common ancestor 1 (of whole Order)
Group 2' (New World Monkeys) most like common ancestor 2
Group 3' (Old World Monkeys) most like common ancestor 3
Group 4' (Lesser Apes) most like common ancestor 4
Group 5' (Orangutans) most like common ancestor 5
Group 6' (Chimpanzees) most like common ancestor 6

Figure 7.1

Cladogram of the order primates.

highest level of intellectual development observed in nonhuman primates; the lesser apes, the next highest, the old world monkeys the next, and the prosimians the least.[2]

Comparative data on great ape intellectual development allow us to infer that our common ancestor with living chimpanzees and gorillas displayed the early preoperational intelligence characteristic of all its nonhuman descendents; that the earliest hominids must have displayed at least the same intellectual level; and that descendents of the earliest hominids displayed increasingly higher levels of intellectual achievement. This logical reconstruction is supported by a Piagetian analysis of archeological data which suggests that *Homo habilis* and *Homo erectus*, the lineal descendents of the first hominids, displayed abilities characteristic of human children during the second stage of preoperations and

Table 7.1 *Piaget's model of cognitive development*

Periods of development	Types of logic	Physical	Interpersonal	Intrapersonal
			Domains of cognition	
Sensorimotor period (birth to 2 yrs)	Sensorimotor trial-and-error; experimentation; discovery of new means	Object permanence; externalised time, space, and causality	Deferred imitation of novel schemes; sensorimotor games	First evoked images
Preoperations period Symbolic subperiod (2–4 yrs)	Nonreversible interiorised action schemes, i.e. preconcepts with transductive reasoning	Object identity; topological space; graphic collections	Make-believe games; unilateral respect for authority	Static evoked images
Intuitive subperiod (4–7 yrs)		Incipient projective and Euclidean nongraphic collections		
Concrete operations period (7–12 yrs)	Reversible interiorised action schemes, i.e., true concepts with deductive reasoning about concrete phenomena	Object quantity; true classification with inclusion	Games with rules; concept of winning and losing	Dynamic evoked images
Formal operations period (12 yrs on)	Abstract reasoning, systematic hypothesis formation and testing, inference concerning hidden variables	True measurement	Universal rules based on abstract concept of justice	Anticipatory imagery of events never witnessed
	INRC group 16 binary operations	Proportionality, conservation of weight and volume, understanding of density, equal action and reaction, etc.		

during the first stage of concrete operations (Parker and Gibson 1979, 1982; Wynn, 1979).

These data suggest that the stages of intellectual development in human children today recapitulate the stages of their evolution in a series of common ancestors of more and more closely related primate species. This recapitulationist argument is also supported by the cumulative nature of human intellectual development in which each stage is constructed from the raw materials provided by the preceding stage (Piaget, 1978). It is important to remember in this context that the evolution of new forms can only come about through the adaptive modification of pre-existing forms through mutation and recombination: ontogenetic recapitulation is the product of a series of terminal additions of new structures or stages during the evolution of lineage (Gould, 1977).

The Nature of Higher Intelligence

The highest stage of intellectual development in the Piagetian sequence is formal operational thought (Inhelder and Piaget, 1958; Piaget and Inhelder, 1975, 1977, 1969, 1967; Piaget, Inhelder and Szeminska 1964; Piaget, 1971), which children develop between eleven or twelve and fifteen years of age. This stage develops out of high or late concrete operational thought which is characteristic of children at nine or ten years of age. In this paper, I take 'higher intelligence' to refer both to formal operational thought and to its late concrete operational precursors.

Formal operational thought is characterised by hypothetical-deductive reasoning involving the mental formulation of all possible combinations of elements, and by systematic hypothesis testing. These abilities allow formal operational children to infer the influence of hidden or confounded variables and hence to understand physical concepts such as weight, volume, density, friction, inertia, and the equal and opposite vector of forces. Formal operational reasoning allows children to anticipate the conservation of weight and volume in materials undergoing various transformations they have never witnessed. Formal operational reasoning is analogic because it depends on proportionality (Lunzer, 1965) and is characterised by a sense of the logical necessity of theoretical conclusions, as for example the infinity of possible subdivisions of a line or of possible numbers.

Formal reasoning is also characterised by the invention and application of rules as universal codes of conduct derived from abstract principles of justice (Piaget, 1965). These rules are of two types: regulative rules pertaining to pre-existing activities, and constitutive rules pertaining to entities created by the rules themselves (Searle, 1972). The existence of rules (and indeed the existence of formal reasoning) implies mental manipulation of abstract elements which must be represented by some symbolic device such as language, (Parker, in press).

Inhelder and Piaget (1958) believe that it is possible to represent all the operations involved in formal reasoning in the concept of sixteen binary operations (on two elements taken two at a time as in penny flipping) of propositional logic, and in the concept of the INRC group (I stands for the identity transformation on a set of elements; N stands for the negation transformation; R stands for the correlative transformation (which is the inverse of the reciprocal).)

Formal operational reasoning is preceded by concrete operational reasoning which is characterised by anticipation and reconstruction of transformations of concrete properties of objects, for example, by conservation of length and of the quantity of 'continuous' substances such as fluids and 'discontinuous' substances such as pennies; by classification of concrete objects according to consistent criteria; by systematic seriation of objects; and by an understanding of transitive relations. Although concrete reasoning yields hypotheses, it does not allow their systematic testing through control of more than two variables, and it does not allow the inference of the operation of hidden variables (Karmiloff-Smith and Inhelder, 1975).

Piaget classifies children by stage according to their highest level of reasoning. This is important because all individuals continue to use logic characteristic of lower stages or levels of reasoning. Regression to the logic characteristic of lower stages of development is common in new situations and under stress. Indeed there is some evidence that people recapitulate the stages of intellectual development from sensorimotor through formal operations during the period they confront and solve a novel problem (Karmiloff-Smith and Inhelder, 1975). Formal reasoning is scientific thinking and is hardly characteristic of all adult mental operations.

Replication studies of Piagetian tasks done on non-Western populations have revealed a universal sequence of developmental stages up to and including concrete operations. The universality of formal operational development, however, has been debated because some studies have failed to elecit the highest level of reasoning (Brainerd, 1978; Pulos and Lynn, 1981). Piaget himself once suggested that formal operational reasoning may be dependent on educational experiences which may occur in all societies.[3]

Despite the well-recognised ambiguity surrounding the achievement of this highest developmental stage, it is my contention that formal operational reasoning is universal and characteristic of our species. I base this conclusion on evidence that this form of intelligence is revealed in a number of cultural inventions common to all living people and traceable in the archeological record. In light of this evidence I suggest that the difficulty students have in eliciting formal reasoning can be attributed to their testing procedures. I am confident that an analysis of the logic involved in rule-making and rule manipulation, in architectural construction, measurement, and the invention of and use of technology will yield more insights into human intelligence than the administration of tests, even sophisticated Piagetian tests. In this case as in others, the investigator's grasp of the native language is a vital factor (Kamara and Easley, 1977).

In the following sections of this paper I will analyse the intellectual operations implied in the invention of a selected set of universal cultural practices including kinship terminological systems and their associated rules, and the technologies of blade-core tool, hafted tool, and engine-launched missile production, and fire making. I will combine this analysis with an argument about the adaptive significance of these activities.

Before I proceed with my analysis I should note that the coexistence of less cognitively demanding practices with more demanding ones does not imply the absence of formal reasoning. In diagnosing the cognitive level of a cultural repertoire we will follow the same rule Piaget follows in diagnosing the cognitive level of an individual: we classify it according to the highest level revealed.

I should stress that the higher levels of mental functioning often are involved in the *invention* and *production* of tools and machines than are involved in their use. This is probably obvious to anyone who has learned to drive a car or use a computer. It is equally obvious that the fact that a young child can use a computer certanly does not imply that he could invent one.

The Unique Cultural Achievements of *Homo sapiens*

By about one-third of a million years ago the first members of our species descended from their *Homo erectine* ancestors. A million years earlier, *Homo erectus* had migrated out of Africa into the old world with the aid of such new technologies as cooperative game driving, cooking, and shelter construction, clothing, and a variety of Acheullian tools which were probably based on concrete operational reasoning (Wynn, 1979). The innovations of their descendants include more sophisticated and varied tool technologies, such as hafted tools, and later simple missile-launching machines such as bows and arrows, and social innovations such as ritual burials and later, artistic renderings. The technologies I shall analyse as revealing formal operations are associated with the Upper Paleolithic cultures of anatomically modern *Homo sapiens*, rather than the Mousterian culture of archaic *Homo sapiens*.

Although it is probably impossible to reconstruct the origins of kinship terminologies and their associated rules, we can infer their presence from the occurrence of technologies requiring similar intellectual operations. If early *Homo sapiens* used formal reasoning in their technology, then we can conclude that they probably had and used such terminologies. This reconstruction is consistent with the recapitulation model and with the fact that these creatures displayed a fully modern brain capacity which presumably correlates with the highest level of intelligence.

The Formal Logic of Kinship Terminological Systems and Associated Rules of Exogamy, Residence, and Descent and their Adaptive Functions

Kinship terminologies are universal features of human society. Peoples living at the rudest subsistence levels with the most primitive technologies have terminological systems as elegant and consistent as those of civilised peoples. Each terminological system classifies kin and marriage partners into comprehensive categories based upon generation, sex, affinity (marriage), collaterality, and a few other principles. The basic distinction between different systems lies in who is classified with whom (Fox, 1967).

Our own terminology is only one of many possible classification systems which can be generated from the few principles enumerated above. While we find it natural to classify our father's brother and our mother's brother together under the term uncle, in some other systems the father's brother is called by the same term as the father (presumably because he can play the role of father by marrying his deceased brother's wife, a custom known as the leverite) while the mother's brother is called by a different term. In other systems, such as an ancient Roman's, father's brother and father and mother's brother are all classified differently (Fox, 1967).

One of the major functions of kinship systems is the specification of marriageable and unmarriageable classes, and of descent groups: 'Kinship systems then, can be seen as assortative mating systems... and kin classification as a flexible means of adjusting the categories of marriageable and unmarriageable kin' (Fox, 1967, p. 127).[4]

Kinship groups are the basis for recruiting members of residential, labour, ritual, and fighting units. Residentail units, for example, are often recruited on the basis of matrilineal or patrilineal descent: patrilocal residence being associated with patrilineal descent and matrilocal residence with matrilineal descent (Fox, 1967; Martin, 1974; Evans-Pritchard, 1967). Different residence patterns generate particular patterns of associations and kin investment which are adaptive under different resource distributions and densities and subsistence strategies

The Genetic Relations Underlying Different Kinship Terminologies

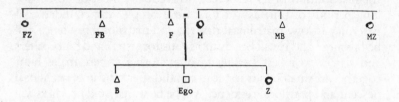

Different kinship terminologies specify different equations between
the same genetic relationships: e.g., in our American terminology
FB = MB (i.e., "uncle,")and MZ = FZ (i.e., "Aunt"); whereas in some
other systems FB ≠ F but MB = F (i.e., father's brother is also
"father", but mother's brother is not); in Rome, on the other hand,
FB ≠ MB ≠ F (i.e., different names were applied to each of these
relationships) (Fox 1967,).

F = father
M = mother
B = brother
Z = sister

Figure 7.2

The genetic relation underlying different kinship terminologies.

(Irons, 1979).

Kinship groups also provide a framework for alliances and
hostilities. This can be seen, for example, among the Nuer whose
territorial units are based on kinship and compose fighting units
from among close kin (Evans-Pritchard, 1967) and among the
Yanomanö who divide their villages on the basis of kinship
(Chagnon, 1979).

In evolutionary terms kinship categories are adaptive because
they 'provide a reservoir of potential recipients of discriminatory
behaviour, in the same way that the categories of "potential
spouse" provide a reservoir of actual mates. Which actual relatives
will be nepotistically or altruistically favoured is another matter
(Fox, 1979, p.143). The actual investment patterns will depend
upon two major factors: the relative reproductive potential of
various candidates of equal relatedness, and their relative potential
for contributing to the actor's reproductive success (Irons, 1979).

The latter factor will depend upon the subsistence mode and on the distribution of its resources: where males must be absent for long periods of time as warriors, for example, and confidence of paternity is low, matrilineal descent and matrilocal residence will be favoured and it will be advantageous for sisters and for brothers and sisters to invest heavily in one another; where males hunt together in small bands for scarce and dispersed game, patrilineal descent and patrilocal residence will be favoured, and brothers will invest heavily in each other.

Rules, including rules of exogamy, residence, and descent, can be viewed as sophisticated devices for making strategic alliances and for gaining scarce resources in the form of parental and other forms of nepotistic investment, as well as food, territory, status, and so on.

It is my contention that the invention and manipulation of kinship terminologies and associated rules of exogamy, descent, residence, and so on, requires formal reasoning, and that such reasoning abilities were selected in part because they facilitated these self-serving inventions. Kinship terminologies apparently involve the following aspects of formal reasoning: (1) the generation of abstract categories and rules which have no existence independent of their invention; (2) universal application of a logically derived rule to (3) an infinity of potential members; (4) the use of analogy.[5]

The Formal Logic of Four Technologies: Core-Blade Tools, Hafted Tools, Missile-Launching Machines, and Fire-Making Machines

Tools and machines increase the efficiency of work and/or make possible otherwise impossible achievements. In other words, they reduce energy expenditure, thereby releasing energy for other tasks. In this respect they are analogous to organic adaptations. Since all animals have a limited amount of energy to expend on the vital activities of reproduction (mating, parental care), maintenance (feeding, sheltering), and defence, any energy-reducing device contributing to these activities will be advantageous to the individuals using them.

Human beings use tools for all their major subsistence activities including shelter construction, transportation, hunting, gathering, horticulture, agriculture, and other forms of domestication, food processing, and so on. They also use many of the same tools in warfare.

Aggressive competition between groups is one of the characteristic features of our species and probably of our family. The rapid increase in brain size (and we presume intelligence) from the time of hominid emergence about four million years ago until about a third of a million years ago may be due in large part to selection pressures of war (Bigelow, 1973). Wars in historic time have been won by superior technology and by the strategic choice of victims (Colvinaux, 1980). It seems likely that these elements have favoured victory as long as war has occurred, and there is evidence for the considerable antiquity of this practice (Bigelow, 1973).

The importance of strategy comes in the appropriate choice of victims, and allies, and in calculations of costs in time, men, travel, equipment, and so on versus the benefit in acquired resources. These strategic calculations also involve speculation about the parallel calculations of potential enemies (*see*, for example, Chagnon, 1977). Strategies of this sort entail hypothetical and combinatory reasoning and attempted control of variables. As I will indicate in the following sections, primitive weapons of warfare, including hafted tools, machine-launched missiles, and fire, are based on formal operational reasoning. This all suggests that higher intelligence was selected by war because it favoured victory through superior technology and strategy.

Hafted Tools

Hafting a tool to a handle was a major technological innovation of *Homo sapiens*. Although hafting is difficult to infer from archeological remains, the prepared-core flakes produced by archaic *Homo sapiens* in Europe (Neanderthal) were probably the earliest hafted tools (Howell, 1968). Microlithic flakes and blades produced by modern *Homo sapiens* in the upper paleolithic were almost certainly hafted (Cole, 1965; Chard, 1975).

The invention and efficient manufacture of hafted tools

apparently involves several aspects of formal reasoning: (1) the analogy between the arm and the handle of the tool; (2) the anticipation of a novel connection between the tool and the handle; (3) the conception of a novel agent of connection (the thong, cement, tongue in groove, and so on) between the two elements; (4) an understanding of the mechanical advantage conferred by the hafting; and (5) systematic experimentation with the materials, shapes, and placement of the elements.

Hafting entails connecting two dissimilar elements in the construction of a new compound entity. It is more complicated than connecting two similar elements: although inserting one stick into the hollow end of another stick to lengthen it may seem impressive (especially when done by a chimpanzee (Kohler, 1927)), it requires only simple topological notions of penetration and enclosure characteristic of early preoperational reasoning in young children and chimpanzees. Simple knot tying is also characteristic of children of this stage (Parker and Gibson, 1979). It is important to note that although knot tying is involved in some types of hafting, its use in this context involves higher mental operations.

Machine-Launched Missiles

Primitive devices of this sort, including the spear thrower, the bow and arrow, and the blow gun, are virtually universal among modern hunter-gatherers. Spear launchers and arrow heads are widely represented in archeological sites associated with modern *Homo sapiens* all over the world and their use is depicted in cave paintings (Chard, 1975). The invention and efficient production of these devices implies the following aspects of formal reasoning: (1) use of hafting; (2) an understanding of the equal and opposite action of forces; (3) an understanding of leverage; (4) an understanding of friction; (5) systematic experimentation with material density, weight distribution, and friction.

Fire-Making Machines

The invention of friction-based fire-making machines such as the fire-plough, the fire-saw and the fire-drill (Mason, 1966) implies the following aspects of formal reasoning: (1) an understanding of friction and its heat-generating effects; (2) the conservation of matter in the transformation of wood into sawdust and of sawdust into smoke and heat; (3) systematic experimentation in the selection and shaping of substances and in the direction of motion.

While it is impossible to reconstruct the origin of fire-making machines, their widespread distribution today combined with archaeological evidence of fire use back into the lower Pleistocene (Gowlett *et al.*, 1981) strongly suggest an ancient history. Of course the use of fire does not automatically imply fire-making machines; many primitive peoples store fire in covered coals, and others create fire through percussion of natural fire-making rocks (Mason, 1966).[6]

(It is fascinating to reflect on the continuity in the nature of weapons of war from the simple torch to nuclear bombs, and from simple bows and arrows to intercontinental ballistic missiles. This continuity suggests to me that the fascination matches, fire crackers, and other explosives hold for young boys may have been shaped by selection for war games.)

The Prepared-Core and the Blade-Core Techniques

The blade-core technique of stone tool production involves preparation of a striking platform on the top of a rock around whose circumference a series of blades can be struck off. This technique apparently involves the following aspects of formal reasoning: (1) anticipatory imagery of a novel transformation; (2) an understanding of equal and opposite action of force; (3) systematic experimentation with the direction of force of the blow.

The blade-core technique involves the conception of a tool whose shape is not implied by the shape of the rock from which it is made, and whose production requires a new level of imagination of possible combinations of sectioning. It is apparently a refinement of the prepared-core tool technique which emerged in the late Acheullean or Early Mousterian tool culture and is well-developed in the Mousterian tool culture associated with archaic *Homo sapiens* (Howells, 1968; Bordes, 1968).

Civilisation and Its Cognitive Contents

Civilisation is characterised by technologies of domestication, metallurgy, architecture, navigation, writing, mathematics, and calendric systems as well as social stratification and specialisation. Virtually all of these technologies and the sociopolitical rules associated with them such as slavery, taxation, tribute, law, and so on, are based on formal operational reasoning.

The invention of domestication and metallurgy, for example, involve hypothesis formation and testing through control of variables. The invention of navigational and calendric systems involve these operations plus systematic measurement. So do taxation and tribute. Architecture involves scaled plans, proportionality, and the use of machines such as the inclined plane, the lever, and the pulley. The invention of mathematics involves the concept of infinity plus the INRC group and the sixteen binary operations.

While these attainments are not universal among living or dead *Homo sapiens*, they apparently arose more or less independently in the Near East, North Africa, India, China, Northern Europe and Mesoamerica under the twin conditions of resource surpluses and heavy population densities. The reasoning abilities common to 'savagery' and civilisation suggest that the attainments of civilisation are simply hypertrophied extensions of pre-existing social and technological inventions. This interpretation is certainly consistent with traditional anthropological arguments for the psychic unity and intellectual equality of mankind (Boas, 1938).[7]

Strategic Object Manipulation: Social and Technological

In the preceding sections I have analysed two applications of higher intelligence: social and technological. In this section I want to emphasise the common function of these two adaptations: each in its own way contributes to differential reproductive success through object manipulation. Technology does this by reducing energy expenditure and garnering otherwise inaccessible resources; social rules do this through social manipulation of competitors in the service of garnering an increased share of scarce resources (Parker, in press). This interpretation of social rules is an extension of the sociobiological concept of communication as a form of social manipulation: social manipulation is advantageous when other individuals are competitors for scarce resources, or are sources of scarce resources (such as parental investment), and/or are potential sources of labour for scarce resources (Dawkins and Krebs, 1978). All these conditions are met in human societies.

In fact, technology also operates in the service of social manipulation: this is true, for example, in warfare. Social and technological object manipulation are means to the same end, and they are based on the same mental operations. The capacity to invent new forms of social and technological object manipulation was favoured by the diversity of resources and resource distribution and densities encountered by a vagal, culture-bearing species.

The emergence of higher intelligence in *Homo sapiens* was associated with entry into a new niche which we can characterise as the niche of *abstract culture* (as opposed to the preceding niche of concrete culture). Entry into a new niche requires physical, ecological, and evolutionary access (Simpson, 1953). In this case evolutionary access to the niche of abstract culture came through terminal addition of formal reasoning onto pre-existing concrete operational reasoning abilities; ecological access through the challenge of a variety of habitats; and physical access came through the geographic mobility conferred by the pre-existing concrete cultural niche.

Postscript

This model for the evolution of higher intelligence is speculative, but I would like to point out that it is logically consistent and within the constraints imposed by evolutionary theory, and that much of it is testable. The interpretations concerning the mental operations entailed in manufacture of various devices could be tested, for example, by interviewing native makers of such devices about the logic involved in their choice of materials and their designs. Similarly, native political leaders could be interviewed concerning the logic involved in their strategies and rules. I am convinced that innovative uses of Piaget's clinical method of interviewing in naturalistic settings will give us the richest data on human cognition.

Notes

1. To satisfy the curious reader, I'll classify these activities in terms of Piaget's stages: the first two imply fifth stage sensorimotor intelligence; the third implies late preoperational intelligence; the fourth implies concrete operational intelligence; and the last three imply formal operational reasoning.
2. Roughly speaking prosimians display stage 1 and 2 sensorimotor intelligence; old world monkeys display stage 4 sensorimotor intelligence with stage 5 object conception; great apes display stage 6 sensorimotor intelligence and symbolic preoperational intelligence (without vocal imitation). One genus of new world monkey the Cebus, displays intellectual abilities comparable to those of great apes (Parker, 1977; Parker and Gibson, 1977; Chevalier-Skolnikoff, 1977; Antinucci *et al.*, 1982; Mathieu *et al.*, 1976).
3. Although it is beyond the scope of this paper to discuss criticisms and replications of Piaget's model, I do want to acknowledge the existence of a vast literature on this subject (see for example Brainerd, 1978; Dasen, 1972; Pulos and Linn, 1981).
4. Marriage systems are of two types: elementary and complex. Elementary systems have positive marriage rules specifying who should be married (for example, cross cousins); complex systems have negative rules specifying who cannot be married (for example, mothers, sisters, aunts). Direct or symmetrical exchange systems are the simplest elementary systems: they stipulate that the men of patrilineal group A give their sisters to the men of patrilineal group B, and that they are given the sisters of group B in exchange. This means that ego marries his mother's brother's daughter who is also his father's sister's daughter, that is, his bilateral 'cross cousin', because his father's sister is married to his mother's brother. The other type of elementary system is the indirect or asymmetrical exchange system which involves several groups and a rule by which men cannot take wives from the group to which they give wives (Fox, 1967).
5. In American kinship terminology, for example, *FZ* and *MZ* are analogous (that is 'aunts'); *FB* and *MB* are analogous (that is, 'uncles'); *FBS, FSS, FBD, FSD, MBS, MSS, MBD, MSD* are analogous (that is, 'cousins').
6. The early use of fire is puzzling because even the storage and especially the transport of fire may imply formal reasoning in the form of systematic experimentation with flammable materials and methods of storage. Perhaps the 'eternal flame' was an early solution, but it may not have been portable.

7. The argument in a nutshell is this: all human societies display cognitive complexity in some domain; people from primitive cultures master the rules and technology of modern society; cultural climaxes have occurred all over the world in different epochs.

References

Antinucci, F., S. Spinozzi, V. Visalberghi, V. Voltera (1980), 'Cognitive development in a Japanese macaque', presented at VIII International Primatological Conference, Florence.
Bigelow, R. (1973), 'The evolution of cooperation, aggression, and self control', in James Cole and Donald Jenson (eds.), *Nebraska Symposium on Motivation*, 1972, Lincoln, Univ. of Nebraska Press.
Boas, F. (1958), *The Mind of Primitive Man* (rev. ed.), NY, The Free Press.
Bordes, F. (1968), *The Old Stone Age*, World University Library, NY, McGraw-Hill.
Brainerd, C.J. (1978), *Piaget's Theory of Intelligence*, Englewood Cliffs, Prentice Hall.
Chagnon, N. (1977), *Yanomonö: The Fierce People* (2nd rev. ed.), NY, Holt, Rinehard & Winston.
Chagnon, N. (1979), 'Mate competition, favouring close kin, and village fissioning among the Yanomanö Indians', in *Evolutionary Biology and Human Social Behavior*, N.A. Chagnon and William Irons (eds.), NY, Duxbury Press.
Chard, C.S. (1975), *Man in Pre-history* (2nd ed.), NY, McGraw Hill.
Chevalier-Skolnikoff, S. (1977), 'A Piagetian model for describing and comparing socialisation in monkey, ape, and human infants', in S. Chevalier-Skolnikoff and F. Poirier (eds.), *Primate Biosocial Development*, NY, Garland.
Cole, S. (1963), *The Prehistory of East Africa*, NY, Mentor.
Colvinaux, P. (1980), *The Fates of Nations*, NY, Simon & Schuster.
Dasen, P.R. (1972), 'Cross-cultural Piagetian research: a summary', *J. of Cross-Cultural Psychology*, Vol. 3, pp. 23–39.
Dawkins, R. (1976), *The Selfish Gene*, Oxford, Oxford Univ. Press.
Dawkins, R. and J. Krebs (1978), 'Animal signals: information on manipulation?' in J.R. Krebs and N.R. Davies (eds.), *Behavioural Ecology: An Evolutionary Approach*, Oxford, Blackwell Scientific Publications.
Evans-Pritchard, E. (1967), *The Nuer*, Oxford, Oxford Univ. Press.
Fox, Robin (1967), *Kinship and Marriage*, Harmondsworth, Penguin.
Fox, R. (1979), 'Kinship categories as natural categories', in N. Chagnon and W. Irons (eds.) *Evolutionary Biology and Human Social Behavior: An Anthropological Perspective*, NY, Duxbury Press.
Gould, S.J. (1977), *Ontogeny and Phylogeny*, Cambridge, Harvard Univ. Press.
Gowlett, J.A.J., J.W.K. Harris, D. Walton and B.A. Wood (1981), 'Early archeological sites, hominid remains and traces of fire from Chesowanja, Kenya', *Nature* (Nov.) vol. 294, pp. 125–9.
Howell, F.C. (1965), *Early Man*, NY, Time-Life Books.
Inhelder, B. and J. Piaget (1958), *The Growth of Logical Thinking from Childhood*

to *Adolescence*, NY, Basic Books.

Irons, W. (1979), 'Investment and primary social dyads', in N. Chagnon and W. Irons (eds.), *Evolutionary Biology and Human Social Behaviour*, NY, Duxbury Press.

Jolly, A. (1972), *The Evolution of Primate Behavior*, NY, Macmillan.

Karmiloff-Smith, A. and B. Inhelder (1975), 'If you want to get ahead, get a theory', *Cognition* 3 (3), pp. 195–212.

Kamara, A. and J. Easley (1977), 'Is the role of cognitive development uniform across cultures? A methodological critique with new evidence from Theme children', in P. Dasen (ed.), *Piagetian Psychology: Cross-Cultural Contributions*, NY, Gardener Press.

Kohlër, W. (1927), *The Mentality of Apes*, NY, Vintage Books.

Lunzer, E. (1965), 'Problems of formal reasoning in test situations', in Paul Mussen (ed.), *European Research in Cognitive Development*, Monograph of the Society for Research in Child Development.

Martin, K. (1974), 'The foraging adaptation: uniformity or diversity?' *Addison-Wesley Module in Anthropology*, No. 56.

Mason, O. (1966), *The Origins of Inventions* (reprint of 1895 edition), Cambridge MIT Press.

Mathieu, M., M.A. Bouchard, L. Granger and J. Herscovitch (1976), 'Piagetian object permanence in *Cebus capucinus*, *Lagothrica*, and *Pan troglodytes*', *Animal Behaviour*, vol. 24 pp. 585–8.

Parker, S.T. (1977), 'Piaget's sensorimotor period series in an infant macaque: a model for comparing unstereotyped behaviour and intelligence in human and nonhuman primates', in S. Chevalier-Skolnikoff and F. Poirer (eds.), *Primate Biosocial Development*, NY, Garland Press.

Parker, S.T. (in press), 'Language and play as adaptations for social manipulation through rules and requests', in S.K. Ghosh (ed.), *Human Language: Biological Perspectives*, Ghent, E. Story Scientia.

Parker, S.T. and K.R. Gibson (1977), 'Object manipulation, tool use, and sensorimotor intelligence as feeding adaptations in Cebus monkeys and great apes', *J. of Human Evolution*, vol. 6, pp. 625–41.

Parker, S.T. and K.R. Gibson (1979), 'A developmental model for the evolution of language and intelligence in early hominids', *The Behavioral and Brain Sciences*, vol. 2 (2).

Parker, S.T. and K.R. Gibson (1982), 'The importance of theory for reconstructing the evolution of language and intelligence in hominids', A.B. Chiarelli (ed.), in *Advanced Views on Primate Biology*, Proceedings of the 8th Congress of the International Primatological Society, Springer.

Piaget, J. (1965), *The Moral Judgment of the Child*, NY, Fress Press.

Piaget, J. (1969), *The Child's Conception of Time*, NY, Ballantine.

Piaget, J. (1974) *Understanding Causality*, NY, W. Norton.

Piaget, J. (1978), *The Development of Thought*, NY, Viking.

Piaget, J., B. Inhelder and A. Szeminska (1964), *The Child's Conception of Geometry*, NY, Harper & Row.

Piaget, J. and B. Inhelder (1967), *The Child's Conception of Space*, NY, W.W. Norton.

Piaget, J. and B. Inhelder, (1972), *Mental Imagery in the Child*, NY, Basic.

Piaget, J. and B. Inhelder (1974), *The Child's Construction of Quantities: Conservation and Atomism*, London, Routledge & Kegan Paul.

Pulos, S. and M. Linn (1981), 'Generality of the controlling variables scheme in early adolescence', in *Journal of Early Adolescence*, vol. 1 (1).

Searle, J. (1972), 'What is a speech act?', in P.P. Giglioli (ed.), *Language and Social Context*, Baltimore, Penguin.

Simpson, G.G. (1953), *The Major Features of Evolution*, NY, Columbia Univ. Press.

Wynn, T. (1979), 'The intelligence of later Acheullean hominids', *Man*, vol. 14, pp. 371-91.

8 Has the Evolution of Intelligence Stagnated since Neanderthal Man? (Commentary on Parker)

KATHLEEN GIBSON

One major contention of Parker's stimulating manuscript is that Piaget's final stage of intelligence, formal operations, is universal among modern human populations. A second is that this stage of intelligence was already manifest as a species-specific characteristic in the earliest *Homo sapiens*. Archaeological and anatomical evidence indicate, however, that Parker is in error on the second point. Far from reaching a plateau in early *sapiens* forms, intelligence continued to evolve at least to the time of Cro-Magnon man.

Parker's argument for the early emergence of formal operations rests on intelligence considered as a pre-requisite for the use and production of several key technologies. However, three of these, blade-core tools, engine-launched missile devices and fire-making devices, were late temporal acquisitions by comparison with the origin of the species, *Homo sapiens*. The earliest unquestioned representative of our species, Neanderthal Man, dates to 100,000 years ago. Other more controversial *Homo sapiens* finds are dated as early as 250,000 years. By contrast, blade-core tools first appeared in the archaeological record 35,000 years ago, while bows and arrows, spear throwers and fire-making devices were invented only in the last 10,000–15,000 years (Oswalt, 1976; Predeaux, 1973). Consequently, these technologies must be considered irrelevant to the question of the universality of formal operations among modern and archaic *Homo sapiens*.

Thus Parker's argument rests primarily on the necessity of formal operational reasoning processes for the invention, generational transmission and daily use of hafted tools. Her assertion that these reasoning processes are required is based on two assumptions: first, that the combination of tool elements requires these systematic thought processes; and second, that the use of a hafted tool demands an understanding of the theoretical physics which can explain its effectiveness.

Neither contention seems warranted. The first hafted tools (250,000 years ago) consisted of the junction of a stone axe head with a wooden digging stick-spear. By this time both items had been in existence for a million or more years. Their mutual junction into one tool would not have required systematic experimentation with large numbers of variables. Further, once invented, manufacturing techniques would have been transmitted by cultural convention for generations. Little or no further experimentation was necessary.

The assumption that the use of such tools demands an understanding of their physics is even more tenuous. Modern human children manipulate physical causality in games of marbles, baseball, see-saw and water sports, long before they can comprehend in formal operational terms the physical principles embodied in Newton's laws, the mechanisms of a lever or Archimedes principle. There is no reason to believe that earlier hominids could not also have observed and utilised cause-and-effect relationships in the absence of any genuine understanding of physical mechanisms.

Fossil Hominids

Earlier anthropologists sharply distinguished the behaviour of Neanderthal Man (100,000–40,000 years ago) from that of Cro-Magnon (35,000–10,000). The former was pictured as dimwitted, brutish, and uncouth while the latter was considered a noble, intelligent creature. Neanderthal, it was thought, became extinct either through his own dullness and warlikeness or at the hands of Cro-Magnon.

More recently, the probable genetic contributions of the Neanderthals to modern populations have been emphasised. Further, though no one doubts a rather rapid flowering of art and material culture with the advent of Cro-Magnon man (Table 8.1), there are many who would credit Neanderthal with equal intelligence. According to this view, the increasing complexity of tools and other artefacts since Neanderthal times has been based on cultural rather than biological change.

Two recent Piagetian analyses fall within this latter tradition. The first by Wynn (1979) suggests that intelligence reached its

Table 8.1   *Time frame of hominid evolution*

Time (yrs)	Genus/species	Mean brain size (cc)	Major cultural advances
4,000,000–1,000,000	*Australopithecus/ Homo habilis*	400–500	Habitation of savannah; extractive foraging with tools; gathering/hunting adaptation; food sharing; stone tool manufacture
1,500,000–300,000	*Homo erectus*	900–1,000	Habitation of temperate zone; cooperative hunting of big game; fire use/cooking; manufacture of symmetrical stone tools
250,000–40,000	*Homo sapiens* archaic and Neanderthal	1,300	Habitation of subarctic and semi-desert areas; exploitation of herd animals; prepared core tools; hafted tools; care for disabled; burial of dead; religious cults
35,000–	*Homo sapiens*	1,400	Habitation of arctic tundra regions; invasion of rain forest; migration to Australia and to Americas; increased exploitation of herd animals; extensive fishing; blade-core tools; bone, ivory and antler tools; kilns; fire making devices; bows and arrows, spear throwers; fishing weirs, fish hooks, harpoons; cave art

modern level even prior to Neanderthal with *Homo erectus* populations 300,000 or more years ago. Although less explicit on this point, Parker's contention of the presence of formal operational reasoning in the earliest *sapiens* forms is consistent with the interpretation that intellectual evolution has stagnated over the last 100,000–200,000 years.

Niether Wynn nor Parker offer concrete suggestions for distinguishing biological from cultural changes. In particular, they both fail to examine the brain, a critical flaw. For, in fact, major changes in brain size and structure occurred during this period.

This suggests that the cultural changes were, in part, biologically based.

From 4,000,000 to 100,000 years ago, the course of human evolution was one of ever increasing brain size (Figure 8.1). For instance, the average cranial capacity of *Homo erectus*, claimed by Wynn to possess modern intellectual skills, was only three-quarters that of modern man. Although Neanderthal brain size equalled that of modern humans, it differed in critical structural aspects. Specifically, in Neanderthals the anterior frontal and superior parietal association areas were less developed than in modern humans, while the occipital region was larger and more protuberant (Kochetkova, 1978). Overall the brain of Neanderthal man also exhibited less rounding and less flexure than modern human brains. Only by Cro-Magnon times (35,000–10,000 years ago) did the brain achieve both modern shape and size.

These evolutionary changes are consistent with only one interpretation: Modern levels of intelligence were not reached until Cro-Magnon times. Functional analyses of these neurological changes also supports the concept that formal operational reasoning, per se, did not fully develop until the Upper Paleolithic. Further, such analysis predicts behavioural changes throughout the course of hominid evolution which are fully supported by the archaeological record.

Functional Analysis of Neurological Changes

Increased brain size primarily reflects increased neocortical processing capacities. Two primary neocortical functions are of interest in this context: differentiation and construction (Gibson, 1977, 1981a, 1981b). Differentiation involves the ability to break whole percepts, actions or ideas into their component parts. Construction refers to the reverse—the ability to construct new percepts, actions or ideas from component parts. Construction may be either simultaneous as in the making of a new object or sequential as in the use of several successive action plans to meet a single goal. Construction in humans is hierarchical in that the final constructed idea, action, or object may subsume a number of previously constructed subcomponents. Intelligent construction is mobile. An individual can combine separate elements in varied ways to make varied constructs.

Increased levels of differentiation and mobile constructional processes form the base of each Piaget's successive stages. His last stage, formal operations, requires the ability to mentally process all possible combinations of events. Consequently, it may be seen as the culmination of the mobile constructional process. As a corollary, each of the developing conceptual abilities discussed by Piaget such as classification, mathematics, kinship terminologies, concepts of physical causality, and morality demands increasing differentiation and construction. Elsewhere, it has also been argued that these capacities underlie both language and tool use (Abler, 1981; Gibson, 1981b, Reynolds, 1981).

Certain neocortical areas function for differentiation and construction within specific modalities only (vision, touch, audition, movement). Others such as the frontal and parietal association areas are cross-modal in function. These cross-modal areas mediate complex intellectual as opposed to perceptual constructs. They also vary in processing mode, the frontal lobe specialises in sequential processing mechanisms, the parietal, the simultaneous (Luria, 1966).

Of two areas exhibiting expansion in Cro-Magnon as opposed to Neanderthal man, one, the superior parietal lobe, is specialised for the construction of complex somatosensory images. The other, the anterior frontal lobes, mediates the twin processes of sequential action plans and mental reversibility. For instance, human patients with frontal lobe damage cannot inhibit one idea or action in order to move on to the next. Lack of mental reversibility is also evident in these patients by their inability to view Necker cubes from alternate perspectives. Since reversibility and mental flexibility are hallmarks of the formal operational stage, frontal lobe patients would be expected to manifest a deficit in these reasoning processes.

Interpretation of these data suggest the following model. The large quantum increase in brain size from *Homo erectus* to Neanderthal man was accompanied by a similar increase in overall intelligence which should be reflected by increased general constructional capacities. The specific increases from Neanderthal to Cro-Magnon imply specific effects. Cro-Magnon's tools and other productions should evidence increased tactile sensitivities and kinaesthetic skills. His behaviours should manifest greater advanced planning and greater numbers of sequential steps. In addition, they should exhibit greater mental flexibility and greater advancement in the formal operational process of looking for all possible combinations of events.

These cognitive changes would have been reflected in behavioural changes most of which are not amenable to retrospective analysis. One, however, is—material cultural. Examination of the archaeological record does, in fact, bear out these predictions.

At the *Homo erectus* level tools exceeded those of great apes in manifest constructional capacity, but fell far below that of early *sapiens* forms and Neanderthal Man. Throughout his one million years, *Homo erectus* tools remained few in number and relatively static in form. The culmination of his achievement was the Acheulian hand-axe. This tool did exhibit a preconceived mental form, hence, some advanced constructional planning, a genuine advance over previous tools. Hand-axe manufacture, unlike that of animal tool manufacture, also required the use of a stone tool to make a stone tool. The hand-axe remained, however, a single-component tool formed by removing parts from a single stone. In all, hand axe manufacture was a two-step process. First a stone was shaped in a roughly oval form, then the sides were chipped to form symmetrical straight cutting edges. A total of approximately sixty-five blows with a stone tool were required.

By contrast with *Homo erectus*, Neanderthal man produced a wide diversity of stone tools—over sixty in all—as well as an occasional tool of bone (Constable, 1973). A major advance by early *sapiens* and Neanderthal forms was the constructed tool: a hafted spear composed by the junction of a stone point with a wooden handle.

Neanderthal stone points, by contrast, with the *Homo erectus* hand-axe required four major steps and 110 blows. Addition of the steps involved in producing the handle and junctional mechanism suggest that the Neanderthal hafted tool required anywhere from seven to ten steps for its production. This evidence of increased constructional capacity and variation, coupled with Neanderthal advances in religion, burial of his dead and brain size, suggest a genuine increase in intelligence as compared to *Homo erectus*.

With Cro-Magnon, however, culture flowered. The speed of

cultural change, the diversity of cultural productions and their manifest constructional capacity all increased dramatically during his 25,000 years of existence (Prideaux, 1973). His cultural advancements took us from a hunting and gathering creature to the brink of agriculture and permitted our species expansion into Australia and the New World.

Cro-Magnon was the first to evidence systematic experimentation with a variety of raw materials. As a result he not only made over a hundred varieties of stone tools but also worked extensively with bone, antler, ivory and even somewhat with clay. His tools were highly diversified and differentiated in form and function, consisting not only of hunting and butchering gear but also of a wide variety of complex fishing apparatus (harpoons, leisters, weirs, fish hooks), tools for the harvesting of grain and miscellaneous items such as needles and baked clay receptacles.

Cro-Magnon tools were not only diverse, they evidenced higher constructional capacity than anything that had preceded them. He was the first to make a compound tool consisting of two or more separate elements functioning together, for example, mortar and pestle, bow and arrow, spear and spear-thrower and fire-making devices (Constable, 1973). Another 'first' was his achievement of producing his own constructional materials by the mixing of two or more separate elements, for example, bone and clay.

As would be expected from the expanded frontal lobes, his sequential constructional and planning capacities were especially well advanced. The basic blade-core tool was produced by a nine-step process, further reshaped after production and often joined with a handle. Bone and ivory working required hafted blade tools for splitting of the materials. Prior to splitting, the material required a complex six-step preparatory process. Subsequently, it still needed to be shaped. These processes required considerably expanded sequential constructional capacity as compared to Neanderthal Man.

Finally, of course, Cro-Magnon intellectual capacities were manifested in his diverse. artistic accomplishment and in his apparent representational notation of seasons, phases of the moon and other elements (Marschack, 1972). Considering all of his cultural accomplishments, the speed of cultural change during his tenure and the changes in his brain, it seems clear that Cro-Magnon was brighter than Neanderthal. Formal operations, or at least the last stages of intelligence, were reached only in the last 35,000 years.

Generalisation and Recapitulation

Examination of brain structure supports the hypothesis suggested by Parker and others that overall levels of intelligence can be judged by studying stone tools (Gibson, 1981b). For the neural areas most concerned with higher intellectual constructs and mental flexibility are multimodal in function. A single lesion of the parietal association area in humans for instance, may interfere with tool using ability, language, mathematics and classification abilities (Luria, 1966).

The analysis presented here suggests, however, that when generalising from tool form to tool use as well as to such items as language abilities (Gibson, 1981b), rule-making capacity, kinship terminology and war-making capacity, one must postulate comparable mental constructional levels underlying each behaviour. To do as Parker does, for instance, and postulate compound fire-making tools in *Homo erectus* forms when no other compound tools are known until 10,000–15,000 years ago (Oswalt, 1976; Prideaux, 1973) is to ignore the very usefulness of Piagetian and constructionist techniques. The only valid interpretation of the evidence is that all tool-making or tool-using behaviours, as well as other cognitive capacities, evolved in tandem and manifested simple constructional capacities in *Homo erectus* times and complex ones by Cro-Magnon.

This critique does not, of course, invalidate Parker's contention that the ontogeny of intelligence recapitulates its phylogeny. The assignment of formal operational reasoning to Cro-Magnon rather than earlier hominid forms merely changes its date of emergence. It still remains the last evolving intellectual level.

Actually, analysis of brain structure and function supports the recapitulationist model and effectively negates Gould's neotony model (Parker and Gibson, 1979; Gibson 1981b). Further, it provides a suggestive mechanism for this recapitulation. The recapitulation of intelligence is basically a recapitulation of cortical processing capacities and, hence, of mental constructional ability (Gibson, 1981a).

Natural Selection and the Evolution of Intelligence

Parker theorises that the various aspects of intelligence evolved in response to specific selective agents: early hominid tool use and proto language for extractive foraging (Parker and Gibson, 1979), advanced language and formal operations for rule-making and complex social manipulation (Parker, 1981) and technology and brain size for war. Others, however, have suggested that intelligence is a generalised phenomenon that cannot be attributed to many specialised selective events (Gould, 1979). Indeed, Parker's own attempts to generalise from tool use to other cognitive behaviours seem inconsistent with her attribution of highly specific functions to individual intellectual capacities.

Analysis of brain function suggests that in some instances selection should be specific, in others general. Specific sensory or motor areas would be expected to evolve in response to sensory specific selective pressures. For instance, the expanded superior parietal somatosensory areas of Cro-Magnon are best viewed as an adaptation to advanced tool-making and artistic endeavours, as opposed to rule making and kinship terminology. By contrast, the association areas which mediate higher intelligence possess general functions and are best considered as responses to generalised selective pressures.

Examination of the fossil record suggests that all aspects of intelligence and brain size were, in fact, evolutionary responses to what must be viewed as one basic hominid adaptation. Throughout its course, the hallmark of human evolution has been the invasion of varied and often inhospitable habitats and the intensive exploitation of these habitats for maximum population expansion through cooperative group endeavours. Early hominds invaded the savannah and survived by gathering and sharing food. *Homo erectus* expanded to temperate zones by the cooperative hunting of big game. Neanderthal man was the first to survive in subarctic and semidesert areas. He did so by group hunting of migratory herds and by cooperative efforts that extended to caring for the disabled and the dead. By Cro-Magnon times man was surviving in the Arctic tundra during the cold winter months, had reinvaded tropical rain forests, and expanded our species to nearly all continents. Ever increasing Cro-Magnon technological and artistic sophistication also suggests increasing specialisation and division of labour.

By itself, expanded group cooperative endeavours selected for expanded intelligence. For a division of labour requires the ability to view both subsistence activities and the population as composed of component parts which can be added together to form a wholistic subsistence base. In addition, as cooperative endeavours increased in complexity, the language based capacities for discussing events displaced in time and space would have acquired functional significance (Gibson, 1981b). Rules would have provided for the smooth functioning of group endeavours while kinship systems provided a logical base of the division of labour and resources. These latter abilities, as Parker suggests, would have also played direct roles in the selection for intelligence and language.

Similarly, increasingly difficult subsistence strategies required increased technological capacity. Hominid tool use began as an adaptation for the extraction of embedded foods (Parker and Gibson, 1979). The chopper tools, flakes and hand axes, which characterised hominid technology from 2,500,000 to 300,000 years ago, can be viewed as multipurpose tools effective for the processing of a variety of vegetable foods as well as for the butchering and capture of game. The utilization of fire by *Homo erectus* served both for production of heat in temperate environments, for the driving of game and the cooking of food.

Neanderthal hafted spears are best viewed as weapons of master hunters. Cro-Magnon tools served many resource needs. Fish hooks, weirs and harpoons harvested water food. Bone needles served for the sewing of clothing. Blade-tools were functional in a variety of butchering and cutting activities. Bows and arrows and spear-throwers permitted long-distance hunting of individual game.

Even improved stone tool production methods and the increased utilisation of bone, ivory and antler by Neanderthal and Cro-Magnon can be viewed as adaptations to harsher environments. For these forms increasingly occupied habitats in which stone was in short supply. Prepared core techniques provided much more cutting surface per pound of stone than earlier techniques. An Acheulian hand-axe, for instance, provided eight inches of cutting edge per pound of raw material; a Mousterian point, 40in, and a Cro-Magnon blade-core tool, 40ft (Constable, 1973). Prepared core techniques also would have served to advantage during long hunting trips as, once prepared, the core provided for rapid tool production.

Together all of these cooperative advances selected for intelligence and brain size. Not only is there no need to postulate, as Parker and Bigelow (1969) do, that brain size increases during the 4,000,000–300,000 year period were primary responses to warfare, there is no evidence for it. Nowhere during this time period do we find tools whose primary purpose must be assumed to be warfare. All ancient tools appear to have functioned in daily subsistence techniques. The first weapon possibly to provide primary benefits to war was the bow and arrow, invented only 10,000–15,000 years ago, by which time the brain had already reached its final size and configuration.

This does not mean that war was non-existent during hominid evolution. Warfare in the form of raids undoubtedly characterised our species from its inception. Troop 'raids' may result in occasional death even among monkeys and apes (Hrdy, 1977; Goodall, 1979) and hominid cannibalism apparently occurred throughout the Pleistocene. Further, early hominid hunting and butchering weapons would have rendered warfare increasingly bloody.

Truly sophisiticated wars of conquest, however, must have been a very late evolutionary development. No evidence exists for mass killing prior to the cannibalised remains of twenty Neanderthals at Krapina, Yugoslovia (Constable, 1973). The first suggestive (and highly controversial) evidence for rapid cultural replacement and change in the physical structure of a population occurs with the replacement of Neanderthal populations by Cro-Magnon man 35,000 years ago. This suggests that sophisticated warfare arose only in Cro-Magnon populations whose brain had already reached modern size and configuration.

Consideration of the requirements of mass warfare support the fact that it could only have been a late evolutionary development. Wars of conquest demand group division of labour as well as food procurement and preservation techniques sufficient to provision armies. The first evidence of provisioning of non-productive members of society comes only with Neanderthal man.

Further, wars of conquest will only erupt when perceived to provide benefits to a wide segment of society. This will occur generally in the presence both of population explosion and of the technology and social sophistication necessary to exploit effectively alien habitats and peoples.

Therefore, contrary to Parker, I would suggest that mass warfare did not directly select for intelligence and brain size. Rather, it is a late emerging by-product of intelligence, technology and cooperative skills which evolved primarily for the maximisation of habitat utilisation. Whenever, however, one group improves its technological skills to the point of population explosion, war will tend to erupt and lead to the spread of cultural inventions and genes to new populations.

This process can lead to increased brain size and intelligence in the subjugated populations only if, in fact, conquerer and conquered differ in these characteristics. This situation may have occurred only at one point; the final stages of hominid brain evolution, the transition from Neanderthal to Cro-Magnon man. Prior to this time, mass warfare was unknown. Subsequent to it, the brain had already reached modern form. The lack of evidence of extensive warfare during this evolutionary transition suggests, however, that Cro-Magnon replaced Neanderthal primarily by out-competing him rather than by killing him.

References

Abler, W. (1981), 'Relationship between linguistic and manual constructional ability in apes and humans, UNESCO Trandisciplinary symposium on Glossogenetics, Paris, August 1981.

Baron, N. (1981), 'From universal language to language origin: the problems of shared referents', UNESCO Trandisciplinary symposium on Glossogenetics, Paris, August 1981.

Bigelow, R. (1969), *The Dawn Warriors*, Boston, Little, Brown.

Constable, G. (1973), *The Neanderthals*, New York, Time-Life Books.

Gibson, K.R. (1977), 'Brain structure and intelligence in macaques and human infants from a Piagetian perspective', in S. Chevalier-Skolnikoff and F.E. Poirier (ed.), *Primate Biosocial Development*, New York, Garland, pp. 113–57.

Gibson, K.R. (1981a), 'Comparative Neuro-ontogeny; its implications for the development of human intelligence', in G. Butterworth (ed.) *Infancy and Epistemology*, Brighton, Harvester Press, pp. 52–82.

Gibson, K.R. (1981b), 'Comparative neurobehavioural ontogeny: the constructionist approach to the evolution of the brain, object manipulation, and language', UNESCO Transdisciplinary Symposium of Glossogenetics, Paris, August 1981.

Goodall, J. (1979), 'Life and death at Gombe', *National Geographic*, May 1979.

Gould, S.J. (1977), *'Ontogeny and Phylogeny'*, Cambridge, Mass., Harvard U. Press.

Gould, S.J. (1979), 'Pan selectionist pitfalls in Parker and Gibson's model for the evolution of intelligence', *The Behavioural and Brain Sciences*, 2 pp. 367–408.

Hrdy, S.B. (1977), *The Language of Abu*, London, Harvard University Press.

Kochetcova, V.I. (1978), *Paleoneurology*, Washington,DC, V.H. Winston.

Luria, A.R. (1966), *Higher Cortical Functions in Man*, New York, Basic Books.

Marschack, A. (1972), 'Cognitive aspects of Upper Paleolithic engraving', *Current Anthropology*, 13, pp. 445–77.

Missakian, E. (1972), 'Genealogical and cross-genealogical dominance relations in a group of free-ranging rhesus monkeys (*Macaca mulatta*) on Cayo Santiago', *Primates* 13 pp. 169–80.

Oswalt, W.H. (1976), *An Anthropological Analysis of Food Getting Technology*, New York, John Wiley.

Parker, S.T. (1982a), 'Higher intelligence as an adaption for social and technological strategies in early *Homo sapiens*', Paper presented at British Psychological Association, March 1982, University of Sussex.

Parker, S.T. (1982b), 'Language and play as adaptions for social manipulation through rules and requests', in S. Ghosh (ed.), *Biology of Language: An Evolutionary Perspective*, E. Story, Scientia, Ghent.

Parker, S.T. and K.R. Gibson (1979), 'A developmental model for the evolution of language and intelligence in early hominids', *The Behavioural and Brain Sciences* 2, pp. 367–407.

Prideaux, T. (1973), *Cro-Magnon Man*, New York, Time-Life Books.

Reynolds, P.C. (1981), 'An age constructional ability and the origin of linquistic structure', UNESCO Transdisciplinary Symposium on Glossogenetics, Paris, August 1981.

Wynn, T. (1977), 'The intelligence of later Acheullian hominids', *Man*, 14 pp. 371–91.

9 Does the Phylogeny of Conceptual Development Increase Our Understanding of Concepts or of Development? (Commentary on Parker)

JULIE C. RUTKOWSKA

Is the type of phylogenetic approach advocated by Parker relevant to developmental psychologists concerned with the nature and acquisition of knowledge? Parker's model is particularly distinctive in its use of Piagetian theory. She believes that Piaget's conceptualisation of formal operational thought provides an objective, reliable index of higher intelligence and can form the foundation for both evolutionary and developmental explorations of the acquisition of knowledge. Simultaneously, she implicitly rejects Piaget's (1971, 1972a) fundamental argument that the orthodox neo-Darwinian or 'synthetic' theory cannot explain either the evolution or the development of knowledge. This commentary will suggest that her evaluations of the Piagetian contribution should be reversed. Piaget's approach has provided a poor route to understanding the psychological mechanisms underlying ability, but Parker would do well to take into account the complex questions he raises about developmental processes.

Parker's model reiterates the central role of genetic mutation and recombination. Formal operational thought, which presumably came into being as a result of such processes, was selected because it made possible particular social and technological adaptations which contributed to differential reproductive success, for example, kinship terminological systems and their associated rules, hafted tools, strategic warfare, and so on. More unusually, Parker resurrects the notion that there is ontogenetic recapitulation, which she considers to be the product of a series of terminal additions of new structures or stages during evolution. This framework's general relevance to developmental theory has been clearly highlighted by K. Gibson: 'more intelligent species achieve their greater intelligence not by altering early developmental processes, but by adding later stages of intelligence to the end of the developmental cycle' (1981, p. 52).

In contrast with this, Piaget views his stages of development as representative of levels of knowledge which are not additive. It is central to his theory that the final stages can only be achieved because of developmental processes which operate from the very outset: 'the last stages ... mark the completion of operational or logical structures, but even the earliest stages are oriented in this direction. The development of cognitive functions consists, above all, of a process of equilibration' (Piaget, 1980, p. 107). On the basis of his formal analysis of the stages, he claims that the mechanisms underlying them are isomorphous in structure and that this is evidence that each level is a reconstruction of the previous one. Thus, his emphasis is on equilibration, the endogenous regulatory process which he claims is responsible for this transformation. Thought is said to be interiorised action insofar as it embodies the general form of the coordination of action, abstracted from its particular content through a process of reflective abstraction. For Piaget: 'the structures of knowledge do indeed achieve necessity: but at the end of their development without having it from the start, and do not involve any antecedent programming' (1972a, p. 56).

Notions such as reflective abstraction and equilibration have been described as identifying important theoretical problems without solving them (Boden, 1982), and are less flatteringly referred to as 'inchoate' (Brown, 1979), and 'surplus baggage' (Bruner, 1959). Given this, Parker's model might appear to offer something more streamlined. In evaluating its relevance to developmental issues, two questions are central: (1) Does it help us to understand *what* is being acquired—the psychological mechanisms underlying ability? (2) Do the evolutionary concepts invoked throw light on *how* phenomena of developmental/ ontogenetic change occur?

Psychological Mechanisms: Product, Process and Structure

From a psychological viewpoint, it is extremely difficult to get at the mechanisms underlying ability (even with living subjects) and the question 'what *is* formal operational thought?' is far from trivial. Yet one of the striking characteristics of Parker's approach is the ease with which it maps between the products or outcomes of ability and the psychological data structures and processes which the subject would need in order to produce them. She not only believes that Piagetian theory provides a standard for assessing the relative complexity of activities and achievements, but also assumes that such a task analysis is virtually synonymous with establishing psychological mechanisms. Furthermore, she confounds the crucial distinction between structuralist and psychological levels of description in Piagetian theory, between 'logical operations' and 'thought operations' (Piaget, 1953, 1968). On the one hand, the mechanisms underlying the subject's task performance can be described in terms of abstract *structure* through a logico-mathematical (frequently algebraic) formalism. On the other hand, the psychological *system* which actually implements these structures can be described in terms of concepts such as Piaget's action schemes and thought operations. It is the latter which is of primary concern to psychologists. While Piaget hypothesises an especially close correspondence between these levels of description at the formal operational stage, they must be distinguished if one is not to misinterpret his aims and methodology.

Parker subsumes both levels under an intuitive notion of 'logic': both are included in the 'Types of logic' column of her table depicting 'Piaget's Model of Cognitive Development' (Table 7.1), and she believes her task analyses can be tested by interviewing native informants about the 'logic' involved in tool manufacture and rule production and use. But although subjects' justifications of their reasoning are important to Piaget, he does not believe that subjects' explicit theories provide a direct link to either logical structure—'completely unconscious' (Piaget, 1953, p. 39)—or psychological process. Contemporary cognitive psychology concurs with Piaget's rejection of searchlight or illumination metaphors for consciousness (for example, Nisbett and Wilson, 1977). Parker's simplified approach to psychological mechanisms is illustrated by her attempt to fit her model to both the late concrete operational and formal operational stages of ability. Piaget claims very significant differences between these two levels, the key characteristic of the structure of formal operational thought being that it constitutes a '*structure d'ensemble*' or 'structured whole'. Thus, it is contradictory to claim that 'aspects of formal reasoning' in some activity provide evidence for the stage of formal operations.

For psychological purposes, a much more differentiated model of mechanisms is needed. Even if Parker were to clarify the distinctions discussed above, it can be suggested that it would be misleading to follow Piaget's example of how to arrive at an account of psychological mechanisms. His structural level of description is too abstract for psychological purposes; his account of actual process in terms of concepts such as schemes and operations lacks the necessary detail; and contemporary research does not find as close a relationship between them as his theory necessitates, even in formal reasoning.

Piaget's structural level of description is intended to capture the abstract form of psychological mechanisms, rather than their actual implementation. Nevertheless, it is primarily derived from analysis of tasks which subjects succeed or fail in doing. For example, in the earlier levels of development, the object movements and transformations with which the infant is confronted are formalised in terms of the 'group of displacements', and the degree of success in task performance is taken to indicate the extent to which the psychological system is similarly structured. This aspect of Piaget's methodology has led developmental psychologists, as well as Parker, to focus on task structure. The consequences of this are evident in a vast literature which purports to show that, when Piaget's tasks are suitably modified, very young children can succeed, revealing that they possess the logical thought processes which Piaget maintains they lack. For example, young children who have been trained to compare the sizes of pairs of coloured sticks from a length series $(A > B; B > C; C > D; D > E)$ can successfully work out that $B > D$ without needing to compare them directly, provided they are trained until they can readily recall each component comparison (Bryant and Trabasso, 1971). 'Conservation' responses will be given in comparing the quantitative properties of two objects, following a perceptual change in their relationship, provided the transformation appears to be an 'accident' perpetrated by a 'naughty' teddy bear (McGarrigle and Donaldson, 1974); or is made to appear incidental to the situation (Light, Buckingham and Robbins, 1979). When presented with a row of 'sleeping' toy cows, young children find no difficulty in answering questions such as

'Are there more black cows or more sleeping cows?', a wording slightly different from Piaget's own (McGarrigle, Grieve and Hughes, 1978).

But quite different psychological mechanisms could underlie tasks which can be considered identical at an abstract structural level of description, and a critique of this type of study could argue that the tasks have been altered in such a way that mechanisms other than those of concern to Piaget have been brought into operation. This is very likely to be the case, and alternative mechanisms can be suggested to challenge the view that the tasks mentioned here actually call upon the child to make 'transitive inferences' (Youniss and Furth, 1974), understand 'conservation' (Neilson and Dockrell, 1982) or manipulate 'class inclusion' relations (Smith, 1982) respectively. It is important to note that, at an abstract level of description, the tasks may be quite identical to those used by Piaget. This does not show that very young children could 'do all along' the things that Piaget believes they cannot. It does reveal that a structural level of description can be so general as to apply to tasks which have little in common in terms of psychological process.

Despite Piaget's admirable emphasis on the active nature of psychological processing, his accounts of psychological mechanisms tend to reify thought operations by stressing the separation between process and content. At the formal operational level, he maintains, thought is 'completely divorced from subject matter' (Piaget, 1953, p. 17). The claim that general-purpose logical processes exist as a component of psychological mechanisms is open to serious objection. It is now well known from cross-cultural and developmental psychological studies that varying the material or content of reasoning tasks dramatically affects the performance of child and adult subjects in a manner which cannot be explained convincingly by concepts such as horizontal decalage (for example, Cole, Gay, Glick and Sharp, 1974; Donaldson, 1978). Essentially, subjects who succeed with ease in familiar knowledge domains may fail entirely with other material which appears to be identically organised and to call on the same reasoning processes, and this finding generalises to formal and propositional reasoning. In the 'selection task' (such as, Wason, 1968), for example, adult subjects are shown four cards and told that each has a letter on one side and a number on the other side (for example, 'A', 'B', '3' and '2' are visible). They rarely make the 'logical' choice of which card(s) to turn over in order to test the truth or falsity of a rule such as 'If a card has an 'A' on one side, then it has a '3' on the other side.' Commonly, they will select the '3' card (erroneously assuming biconditionality of the A-3 relation) and fail to select the vital '2' card which could falsify the rule. These mistakes are not made with more 'realistic' material. Logically correct choices are made in testing rules, such as 'Every time I go to Manchester, I travel by train' when the cards feature destinations and modes of transport; or rules such as 'if a letter is sealed it has a 50 lire stamp on it', using envelopes instead of cards (Johnson-Laird, Legrenzi and Legrenzi, 1972).

Viewing the effect of content as merely altering the likelihood of the subject applying their logical processes or the ease with which they do so may be an erroneous reification. In computational terms, the way in which information is represented within our data structures, together with the nature and order of processes manipulating it, may be generating what look like logical performances without using a system of logical rules. For example, the form in which the terms of syllogisms are introduced affects which of the possible valid conclusions subjects will tend to draw, and Johnson-Laird and Steedman (1978) have shown that this can be modelled by a system in which quantified assertions receive analogical mental representations. Potential conclusions are generated by a heuristic combination of these representations. To the extent that a system of logical rules can be said to exist in such a system, it is *implicit* or inherent in the mental modelling of objects and their relations. Thus, there appears to be little evidence for Piaget's notion of formal thought as interiorised, content-free process. In this context, it is interesting that, more lately, Piaget (1972b) appeared to reject his content-neutral position on formal operational thought in favour of a view which saw it as a development specific to those domains of knowledge with which the subject had the greatest involvement, for example, carpentry in some cases, mathematics in others.

The question of whether logical processes exist as independent entities which confer distinct levels of functioning on the subjects who possess them or, alternatively, are emergent properties of the organisation of human representational systems has important implications for developmental psychology, and must be addressed by Parker's model if it is to claim to explain formal operational thought. However, Parker's approach seems most closely allied to the 'general-purpose' viewpoint criticised above.[1] For example, she argues that the presence of kinship terminologies and associated rules can be directly inferred from the existence of certain technologies because, on her analysis, both would require formal operational reasoning. However, as has been noted, similarity of task structure does not justify the assumption of common mechanisms and psychological studies point to the lack of generality of whatever processes actually underlie logical reasoning.

Additionally, Parker repeatedly appears to assume that formal reasoning abilities came into being prior to their adaptive use in certain activities, that is, they were necessary precursors of their 'invention'. But because a kinship terminological system, say, may be described in formal structural terms, it does not follow that formal operational reasoning was implicated in its genesis. Nor need technologies such as domestication require an ability to formulate all possible hypotheses and test them through systematic control of variables. As Humphrey notes in discussing ethological evidence for 'the' original function of higher intellectual faculties: 'even when a technique could in principle be invented by deductive reasoning there are generally no grounds for supposing that it has been' (1976, p. 306). Piaget's developmental studies are compatible with this viewpoint.Rather than providing independent confirmation of his theory, Parker ignores his constant reiteration of the necessary precedence of 'practical success' over 'conceptual understanding' and the fact that his stages refer not to any specific domains but to *levels* of knowledge.

Developmental Process and the Recapitulation Hypothesis

In biology, the biogenetic principle of recapitulation is no longer accepted. From embryology, for example, it is clear that the gill pouches of an embryo mammal are not like the gill slits of an adult fish; they are more like the gill pouches of an embryo fish (Maynard-Smith, 1975). However, the principle might have some utility—if only as a heuristic—in the domain of behavioural and mental development. For the claim that 'ontogeny recapitulates phylogeny' to be more than loosely metaphorical, it must say something about developmental process. Obviously, there is no necessity for ontogenetic and phylogenetic mechanisms of change to parallel each other precisely. In principle, processes which produce developmental phenomena quite unlike adaptation through natural selection could be selected for during the course of evolution via neo-Darwinian mechanisms. However, Parker implies a close parallel between 'terminal addition' and ontogenesis—rather than some more radical change to developmental processes—by arguing that the adult abilities of species with whom we are assumed to have shared a common ancestor are homologous with early human abilities. This views the 'stages' of development as a simple ladder—even if complex genetic changes are considered necessary to add a rung to that ladder—and the only developmental mechanism in evidence is maturation.[2] The main consequence of this is that her model does no more than predict an already well-known order of acquisition of certain behaviours.

Studies of cognitive development in the infant sensorimotor period are of relevance since they do appear to show comparable patterns of change among human infants from differing societies and in a large number of other species (Jolly, 1974; Scarr-Salapatek, 1976). This is true so long as we consider the *order* of success on Piagetian tasks. However, we know that a notable finding in cross-species comparison is the great difference in rates of development (for example, Etienne, 1973), and it should be recalled that Piaget considered human infants to be slower precisely because they were, in his terms, 'going further'. This relative slowness of human development provides part of Gould's (1981) evidence for the role of neotony in human evolution. The notion that it is the juvenile form of ancestors which is retained in the adult form of descendants—the converse of recapitulation—seems more compatible with the evidence that humans retain behavioural characteristics of exploration, play and flexibility of behaviour which disappear in the adult form of many mammals. Notions such as 'exploration' and 'flexibility' are too molar to support detailed psychological explanations of ontogenesis, but Gould's general perspective is relevant in showing that, in principle, the developmental psychologist's concerns may prove compatible with some type of phylogenetic approach. The question which must be addressed is why human infant development might be slower: what different processes might be in operation? Two important areas concern the role of the social in development and the nature of the processes which reorganise the representational systems underlying the infant's knowledge of the world. The suggestions which are sketched below are compatible with theoretical directions in contemporary developmental psychology and suggest a basis for further theoretical and empirical investigations.

The differential degree of maturity of social and cognitive abilities in different species during infancy (Jolly, 1974) could provide the opportunity for different modes of acquisition of the object knowledge which characterises early development. This could result in differences in the psychological mechanisms acquired, and would make it necessary for those concerned with cognitive development to take more seriously the implications of Trevarthen's (1974, 1980) claim that 'human intelligence develops from the start as an interpersonal process... the maturation of consciousness and the ability to act with voluntary control in the physical world is a product rather than an ingredient of this process' (1974, p. 230). The issue of how social and cultural factors may affect the actual nature of early knowledge is yet to be clarified, but it is interesting to consider Nelson's (for example, 1980) argument that Schank and Abelson's 'script' formalism may provide us with the most useful conceptualisation of young children's knowledge of the social and physical world. 'Script theory' maintains that much of our knowledge of the physical as well as the social world is represented or encoded in terms of stereotyped situations and the activities associated with them. These aspects of the infant's knowledge would not show up in standard Piagetian tasks, which are more informative about outcomes than about the subject's representation, hence the apparent uniformity of humans and other species. In this context, it is interesting that Freeman, Lloyd and Sinha (1979) have found canonical usage of objects to influence whether or not infants make the classic AB error on the Piagetian Stage-4 object hiding task. This also points in the direction of a potentially interesting relation between the social and the acquisition of knowledge at this early age.

Recently, microanalytic studies have provided developmentalists with an empirical methodology which is complementary to the representational concerns expressed in the first part of this paper, enabling them to get closer to the nature of subjects' representations and to effective conceptualisations of processes of change. Such studies concentrate on detailed description of the behaviours which lead to the outcome in a task—'success' or 'failure'—and on interpreting this behaviour by considering how it changes as the subject repeatedly works on the same task. Excellent examples are provided by Karmiloff-Smith's studies of language and other naturalistic representational systems (Karmiloff-Smith, 1979, 1982; Karmiloff-Smith and Inhelder, 1974/75). Interestingly, Parker refers to Karmiloff-Smith and Inhelder's study of children's changing performance on a block balancing task as evidence for a recapitulation of the stages of intellectual development from sensorimotor to formal operations when people confront a novel problem. But this misses the significance of such 'microdevelopmental' changes.

If we take this task as an example, three levels of performance are found in children (ranging from just over four years of age to just over nine years) attempting to balance blocks which are either of uniform density or weighted, conspicuously or inconspicuously: two levels of 'success' with intervening 'failure'. At the first level, even the youngest children succeed in balancing the blocks. They rely primarily on a kinaesthetic representation, moving individual blocks around until the point of balance is found. Following this, the child characteristically moves to a second level which, from the viewpoint of an outcome-oriented observer, may appear to be a regression: many failures occur. At this level, the child appears to formulate the notion that 'blocks balance at their geometric centre', places each block at its centre and does not manage to balance any weighted blocks. The child appears to overgeneralise the new theory ruthlessly, and fails to use the previously successful kinaesthetic representation (interestingly, this may be accessed if the child is forced to perform the task with closed eyes). At this level, Karmiloff-Smith argues, the child has moved to a new 'metaprocedural' level of processing. Here, processing is oriented not to external success but to representational reorganisation, and the child's initially successful procedures have, themselves, become the 'problem-space' for the child. The child's behaviour provides external evidence that s/he is beginning to represent new information which was only implicit at the first level. At a third level, success is again seen, but blocks are treated very differently. The child first attempts to balance a block at its geometric centre, but moves to the use of proprioceptive feedback if this does not succeed. Additionally, if one unevenly weighted block is balanced, the child will look for a similar block to balance next in the series.

Therefore, what appears to be a regression in terms of behavioural outcomes is, in fact, an improvement from the viewpoint of the child's representational system. At the first level, each block was treated as a separate problem, but, at the third level, their treatment is related via the child's theory. Procedures which were, at first, merely juxtaposed and used independently in a data-driven way have become part of an integrated system in which data and theory interact. These three levels reveal a sequence in which implicit knowledge appears to become explicit through reorganisation of the child's representation. The vital link in this development is the 'metaprocedural' level where the child's behaviour appears to be solely theory-driven. A spontaneous endogenous process is suggested by the fact that the child's 'metaprocedural behaviour' is not motivated by failure to perform the task.

These patterns of developmental change are difficult to capture effectively within a recapitulationist framework. Many of the children with whom Karmiloff-Smith and Inhelder are dealing are either preoperational or concrete operational, so how can they be recapitulating the stage of formal operations? Such changes are found in a wide range of task domains (for example, language acquisition; the construction and use of maps as external memory devices), suggesting that a general process of change is at work and that we may legitimately refer to three 'phases' of development within representational systems. Most significantly, such processes may also be operational during infancy. This supports the view that the developmental processes characteristic of humans influence and are necessary to the development of abilities which Parker assumes to be prior to acquisitions, held in common with other, 'less intelligent' species.

Redshaw's (1978) comparisons of the performance of human

and gorilla infants on Piagetian sensorimotor period tasks suggest limitations to Parker's claim that the great apes show the same abilities as human infants to the final sub-stage six of sensorimotor intelligence. They reveal a unique preoccupation on the part of the human infant with the nature of object, means-ends and causal relationships. For example, the gorilla is ahead of the human infant in achieving simple means-ends behaviours which involve direct action to a goal, such as pulling a support or a string to obtain a toy. But, it does not use a stick as an implement, a situation where the relation between the intermediary and the goal-object must be established by the subject. Human infants readily demonstrate interest in object spatial relations such as 'containment', going beyond placement and retrieval of objects to sustained 'in and out' games; they build towers of two objects; and they will release a wheeled toy appropriately on an incline. Significant differences emerge on tasks testing the infant's understanding of causal relationships from the point at which infants cease acting as though the causes of events lie within themselves. Here, the human infant actually overtakes the gorilla, and there is evidence that only the human infant is able to use other individuals as agents of action, handing a mechanical toy back to an adult following a demonstration while the gorilla's energies always centre directly on the toy.

Unlike the gorilla, the human infant is not merely concerned with successful performance, but appears to explore the behaviour and object relations involved for their own sake (cf. McNeill's (1974) discussion of chimpanzees), ultimately revealing a more sophisticated grasp or understanding of means. Independent support for this viewpoint comes from Koslowski and Bruner's (1972) study of human infants manipulating a centrally pivoted rotating board to attain a 'goal' toy placed at the end farthest from the infant. At about two years of age, they generally manage to gain the toy by rotating away the end of the board which is within their reach. However, they may then become so preoccupied by varying their behaviour and observing its effects that they will ignore the toy when it comes into reach. Such phenomena are compatible with Karmiloff-Smith's emphasis on the human going 'beyond success' to a metaprocedural level of processing, and future microanalytic studies of infant performance on such tasks should provide valuable insights into the characteristics of representational systems. Piaget's notion of equilibration is too underspecified to explain these changes. However, he appears to be correct in claiming that, at all ages, the human subject's conscious grasp or 'cognizance' moves from the periphery to the centre of action systems, from an elementary consciousness of acts and goals to consciousness of the structure of action itself.

The issue of whether or not there are 'stages' in development invokes too global a level of analysis. Rather than the phases of development discussed above recapitulating the stages, the stages themselves may be evidence of a complex development in which the representational systems which underlie ability in various domains are successively reorganised via regulatory processes. The comparative study of representational systems may enable us to get beyond the stages issue to a more fine-grained analysis of development and a deeper understanding of the sense in which it is cumulative. While this does not simply invalidate Piaget's theory, it does direct us towards novel concepts which were unavailable to him. It is significant that both the 'mental models' approach noted in the first part of this paper and Karmiloff-Smith's work locate the study of human ability within the new discipline of cognitive science with its focus on sufficient models of mechanism. From this perspective, the approach eleborated by Parker fails to go beyond the description of effects to an explanation in terms of the processes which could produce them. This appears to be the case for both synchronic and diachronic levels of analysis. However we eventually conceptualise the processes of human development, their clarification is essential if we are to understand either conceptual development or its phylogeny.

Notes

1. Parker's speculations about young boys' fascination with fire-crackers and selection pressures for war games notwithstanding, it is assumed here that she would not want to claim that what was acquired was, literally, the ability to execute specific behaviours.

2. Late evolving mechanisms could begin to mature early in development (as in the case of language ability). However, Parker's model of the psychological system remains additive, unless such mechanisms are in some way implicated in the development of those evolutionarily earlier abilities which she assumes to be shared by humans and other species.

References

Boden, M.A. (1982), 'Is equilibration important?—A view from artificial intelligence', *British J. Psychology*, 73, pp. 165–73.
Brown, A.L. (1979), 'Theories of memory and the problems of development', in L.S. Cermak and F.I.M. Craik (eds.), *Levels of Processing in Human Memory*, Hillsdale, NJ, Lawrence Erlbaum.
Bruner, J.S. (1959), 'Inhelder and Piaget's *The Growth of Logical Thinking*', *British J. Psychology*, 50, p. 365.
Bryant, P.E. (1974), *Perception and Understanding in Young Children*, London, Methuen.
Bryant, P.E. and T. Trabasso (1971), 'Transitive references and memory in young children', *Nature*, 232, pp. 456–8.
Cole, M., J. Gay, J.A. Glick and D.W. Sharp (1974), *The Cultural Context of Learning and Thinking*, London, Methuen.
Donaldson, M. (1978), *Children's Minds*, London, Fontana/Open.
Etienne, A.S. (1973), 'Developmental stages and cognitive structure as determinants of what is learned', in R.A. Hinde and J. Stevenson-Hinde (eds.), *Constraints on Learning: Limitations and Predispositions*, London, Academic Press.
Freeman, N.H., S. Lloyd and C. Sinha (1980), 'Infant search tasks reveal early concepts of containment and canonical usage of objects', *Cognition*, 8, pp. 243–62.
Gibson, K.R. (1981), 'Comparative neuro-ontogeny: its implications for human intelligence', in G.E. Butterworth (ed.), *Infancy and Epistemology: An Evaluation of Piaget's Theory*, Brighton, Harvester.
Gould, S.J. (1981), *The Mismeasure of Man*, New York, W.W. Norton.
Humphrey, N.K. (1976), 'The social function of intellect', in P.P.G. Bateson and R.A. Hinde (eds.), *Growing Points in Ethology*, Cambridge, Cambridge University Press.
Johnson-Laird, P.N., P. Legrenzi and M.S. Legrenzi (1972), 'Reasoning and a sense of reality', *British J. Psychology*, 63, pp. 395–400.
Johnson-Laird, P.N. and M. Steedman (1978), 'The psychology of syllogisms', *Cognitive Psychology*, 10, pp. 64–99.
Jolly, A. (1974), 'The study of primate infancy', in K. Connolly and J.S. Bruner (eds.), *The Growth of Competence*, London, Academic Press.
Karmiloff-Smith, A. (1979), 'Micro- and macrodevelopmental changes in language acquisition and other representional systems', *Cognitive Science*, 3, pp. 91–118.
Karmiloff-Smith, A. (1982), 'Modifications in children's representational systems and levels of accessing knowledge', in B. de Gelder (ed.), *Knowledge and Representation*, London, Routledge & Kegan Paul.
Karmiloff-Smith, A. and B. Inhelder (1974/75), 'If you want to get ahead, get a theory', *Cognition*, 3, pp. 195–212.
Koslowski, B. and J.S. Bruner (1972), 'Learning to use a lever', *Child Development*, 43, pp. 790–9.
Light, P., N. Buckingham and A.H. Robbins (1979), 'The conservation task as an

interactional setting', *British J. Educational Psychology*, 49, pp. 304–10.

Maynard-Smith, J. (1975), *The Theory of Evolution*, 3rd., London, Penguin.

McGarrigle, J. and M. Donaldson (1974), 'Conservation accidents', *Cognition*, 3. pp. 341–50.

McGarrigle, J., R. Grieve and M. Hughes (1978), 'Interpreting inclusion: a contribution to the study of the child's cognitive and linguistic development', *J. Experimental Child Psychology*, 26. pp. 528–50.

McNeill, D. (1974), 'Sentence structure in chimpanzee communication', in K. Connolly and J.S. Bruner (eds.), *The Growth of Competence*, London, Academic Press.

Neilson, J. and J. Dockrell (1982), 'Cognitive tasks are interactional settings', in G.E. Butterworth and P.H. Light (eds.), *Social Cognition: Essays in the Development of Understanding*, Brighton, Harvester.

Nisbett, R.E. and T. de C. Wilson (1977), 'Telling more than we know: verbal reports on mental processes', *Psychological Review*, 84, pp. 231–59.

Nelson, K. (1980), 'The conceptual basis for language', Paper presented to the annual meeting of the British Psychological Society Developmental Section, Edinburgh, 6 September.

Piaget, J. (1953), *Logic and Psychology*, Manchester, Manchester University Press.

Piaget, J. (1968), *Structuralism*, London, Routledge & Kegan Paul.

Piaget, J. (1971), *Biology and Knowledge*, Edinburgh, Edinburgh University Press.

Piaget, J. (1972a), 'Intellectual evolution from adolescence to adulthood', *Human Development*, 15, pp. 1–12.

Piaget, J. (1972b), *The Principles of Genetic Epistemology*, London, Routledge & Kegan Paul.

Piaget, J. (1980), *Six Psychological Studies*, Brighton, Harvester.

Redshaw, M. (1978), 'Cognitive development in human and gorilla infants', *J. Human Evolution*, 7, pp, 133–41.

Scarr-Salapatek, S. (1976), 'An evolutionary perspective on infant intelligence: species patterns and individual variations', in M. Lewis (ed.), *Origins of Intelligence: Infancy and Early Childhood*, New York, Wiley.

Smith, L. (1982), 'Class inclusion and conclusions about Piaget's theory', *British J. Psychology*, 73, pp. 267–76.

Trevarthen, C. (1974), 'Conversations with a two month old', *New Scientist*, 62, pp. 230–35.

Trevarthen, C. (1980), 'Neurological development and the growth of psychological functions', in H.J. Sants (ed.), *Developmental Psychology and Society*, London, Macmillan.

Wason, P.C. (1968), 'Reasoning about a rule', *Quarterly J. Experimental Psychology*, 20, pp. 273–81.

Youniss, J. and H.G. Furth (1973), 'Reply to Bryant and Trabasso', *Nature*, 244, pp. 314–15.

PART IV

THE FUTURE OF GENETIC EPISTEMOLOGY

10 Divergence in Evolution and Individuality in Development

HOWARD E. GRUBER

On page one of the first number of the *Etude d'Epistémologie Génétique* (a series of publications of Piaget's Centre of the same name, beginning in 1956), Piaget says:

genetic epistemology is the study of the successive states of a science as a function of its development. A science being a social institution, an ensemble of psychological conducts and a system *sui generis* of science and cognitive activities, a rational analysis of the development of science involves all those things.[1]

So we are discussing the extension of ideas about development to the growth of scientific thought.

It would not be doing violence to Piaget's thinking to speak, not of one science, but of the ensemble of the sciences. Over many years, in elaborating the idea of genetic epistemology, Piaget wrote much about interdisciplinary relationships. The image of the 'circle of the sciences', conveying his lifelong passion for the unity of knowledge, appears first in his novel, *Recherche*, written when he was twenty-one years old.[2]

So we are discussing both the extension of ideas about development to the growth of scientific thought and the relation between ideas about individual development to ideas about organic evolution.

At a recent meeting on ontogeny and phylogeny, I asked two ethologists whether their work depended on evolutionary thought. One answered in the negative: logically, one can study the behaviour of animals without considering their origins. The other answered in the affirmative: the most fruitful ethological questions arise out of evolutionary thought. Both agreed that in their actual studies of ethology , evolutionary theory was hardly mentioned. And yet a third ethologist might well claim that the history of ethology is embedded in evolutionary thought, and that it is indeed indispensable both heuristically in raising useful questions and theoretically in providing the conceptual tools for synthesising a complex domain.

Such differences in outlook arise from the convergence of two quite different factors. Materially, the separate sciences of evolution, genetics, and behaviour have each grown so large and complex that it is quite possible for many workers to tackle empirical questions without ever returning to a theoretical base, or without attempting to synthesise knowledge in these diverse areas. Theoretically, with the elaboration of genetics and molecular biology, it has often been quite tempting to adopt a reductionist perspective. This means to insist on and settle for explanations of the behaviour of different organisms solely in terms of their genetic make-up. Even though modern genetics is closely linked with evolutionary theory, in the history of biology this linkage has been quite variable. For example, when Mendelian genetics first appeared in 1900, there was about a twenty-five year period in which the new science of genetics was seen as opposed, and in some quarters the welcome answer, to Darwinian evolution.

It is important to separate the idea of serial orders in the taxonomic arrangement of living organisms from the idea of evolutionary change as the process producing such orders.

Let us consider only two among many possible taxonomic arrangements, the strictly linear *scala naturae* and the irregularly branching tree of nature. The *scala naturae* is an arrangement of organisms from 'lowest' to 'highest'. The meaning of 'low' and 'high' may vary. The continuum might refer to chronological order of appearance, to degree of complexity, or to level of intelligence. Chronological order of appearance need not refer to a natural evolutionary process. For example, in the Judeo-Christian Bible, in the Book of Genesis, the story is told that God first created the sun, the earth and the oceans, and then created the species in a certain order—plants, animals, man. So the idea of the interdependence of all living things with each other and with their milieu predates not only evolutionary theory but all of modern science.

Nevertheless, it should be recognised that, historically, such ecological thinking came into psychology mainly via the route of evolutionary thought. More generally, much of our thinking in the sciences of growth is modelled after evolutionary theories. But such theories present us with a set of alternative images to guide our thought. It is important that we explore these interdisciplinary relationships, because they often provide the unconsious assumptions, conceptual and metaphorical tools, that regulate our scientific work.

When Piaget was asked 'what is truth?', he answered with the image of truth as a character, presumably a woman, probably somehow like an angel, always running away from you: you're always getting nearer and nearer but never quite catching up. Now that is a very linear image. There's no suggestion there that truth dodges about so that you have to go this way and that way to pursue it. You just have to go faster in the same direction. That linearity in much developmental thinking is the theme that I want to explore here.

In Darwin's notebooks, the notebooks on evolution that he kept in the years 1837 and 1838 when he was working out the theory of evolution for the first time (although he didn't publish until twenty years later), there recurs six times a mysterious idea. Darwin wrote: 'If all men were dead, monkeys [would] make men, men make angels.'[3] In the context of a very rich set of notebooks his meaning is reasonably clear. He is talking about a concept something like an ecological niche and a creature something like man; if man, if Homo sapiens himself were to disappear, then our niche would be filled by some other very intelligent creature. Darwin probably had some idea that niches do not exactly pre-exist but are formed by the evolving creature itself. The phrase 'men make angels' is a sort of afterthought meaning that the future of human evolution is not closed. This very way of putting it (monkey-man-angel) almost suggests something a bit linear in Darwin's own imagery, if you look only at that one quotation by itself. Here is another recurrence of the same idea: 'What a chance it has been (with what attendent organisation of hand and throat) that has made a man. Any monkey probably might, with such chances be made intellectual, but almost certainly not made into man.'[4]

The phrase 'almost certainly not ... man' is an expression of the idea of branching evolution, of divergence. Evolution does not yield exactly the same form repeatedly in nature. When there is room in the world for something like man, an earlier primate may evolve into a more intellectual being ... something like man. Here is another version of the angel theme: 'Our descent, then, is the origin of our evil passions!! The Devil under form of baboon is our grandfather!'[5] He is talking about the expression of emotions, the fact that our affective lives express our animal origins in a very clear way. You can make whatever you like of the grandfather image.

The final form in which that idea appears is in his autobiography where he is discussing religion—his own loss of religious belief and becoming an agnostic. He writes, in conclusion of the advantages and disadvantages of his personal religious developments. On the side of disadvantages he has this to say: 'Believing as I do that man in the distant future will be a far more perfect creature than he is now, it is an intolerable thought that he and all other sentient beings are doomed to complete annihilation after such a long continued slow progress.' And he adds: 'To those who fully admit the immortality of the human soul, the destruction of our world will not appear so dreadful.'[6]

There are, then, two quite different images of the shape of evolution. One image the *scala naturae*, going all the way from the lowest to the highest, from the Devil to the angels, with man somewhere in between. The other image, profoundly different, is the irregularly branching tree of nature. This latter, of course, is the one that we now consider to be typically Darwinian. Any representation of the divergent character of evolution must be some sort of irregularly branching tree and not a Lamarckian ladder simply going onward and upward with minor deviations off to the side.

As I have written elsewhere, Darwin's very earliest theoretical notes and first diagrams of the panorama of nature insisted on the idea of an irregularly branching evolutionary tree.[7] At this stage in his thinking, the tree model seems to have been both an intuition and a characterisation of certain contemporary taxonomic ideas. But it was important enough to him that he searched persistently for a theoretical justification of the idea of divergence as a necessary consequence of evolutionary processes. The solution of this riddle did not come to him until twenty years later, in 1857.[8] It is so important that some scholars rank divergence and natural selection as the two equal and most important theoretical achievements of Darwin's life.

But when we turn to our thinking about developmental psychology, we run into a curious paradox. We all think in terms of evolutionary models, Piaget not least. But our developmental models are unilinear. In their linear character, they are very like the *scala naturae*. Although Darwin put enormous emphasis on individual differences, on variation as grist for the mill of selection, there is no comfortable theoretical place in our most general developmental theories for individual differences. That is true not only of theories derived from Piaget's, but also of Freudian theory and its derivatives, such as Erikson. They are all unilinear models, they all have the form that, in a series of developmental stages, A, B, C, D, E, F, the later stages imply the earlier ones. The earlier stages may not cause the later ones but they do open the way for them: you cannot get to a later stage without having passed through an earlier one. So D implies the pre-existence of C, C implies the pre-existence of B, and so on. Now, there is a particular peculiarity in the way Piaget developed this subject, because he borrowed so heavily and willingly from Waddington's notion of the epigenetic landscape.[9] Waddington introduced this idea and the term *homeorhesis* to refer to the processes that keep development on its normal course. In this approach, minor deviations are possible, but it takes enormous energy or a very unusual confluence of circumstances to disturb the normal course of events, to get you out of the epigenetic valley. If nothing extraordinary happens, you are going down Peaceful Valley and up the ladder of development. Oddly enough, when Waddington developed the notion of the epigenetic landscape, there wasn't just one valley. Half the point of Waddington's idea is that there *could* be alternative developmental pathways. The other half is his notion of a regulatory system that maintains certain develop-mental regularities. In contrast, in the Piagetian picture of the course of development, there is only one way to go: up! You may not make it, but if you go at all that's the way you have to go.

Piaget's use of Waddington's work is a good example of what I have called 'differential uptake of ideas'. Waddington proposed the concepts, homeorhesis and epigenetic landscape, to account for *both* the regularity of development and the occurence of alternative developmental pathways. It was essential to his thought that these ideas co-exist. Piaget emphasised the regularity and neglected almost entirely the alternative pathways.[10]

Of course, the development of certain cognitive universals was Piaget's central concern. If these universals are to be achieved, there are certain constraints on any possible course of development, imposed by the environment, dictated by the kind of world we live in. If you're going to communicate you must have language. If you are going to have a sensible language, you must have something like object permanence so that there can be stable relationships between words and things, and so on. So there must be some cognitive universals.

It is possible to imagine that some of these universals are both logically and psychologically prior to others, so that at a certain low order of magnification, developmental outcomes are indeed organised in a more or less linear fashion. But if we look more closely, we see that these outcomes are not arranged like beads on a string, for there are different pathways between any two points.

This closer look, this more finely grained examination, is now taking place in Geneva under the aegis of Inhelder's studies of strategies and Gillerion's work on procedures, both of which focus on within-stage variations in cognitive processes.

In my own work, now in progress, on adult problem-solving and on adult textual comprehension, we look closely at actual cognitive processes, not focusing on successes and failures, but on the pathways taken. In one case, we gave an elementary problem to professional physicists, requiring the explanation of a fundamental phenomenon in mechanics, something found in any first-year physics textbook. We found at least sixteen different pathways. Moreover, the variations are in a sense private, since the level of thinking involved need not be shared. Consequently, close colleagues were often surprised and sometimes dismayed at each other's approaches. I believe that if you look closely enough at any human activity you will find a similar array of significant variations.

Modern research on problem-solving demands exploration of the structure of the problem space, or studying the ensemble of possible pathways to solution. Only such a study of alternatives permits you to understand the pathway chosen. This idea can be applied to the developmental problem of getting from one stage to another. That would mean that different individuals might all arrive at the same places—developmental way stations—but by different routes. The type of theory I would hope for is one that would not make us all alike even for one developmental instant. If we relax the idea of multiple pathways to common way stations only a little, we might achieve that heterogeneity. Suppose people don't arrive at exactly the same place but they do arrive in a certain zone so their solutions are similar enough to make future communication possible. From a number of interviews I've done with adults about conservation, that is not a bad description of what happens. There are interesting and subtle differences that actually become important in an interchange between people if they focus on certain problems: differences in the way they go about justifying the notion of conservation, differences in the way they make use of the notion. On the whole, most people don't deliberately apply an idea like conservation, although it's in the background—implicit in the texture of the environment. Scientists, on the other hand, typically ask, when they are confronted with a puzzling phenomenon: 'Let's see, what is it that remains invariant?' The very abstract notion that 'something' is conserved becomes an important part of the scientific discourse, so the idea of conservation is never finished and is not really as homogeneous as it seems in a lower magnification. What I would hope for is the construction of a theory that retains our notion of development modelled after branching evolution, and at the same time permits the amount of commonality, the amount of regularity necessary for life in society.

On the one hand, if divergence knew no bounds, no social system would be possible. So a plausible theory must include some account of the constraints on the amount of divergence that can take place. Developmental theorists have not given enough attention to this. On the other hand, the more closely we look, the more potential for variation we see—stemming from differing cultural and historical pressures, from ego needs, from momentary situational factors. Most important of all, there is a sheer human need to create new psychological niches and to occupy them for a while.[11]

I turn now to a rather different aspect of what is really the same problem. As compared with real biology, when psychologists get hold of the idea of variation in selection they do something funny with it. You can find this expressed in one form by Donald Campbell,[12] reflecting Popperian ways of thought, and in other forms by a host of experiments on so-called original or divergent thinking. Experiments on divergent thinking represent a conscious effort to apply the evolutionary schema of blind variation and selective retention to human creativity. In the paradigmatic experiment, a problem is presented to the subject; the problem probably comes from some alien being like the boss, or the teacher, or the Paradigm. In other words, it is not something that grows organically out of the person's own activity. Alternative solutions are emitted haphazardly. Then one of them is selected and the others are all thrown away. That seems to me to be a very wasteful way to work and not necessarily the way things happen; although they may happen that way some of the time. Another possibility (one that I have explored experimentally) would be that someone or some group generates a number of possible solutions, and then examines the ensemble and reflects upon it. That notion of reflectivity is part of what is absent from the usual notion, the usual way of thinking about blind variation and selective retention. Now, a highly efficient system for generating variations, whether a social system or a biological system at any level, would want to retain the variants, and not only in the sense that is commonly spoken of in evolutionary theory—as a pool of genetic variability to be selected from just in case circumstances change later on. More than that, all the organisms forming the population in question, or all the ideas forming the ensemble of ideas being considered together, have some potential value for the system as a whole.

Finally, in the most common applications of the supposedly Darwinian model of variation and selection to the psychology of creativity, there is a strong emphasis on producing a large number of variations. The experimental subjects are explicitly invited to participate in this quantity ethos. This is experimentally feasible because, in these experiments, the subjects are deliberately encouraged to act in an irresponsible way. They are not involved in setting the problem, or in weaving together a workable solution out of their many suggestions, or in reflecting upon the meaning of what they have done. All energy is focused on the production of many variant solutions. How different this is from genuine evolutionary processes in which the very mechanism of variation operates under severe constraints imposed by the total living context in which it takes place!

The point, then, is not that evolutionary epistemology is a poor guide for understanding cognitive development and creativity. But when this effort is someday made, the investigator ought to acquire a good feel for evolutionary theory as a whole, and not just borrow snippets.

Ironically, after all the mountains of research on divergent thinking, there is hardly a shred of evidence that validates divergent thinking tests against real creative performance.[13] Moreover, in my own studies of creative people at work, it does not seem to be the case that they devote much energy to the blind production of a large number of alternative solutions to a problem. Often, one idea is hard enough to come by.

The idea of blind variation and selective retention is closely linked to Popper's insistence on disconfirmation of false hypotheses as the royal road to scientific progress. Although Popper called his work 'The Logic of Scientific Discovery', it does not deal with the construction and discovery of new ideas, but rather with the making of warranted choices among them: no idea can every be perfectly confirmed, but given a set or series of choices, some ideas can be disconfirmed.

Notice that in this view, the rejection of some alternatives must logically be preceded by constructing or proposing them. But if I am right, in the thinking of some very creative scientists, there may not arise very many alternatives. Moreover, if an idea is plausible enough to warrant the effort of testing it, then it may not be entirely false. All the interest, then, really lies not in winnowing out the good ideas from the bad ones, but in understanding how people come to construct the ideas in the first place.

Popper's disconfirmation model entails Campbell's insistence on blind variation and selective retention. They both saw this connection and have acted as intellectual allies. My scepticism about this way of thinking owes much to Piaget's constructivism, as well as to my own detailed case studies of scientists at work. To be sure, the construction of ideas requires some selection and disconfirmation. But any new idea worth talking about is bound to be complex, composed of many components fitted together in special ways. Many acts of confirmation are required in this process of construction. To any disconfirmationists present, I confess that I seek confirmation of the foregoing ideas. This can be found in the work of Ryan Tweney and his collaborators at Bowling Green State University. They have made a good, careful and detailed study of the so-called disconfirmation—confirmation bias problem. It seems very clear from their work that real scientists typically suffer from 'confirmation' bias.[14] Most of their effort goes into the construction of ideas, and hypothesis-testing strategies are mainly aimed at confirmation of the lovelies. It is a very rare moment to arrive at a point where the issue of disconfirmation becomes a serious question. I would add that I have noticed the same thing, of course, in studying Darwin's notebooks. He's not choosing among hypotheses most of the time or disconfirming them. Most of the time, he's trying to make one that seems even worth entertaining. Another point must be added. Scientific work does not take place in a vacuum. It always occurs under conditions of social interaction, often circumstances of controversy. The individuals involved regulate the ground of their work so that there will be some suitable level of controversy. It is part of the job to find the level that you can argue at. In that context, one man's confirmation is another man's disconfirmation and, by the same token, one man's disconfirmation is another man's confirmation.

Scientific work invariably wears this double aspect. It is both the thinking of individuals and a set of social exchanges. At both levels it is a process of construction. Criticism and selection play their roles, but they make sense only within the context of construction.

But there is a difficulty with our present understanding of the process of social exchange as it affects the getting of knowledge. Almost unwittingly, most of the discussion and research on group processes involved in knowing the world are reminiscent of Plato's parable of the cave and are governed by images of power and powerlessness. In Plato's cave, each person is chained in place and can never act on the world so as to find the right meaning of the shadows on the wall. To make matters worse, all of those present see the same shadows, projected by the one light source penetrating through the single entrance to the cave. If the viewers disagree as to the meaning of the shadows, they have no way of deciding who is right. They are condemned either to mutual doubt and mistrust or to allowing the play of power to decide which view shall prevail. This is a gloomy picture, and the affective tone of Plato's parable is dark.[15]

The image of the cave seems to have governed most social psychological research on the effects of group life on knowledge processes. The subjects are led to believe that they are looking at the same scene in the same way. Consequently, any difference in their reports necessarily entails disagreement. Since the experimental situation sharply constrains the subjects' freedom of action, such disagreements can only be settled by the play of power (with the more prestigious person or the majority prevailing), or only a little better, by a weak compromise.[16] In this view of social life we have either the powerlessness of unresolvable ambiguity or the resolution of differences by acts of domination and yielding. Historical and sociological research on the growth of ideas often presents a similar picture of the role of 'influence'. The beneficiary of influence is treated as a passive recipient; his or her benefactor is seen as a powerful agent. This agent may be a powerful mentor, an impersonal paradigm, or an idealised *Zeitgeist*—or in some recent trends merely a passing fashion. But where is the person acting as a vigorous, thoughtful partner in a continuous process of social exchange?

Piaget and Inhelder have provided us with a different, somewhat more hopeful image.[17] In their three-mountain problem, the child looks at a scene from one point of view and is asked to form an idea of how the world looks from the point of view of another. As compared with the group pressures experiments, two profound differences have been introduced. There is now not one station point but a couple; two positions from which the world is viewed. Moreover, both perspectives have equal standing. One view is not right and the other wrong; rather, the task is to understand the point of view of the other. True, knowledge of the other is not directly given and must be constructed; true, also, the child's mastery of this construction must develop over a period of some years (there is controversy now over the exact course of this growth). But still, in Piaget's image the outcome in adult cognition is not a hopeless gulf between knowers: each comes to know the other. And yet it must be admitted that in work on perspective-taking stemming from this Piagetian tradition the task is *only* to know the point of view of the other; the world is taken as given. Nor is the child invited to construct the point of view of the other by an active process of exploration. The aim is only to see what repertoire of operations (such as mental rotation) the child has brought with him, that can be applied while sitting still. Something has been gained here, the introduction of the distinct points of view of two people of equal standing. Nevertheless, something is missing still. Where is the process of social exchange? And where is the task of coming to know the world?

We can turn this model around, let the world be the unknown. Then a path toward knowing it, or of knowing it more deeply than any subject can from a single station point, lies through social exchange, sharing knowledge, cooperation and synthesis of diverse perspectives.

This line of thought leads to another way of looking at relations between individual and social, individual scientist and working group. It also provides a promising approach to the task of rescuing the variants that might otherwise be thrown out with the garbage in the process of blind variation and selective retention.

Imagine that we have a box with an unknown object in it, and a system for casting shadows—one shadow on one screen and another shadow on a second screen at right angles to the first. Thus, if we have two light sources and two screens we have two different shadows. We put an unknown object in the box—I'll let you in on the secret, it's a cone—and orient it so that on one screen a circle is visible and on the other screen a triangle.

Now, in our idealised image of scientists at work, two observers—one seeing the circle and the other the triangle—don't fight it out to decide which one is right. Nor do they strike a compromise agreement on some lozenge midway between triangle and circle. What our scientists say is: 'I see a circle, you see a triangle. How can that be? What could there be in the box that would account for your honourable perception and for mine?'

Of course, the shadow box is intended as a metaphor for our ways of handling the many different views we can have of the same piece of the world—low magnification and high, workers with different disciplinary backgrounds, and so on. But I have, in fact, built a shadow box like the one described, and done experiments with people observing their different shadows and talking to each other. Our subjects have been well-educated adults. The situation is made completely understandable to them. There are no tricks in this at all. I regret to inform you that we call our first finding the '*You're crazy!*' *phenomenon* for that is the first thing people say to each other.

However, we give them time, and we encourage them to go on working together. They eventually develop a language in which they can actually communicate. Often, they take somewhat different roles. For example, one person will be the minute describer and the other will be doing more of the synthesising. They naturally develop different roles because they bring different skills to the situation, both interpersonal and cognitive in kind. Perhaps more important, with some of our object-shadow combinations, different station points provide varying challenges to the subjects' descriptive powers. Drawing on the subjects' communicative, analytic, and synthetic skills, even simple geometrical objects like cones and cylinders turned out to be harder than we had expected.

Unilinear developmental theories appear everywhere in the social sciences. In nineteenth century economic thought there was a proliferation of stage theories not so different from today's theories of psychological development. In contemporary economic thought, we range countries on a spectrum from underdeveloped to developed (with not a little suspicion that some may be overdeveloped). In psychometrics, individuals are ranged on a continuum from low to high intelligence, with little regard for the fascinating, ever-branching ways that individuals can play their part in human society. In such unilinear theories one end of the scale is always most advanced, most effective—'highest'.

We need to dwell on the idea that individual differences are valuable, not only because they can produce the one best type, but because everyone has a role to play. Let us consider an imaginary situation in the history of epistemology. We have our shadow box and two observers, one of whom is reporting 'circle', and the other 'triangle'. But a power structure prevails. The quiet fellow saying 'circle' is being ignored and the one shouting 'triangle' is getting all the attention. Along comes a new person who listens better—'Why is that one saying circle?' Someone else, a gifted synthesiser, overhears the question and thinks a while: 'Aha! It must be a cone.' With a little encouragement from yet another party she announces her solution. Mr Circle soon sees the point and is relieved to escape from his isolation, and finally Mr Triangle must accept the new synthesis. To be sure, the system is much noisier than the idealisation with which we began; but the solution does not come through yielding or compromise. Both initial points of view are conserved in the outcome.

The organisation of work for productive and humane outcomes is, of course, far more complex than the parable of the shadow box.

Not only must the unknown object be constructed, but the set of points of view from which to study it must be invented. Shadows are fine for seeing convexities, but useless for detecting inner textures and concavities. On a larger scale, purely perceptual and other cognitive projections are not enough. Even in scientific work, aesthetic, affective, and moral questions and perspectives are inescapable and inform our thought.

In recent years, concern for epistemological questions has been growing vigorously on a world scale. This growth has taken different forms—in the history and philosophy of science, in the cognitive sciences, and among students of development. Participants in this effort have often been attracted, not only to higher and higher abstractions, but to more and more social formulations. Piaget himself pursued the image of the *scala naturae* in a way that lost contact with his own starting point. In making the future of genetic epistemology, we ought to reinfuse it with the social content that it had before this long process of dessication set in.

A good way to begin would be to insist upon the importance of individual variation and branching evolution as fundamental components of the evolutionary theory we take as our metaphor. But in attending to the individual thinking as a person in society we must be careful not to confuse respect of human individuality with the ideology of individualism.

A long time ago, Piaget said it well, in the closing passage of his poem, *La Mission de L'Idée*:

the rebirth of the idea requires the help of everyone. Metaphysics is not an aristocratic art.... The special mark of each man must be his idea and from these ideas, numerous as the cells, the true idea will come forth, like the soul from the body.[18]

Notes

Work on this paper was completed at the Institute for Advanced Study. I thank Doris B. Wallace for a critical reading and helpful comments.

1. Jean Piaget (1956), 'Le Centre international d'Epistémologie génétique et les Etudes d'Epistémologie génétique', in E.W. Beth, W. Mays and J. Piaget, *Etudes d'Epistémologie Génétique*, Vol. 1: Paris *Epistémologie génétique et*

recherche psychologique, PUF, pp. 1–13.

2. Jean Piaget (1918) *Recherche*, Lausanne, Edition la Concorde (see Gruber and Voneche, *The Essential Piaget*, for a complete summary).

3. Charles Darwin in his First Transmutation Notebook, p. 169, written about November 1837. See Howard E. Gruber (1981) *Darwin on Man, a Psychological Study of Scientific Creativity*, 2nd ed., University of Chicago Press, p.2.

4. Charles Darwin in his Fourth Transmutation Notebook, pp. 68–9, written in December 1838.

5. Charles Darwin in his *Notebooks on Man, Mind and Materialism*, M notebook, p. 123, written 30 or 31 August 1838; published 1980 in Paul H. Barrett (ed.), *Metaphysics, Materialism and the Evolution of Mind* (with commentary by H.E. Gruber), University of Chicago Press p.29.

6. Charles Darwin (1958), *The Autobiography of Charles Darwin*, ed. Nora Barlow, London, Collins, p.92.

7. Howard E. Gruber (1978), 'Darwin's "Tree of Nature" and other images of wide scope', in Judith Wechsler (ed.), *On Aesthetics in Science*, MIT, Press.

8. Janet Browne (1980), 'Darwin's botanical arithmetic and the "Principle of Divergence," 1854–1858', *Journal of the History of Biology*, 13, pp. 53–89.

9. Conrad H. Waddington (1957), *The Strategy of the Genes*, New York, Macmillan.

10. Jean Piaget (1971), *Biology and Knowledge*, University of Chicago Press.

11. *See* David H. Feldman (1980), *Beyond Universals in Cognitive Development*, Norwood, NJ, Ablex.

12. For a recent statement of this position *see* Donald T. Campbell (1982), 'The "Blind-Variation-and-Selective-Retention", Theme', in John Broughton and D. John Freeman-Moir (eds.), *The Cognitive Developmental Psychology of James Mark Baldwin, current theory and research in genetic epistemology*, Norwood, NJ, Ablex.

13. For a recent review of this literature on the experimental study of divergent thinking *see* F. Barron and D.M. Harrington (1981), 'Creativity, Intelligence, and Personality', *Annual Review of Psychology*, 32, pp. 429–76.

14. Ryan Tweney, personal communication.

15. Plato, *The Republic*, Book VII.

16. Solomon E. Asch (1952), *Social Psychology*, Englewood Cliffs, NJ, Prentice-Hall.

17. Jean Piaget and Barbel Inhelder (1956), *The Child's Conception of Space*, London: Routledge & Kegan Paul.

18. Jean Piaget (1916), *La Mission de l'Idée*, Lausanne; Switzerland, Edition de la Concorde, translated by H. Gruber and J.J. Voneche (1977) in H.E. Gruber and J.J. Voneche, (eds.), *The Essential Piaget*, New York: Basic Books.

11   The Future of Genetic Epistemology (Commentary on Gruber)

LEO APOSTEL

What I have to say comes very close to Gruber's general point of view. I sympathise with many of his points. I believe, as he does, that cognitive development has no end points, that it may reach the same state by different roads, that individual equilibria may be structurally different and that temporary or irreversible regressions may occur, on the cognitive as on the emotional level. But, trained as a philosopher, I feel that I should ask a few questions not yet put forward.

My first question refers to the appearance, during the past twenty years, of a second attempt to give to philosophical epistemology a scientific status (the other one being Baldwin's and Piaget's genetic epistemology, so widely known, so deeply successful and so rarely noticed by professional philosophers). This second attempt is the so-called 'science of science': the sociology of scientific groups, the economy of scientific action, the clinical psychology of scientific persons, the computer simulation of scientific behaviour, the political theory of scientists fighting for power. This second attempt (as unnoticed by professional philosophers as was Piaget's) tackles the business of knowledge acquisition from a very different point of view. I shall presently explain the difference. But obviously, as I believe that much truth is to be found in Piaget's biologically inspired synthesis, and as I also believe that much truth is to be found in this 'science of science', my problem as a philosopher is: how can I bring these different truths together?

This second perspective also considers scientists without any doubt as organisms, as living beings. However, they are acting in groups, small or large, and networks of communication exist between these groups. The groups are not homogeneous at all: there are very many of them, with different hierarchies and divisions of labour, and their members, the knowing organisms, have specific cognitive styles. All these groups of organisms belong to one species: Home sapiens. Scientists have been children, they are adults and they also die. The time budget of their careers is not entirely unknown to them and they manage it to a certain extent. Their groups, as such, also have their biographies; these collective biographies are brought to self-awareness by a fast-growing history of science (unhappily not strongly assimilated by present workers, but at their disposal anyway). All these human organisms are capable of making decisions and pursuing ends. They are beings with intentions. Some of these purposes are purely personal ones, others are collective; some are conscious, others are unconscious. Many of them exist; these scientists are not 'epistemological subjects': they love and hate, play and sleep, and are politically and economically active. Among all these different *purposes* (and not unconnected with them) we discover the desire to '*improve*' (this value-laden term is very important in our description) in given '*directions*' (directions that may well diverge from period to period, from group to group, and from individual to individual) the '*quality*' of the *representations* they have of parts of their environment. Let me stress this desire intentionally to improve the quality of representations. To be even more explicit: their strategies and tactics to do so, in all their multiplicity, are not invariant either. Our groups of intentional adults are also trying to improve their strategies and even (supreme paradox) trying to improve their criteria for improvement.

When I say all this, I stress that the groups I mention are not at all coincident with classical 'disciplines' (physics, biology and so forth). The really living tribes, with actual interaction among their members, are much smaller. But they produce 'manuals' to be used as instruments for the acculturation and socialisation of their future members and institutions to defend their interests, and these manuals and institutions create the real but only subordinate existence of the so called 'grand disciplines', which are studied by philosophical reconstructions.

Having made these remarks (obvious and trivial to the empirical student of science who is the twentieth-century successor of the speculative epistemologist) I now come back to the fascinating topics in the domain from which Piaget's genetic epistemology has borrowed its theoretical framework. You have studied the development of living things before birth: embryology. You have studied the growth of organisms from birth to adulthood. You have studied the development of new species. And it is alluring (and, for Piaget, a dominating thought) to see the development of knowledge as similar either to embryogenetic development, or to organic growth, or to the general processes of speciation in macro-evolution. The present 'vogue' of evolutionary epistemology shows that, finally, other people have also discovered what Piaget practised so consistently from 1917. I share this enthusiasm, being a materialist. As Piaget, I cannot even begin to explain the adaptation of our mathematics to our physical world without believing that this mathematics is part of the evolutionary adaptation of our species to this world. I am thus willing to share your aims and to work in the same direction.

So, we are not enemies but allies. But, in agreement about what we are aiming at, we must know what we are doing. *The history of science is not evolution*. Evolution is not the result of intentionally acting beings. *History of science is not growth*: adults are creating it. And *history of science is certainly not embryogenesis* (ideas are not cells). We have been making enormous jumps.

But biology is more than embryology, theory of growth or theory of embryogenesis. There begins to exist an evolutionary ethology: behaviour is a biological characteristic and—as Piaget has noticed—is one of the motors of evolution. So, being well aware that producing science is behaving in certain ways, and remaining strongly non-reductionist (we have no right, if the contrary is not proven, to derive theorems about the behaviour of one species from theorems about the behaviour of other species), this behaviour is still a possible subject of ethological research. The behaviour of the scientific subtribes of the species Homo sapiens belongs to the field of the ethology of that species, and the characteristics of this specific ethology can certainly be understood if laws and causes of evolutionary ethology are known and applied to this specific pattern of behaviour. This can be done without abandoning for one second the strong non-reductionist and humanistic stress I share with Gruber. In the same direction, we see that a 'sociobiology' (or should we rather say: a biological sociology and a sociological biology?) is growing in influence. Some of its representatives defend a reductionism that I strongly and completely reject. I even hesitate to mention this development, feeling so hostile towards some of the ideological and political consequences some of its practitioners have drawn.

Still, I do believe that it is here to stay, and that it can be liberated from its ideological deviations. In the light of this sociobiology, we can certainly look at the sociology of scientific groups (again not forgetting that our species is a very particular and special one). And finally, when scientists are trying to improve their representations of their environment, they are not indeed objects to be studied by ecology, the study of species in their habitats and biotopes?

Even if the history of science is history, and is as such '*sui generis*', I am convinced that a combination of *evolutionary ethology, ecology and sociobiology* can and should join the 'science of science' movement from which it is, at the moment, conspicuously absent. And I would recommend—even if recommendations coming from philosophers are somewhat ridiculous exercises—that sociologists and historians, as much as methodologists of science, join forces with biologists in this spirit. Piaget could, in his lifetime, before the real 'take-off' of ethology, ecology and sociobiology, only anticipate to a certain extent this necessity. But reading *Biologie et Connaissance* (1967) and *Le Comportement Moteur de l'Evolution* (1976), we can be sure that the dominance of the ontogenetic and embryological metaphor would have faded away with time in his mind, and that his rightful aim, the constitution of a biological epistemology, would have taken up the topics I am talking about here. Even though we know so little about the brain, should not *evolutionary neurology* join forces with evolutionary ecology, ethology and sociology in order to reach our common aim? Perhaps the present state of biology, where molecular biology has accustomed us to consider the reproduction of forms as transmission of information, where new light is thrown on—and new doubts arise about—the mechanisms of macro-evolution, creates a biological environment more willing to pay attention to Piaget's unorthodox suggestions about evolution, suggestions he could not avoid if he was willing to defend his (sometimes too strong) analogies between learning and evolving. Even though I am an outsider, I cannot avoid Brian Goodwin's conclusion that wherever there is life there is, in some sense of that difficult word, 'knowledge'.

I have now finished making my first point and asking my first question. We are no strangers in this universe: we are living physical systems. But, in order to feel at home, we don't have to hide our identity: we are very special (I am not saying 'important') creatures. And only by recognising that history (though it continues evolution within one specific species) cannot be reached by biology unless an 'evolution of evolution' is taken into account, can the irreducible specificity of humanity be preserved. My challenge to the biologists is: how, by means of biological methods, can (a) purposeful, intentional action and (b) purposeful, intentional representation be described and causally explained as a probable product of ethological, sociological and neurological interactions? Analogies and metaphors are crucial for the development of science, but we should be aware of their nature. The jump made by Piaget is—to my mind—justified, enormous but yet to be made biologically concrete. As I see it, we should neither copy him nor reject him, but repeat, with our present tools, what he tried to do with those of his time.

As a philosopher interested in the philosophy of logic, I am struck by the fact that Piaget's logic (even though it analyses important issues, neglected by the mainstream of the science) 'presents' itself badly to the reader. Many people have been trying to 'clean' it up, understanding its value (my last attempt will appear in the *Revue Internationale de Philosophie* (1983) special issue on Jean Piaget). But, even when cleaned up, it is still not what he needed. And yet, the logic of our period has been coming closer and closer to meeting his demands. But he, himself, fascinated by the great French 'Bourbakian' tradition did not make use of it. Even though (among others) Jean Blaise Grize, Henri Wermus, Rolando Garcia and myself urged him to do so. I want to make some suggestions about the logics he needed and did not use. Piaget studied the development of knowledge. Developing knowledge is obviously either incomplete *or* inconsistent *or* fuzzy (and, in general, incomplete *and* fuzzy *and* inconsistent). We think in such systems. In our time, logic has developed systems for thinking usefully about inconsistent systems (Da Costa and others), about fuzzy systems (Zadeh) and about incomplete systems (here there was no problem: most classical logics are so). Moreover, the working scientist is working with contents and meanings; he is never a formalist. Even if he is a mathematician, he needs models and intensions. Intensional logics have also been forthcoming (Anderson). It is obvious that Piaget's children function similarly and that he needs *at least* these tools. But he needs *more*!

He is trying to study systems that are modifying themselves as the result of their functioning. Here logicians are also making some initial efforts. (Non-monotonic logic and dynamic paraconsistent logics are cases in point.) In order to represent the facts that Piaget and his teams observed in a precise logical way, all these tools should be brought together and used. This work can be done; he has not done it. This is not an accusation: logicians themselves had committed what Yehoshua Bar Hillel called 'the betrayal of the logician'. They had been so fascinated by the foundations of mathematics that they neglected their own task (the elaboration of norms for the real tools of thought, as it is, and not as some abandoned ideal unification and mathematics imagined that it should be). More astonishing than Piaget's not using the tools I just described—they appeared only recently—is the fact that he did not realise that he needed systems of logic in which a thinking subject capable of action and of the self-representation of strategies and the results of its actions is present. The intuitionists who, with Brouwer, greatly emphasised the constructing subject are much closer to Piaget's thought than his own French algebraic formalist Bourbakian tradition. These last ten years Kreise, Troeltsma and others have developed formalisms in which 'the mathematical subject' is explicitly present. They never brought them into contact with the problem of growth and evolution, but we should do that.

One of the greatest intuitionist mathematicians, Freudenthal, making numerous contributions to the pedagogy of mathematics, claims that he rejects Piaget's work utterly. One can understand him when one knows Piaget only superficially; in fact, it is a minor tragedy for the pedagogy of our time that Freudenthal and Piaget did not recognise that they were inspired by the same ideal: an activist foundation for mathematical thought. A logic of action has also come into being; it has only been connected with intuitionism in a short article of mine ('Is Pragmatics or Praxeology the Foundation of Logic?' *Philosophica*, Ghent, 1981, pp. 3–45 of issue 28, edited by Asa Kasher and Leo Apostel). The application of Gödelisation to a constructivistic action logic has never occurred. Yet, what Piaget calls 'abstraction reflechissante' is the development of a model of a system of actions within that system of actions, developing its own possibilities by means of this self-referential process (which also has biological counterparts).

I am thus proposing a new alliance between the future genetic epistemology and new logic. In doing this I am fully aware of the fact that many other suggestions have been made. Margaret Boden, who had done much to make Piaget's work known and appreciated in England, is of the opinion that the best tool to represent Piaget's findings is the theory of programming. I think her suggestion has much to be said for it if (a) the link with biology is not lost and (b) the unity between evolutionary programming systems (for instance, non-monotonic logic) and parallel programming systems (models for interacting scientists) is truly realised (a demand first realised and formulated by two of our people in Ghent, Werner Callebaut and Jean Paul van Bendgem). Yet we should finally recognise that there are many types of mathematical thought: the geometric, the algorithmic and the algebraic being only three basically different examples. My own intuition is no longer monist, and I recommend modelling self-modifying and growing thought systems in algorithmic, geometric and algebraic ways.

Finally—and here I feel myself again very close to Gruber—sciences do not develop in a social vacuum. Sciences are, among other things, instruments in the struggle for power. Some sciences are 'dominant' in every society we have known, in the sense that they offer most power and prestige to their practitioners and that they stand closest to the higher strata of those societies. During Piaget's life, the physico-mathematical sciences were dominant and this had two major effects on his work. First, his topics of investigation are the basic concepts of the dominant sciences (space, time, number, and causation). Second, his method of investigation tried to come as close as possible to the parts of the dominant sciences he could apply (logico-mathematics). There is no reason for us, who have become aware of the fact that we are not compelled to remain the assistants of those in power, to continue this practice. In our genetic epistemology, we may also study the basic concepts of the non-dominant sciences: life, other biological concepts, language, work and exchange, power, the self, the group, class. And we are also allowed to recognise the hidden authoritarianism in the classical experimental method: Piaget takes a child away from a classroom, puts it in the presence of a few friendly adults and, asking pointed questions, compels the child to perform at the upper limit of its cognitive capacities on tasks imposed by adult interest. And yet, his clinical method also exhibits a tendency towards equality and dialogue. Why not introduce the ecological psychology of Barker and Wright into genetic epistemology? Why not first observe the child in its natural surroundings (Piaget did a lot of this when studying his own children) and then try to analyse the causes of this natural behaviour by participant observation? And we could apply this same ecological, participant interaction, that I have sketched in the case of the child, to our study of the community of scientists.

But the social environment of Piaget had an even deeper influence on him than those I have been describing. To be sure: he did work only on the 'dominant sciences' and we understand why (a biologist-psychologist trying to become part of the elite himself, and reaching his aim). But he also excluded from his attention all the basic concepts of the applied sciences (engineering, medicine, law). We can, again in terms of power structure in our society, understand the reason. But his deepest decision was to reduce epistemology to the theory of science. Yet there is so much non-scientific knowledge used in everyday skills and in all specialised professions that genetic epistemology has a much wider scope. And Piaget's other decision to compare the child and the scientist shows precisely that he did recognise this wider scope but, inhibited by the spirit of his class and of this epoch, was prevented from taking seriously what his own inclinations entailed.

To conclude, the individual subject, Jean Piaget, was a very solitary and lonely person. From the viewpoint of a biological epistemology, the thinking of this solitary intellect could only be decidedly *realist* in philosophy. He views the acquisition of knowledge as the construction, by an already very complex and organised subject (the organism: result of history and evolution, embedded in society), of interior models of an also very highly organised and structured environment, for use in future action. Still, in contradiction to his deepest intentions, he was inclined to neglect the information and stucture present in the environment (here Gibson's theory of perception, generalised to a general theory of knowledge, should merge with the constructivism of Piaget), and he was equally inclined to neglect the full complexity of the genetically endowed and psychologically as well as sociologically enriched knowing subject. In the future of genetic epistemology, the full subject (always an individual and concrete one, not an epistemological entity) should be seen as constructing in interaction (here Piaget's emphasis is fully correct) partial representations of fully organised environments (here Gibson has much to contribute) in the service of practical and theoretical action. Here, the future genetic epistemology, no longer aloof and neutral as the nineteenth-century intellectual was supposed to be, should take seriously the fact that thinking is acting and that the scientist, as a human, is a political and emotional being.

References

Piaget, J. (1967), *Biologie et Connaissance*, Paris, Editions Gallimard.
Piaget, J. (1976), *Le Comportement Moteur de l'Evolution*, Paris, Editions Gallimard.

PART V

DEVELOPMENTAL PSYCHOLOGY AND SOCIETY

12 A Socio-Naturalistic Approach to Human Development[1]

CHRIS SINHA

Introduction

In this chapter, I shall argue for an interpretation of evolutionary and human developmental processes which departs significantly from both of the two 'modern syntheses' which currently hold sway in the disciplines of evolutionary biology and cognitive science respectively. The first of these dominant paradigms, is familiar to biologists and psychologists as Neo-Darwinism. That is, the central dogma that the only source of evolutionary change is natural (and sexual) selection. The second dominant paradigm, in cognitive science, originates in the debate in psychology, between the nativist and rationalist camp, as represented for example by Noam Chomsky and J.A. Fodor, and the environmentalist-associationists in the tradition of J.B. Watson and B.F. Skinner. The demise of 'behaviourism', and the rise of a new, synthetic cognitive science, embracing linguistics, philosophy of mind, neuroscience and artificial intelligence, as well as psychology, has led to a fundamental paradigm shift, in which the 'old' reflexological synthesis has been replaced by a modern synthesis which I propose to call the *Neo-rationalist* paradigm.[2]

The term 'Neo-Rationalism' highlights the historical filiation of modern 'rational psychology' (Fodor's term) with the dominant tendency of Western thought, which has oscillated between 'empiricist' and 'rationalist' solutions to the same *sort* of questions approached within the same presuppositional framework. As Fodor (1980, p.64) himself notes, 'there's a long tradition including both Rationalists and Empiricists, which takes it as axiomatic that one's experiences (and, a fortiori, one's beliefs) might have been just as they are even if the world had been quite different from the way that it is'. This 'contingency assumption' lies at the heart of both empiricist and rationalist theories, and is, I shall argue, enshrined in the modern synthesis in the guise of the

159

competence-performance distinction. Neither Neo-Darwinism nor Neo-Rationalism, however, commands total consent within its own discipline. Furthermore, one consequence of the demise of classical reflexology as an adequate theory of human behaviour, and its replacement by Neo-Rationalism, has been a widening gulf between psychological and biological frames of explanation. In this chapter, I shall propose that the prospect of a reintegration of the theoretical frameworks of these two disciplines is offered by an alternative paradigm, unifying phylogenetic and ontogenetic explanations of behavioural and mental evolution and development. This general alternative paradigm can be termed epigenetic naturalism, and with respect to human development it accords, unlike the dominant paradigm, a significant and formative role to social life in the evolution of mind.

Neo-Rationalism: From Reflexology to Representation

The nature of cognitive science's 'modern synthesis' can best be explained by outlining the presuppositions and goals of its research programme. This has as its goal the understanding of human mental processes, and of the neural mechanisms underlying their translation into behaviour. Against classical reflexology, which proposed a direct causal link between brain/nervous system and behaviour, the modern synthesis asserts the necessity of the study of *mind* as an autonomous level, possessing causal efficiency with respect to behaviour, and circumstantially constrained to, rather than epiphenomenal of, lower level neural and biochemical processes. Cognitive science is anti-reductionist and mentalistic. It studies human behaviour in order to reveal the workings of mind, the structures and processes permitting the operations of reasoning and the manipulation of symbolic information. Its fundamental premise is that human behaviour is *rule governed* and *generative*. That is to say, transformation rules intervene between different stages in coding processes in order to permit goal-directed problem-solving.

Representation and Computation

A central concept in cognitive science is representation. Information may formally be represented in different ways, in order procedurally to effect various strategies directed to specified goals. The mode of specification of the goals of strategies and procedures is itself representational: an end-state in a chain of transformations which may lawfully be derived from the properties of the formal system constituting the representational 'store'. The human subject is conceived of as possessing a 'mental model' (Johnson-Laird, 1980) of the world, or world sectors, and cognitive processes consist in operations carried out upon the model(s).

The concept of representation is extended, in the modern synthesis, in two further ways. First, the representations constituting the cognitive subject are assumed themselves to be *represented*, or instantiated, in the functional architecture of the brain and nervous system, and in neurochemical processes. Thus, the brain itself is seen as a *representation* of mind. This inverts the traditional reductionist view, in which 'mind' was seen as a mere trace of *neural* process. In the modern synthesis the brain is rather an embodiment or representation of *mental* process. Further, it is no longer assumed that the *particular* instantiation of mental processes embodied in human brains is either necessary, or constitutive of mind. Mental processes may equally be instantiated in artificial physical systems, such as computers. I shall refer to the autonomy of cognitive from neural process as the *contingency assumption*.

The extension of the concept of representation to include the brain-as-a-representation is closely linked, therefore, to a second extension of representation to include, or be synonymous with, *computation*. An essentially computational model of mental representation is presupposed by much work in cognitive science, in which, to put it simply, representational content is subordinated to computational form. The representational system is seen as being constituted by *rules*, of a formal and computational nature, and the elements upon which the rules operate are symbolic values, or strings of symbolic values, which are themselves defined over the formal rule-system.

Computational modelling, though it is bound by formal and

theoretical considerations with respect to cognitive processes, is not bound to *behaviour* in a direct fashion since it is assumed that (contingent) processing limitations, inherent in human neuro-biology, intervene between mental processing and behavioural outcome. Thus, the contingency assumption also underpins the distinction between *competence* (constraint to a formal object guaranteeing internal consistency), representing the 'ideal' speaker-hearer, or more generally cognitive subject; and *performance* (constraint to 'contingent' limiting conditions on processing), representing the 'actual' human subject.

Growth and Learning

The Neo-Rationalist paradigm is best typified by its answers to two perennial questions. The first is: what is the relationship between mind and brain? The second is: what is the relationship between experience and knowledge? To these two questions, the modern synthesis answers, respectively, *modularisation* and *maturation*.

The computational models which have the widest currency within the framework of the modern synthesis are (ideally) constrained to well-formulated theories of particular domains. The paradigm for such theories is provided by natural language grammars. The logical next step is to search for quasi-grammatical, generative formalisations of non-linguistic domains. Thus, the programmatic evolution of cognitive science has been dominated by the search for self-consistent, autonomous and generative 'grammars', of action, of vision and so forth.

The result is a *modular theory of mind* which, when given a physicalist interpretation according to the principle of the brain-as-a-representation, assumes the form of a modular theory of brain function. Such a perspective is articulated by, amongst others, Chomsky (1980) who explicitly advances a 'faculty' theory of mind and a modular theory of brain function. Marshall (1980), in his response to Chomsky's proposal, notes the similarity between this and the eighteenth century 'organology' of Franz-Joseph Gall.

The new organology of Neo-Rationalism is also a maturationist theory of development, in which there is little room for *learning* in the traditional sense. Chomsky (1980, p.14) goes so far as to state that, at least as far as *knowledge* is concerned, 'it is rather doubtful, in fact, that there is much in the natural world that falls under learning'. He relegates learning theory, as traditionally understood in psychology, to 'the study of tasks and problems for which we have no special design, which are at the borders of cognitive capacity or beyond, and are thus guaranteed to tell us very little about the nature of the organism'.

I shall return to the problem of evolutionary design which this theory poses. To continue, however, the appropriate model within the theory for cognitive development is growth, rather than learning. This maturationist position appears, at first sight, to fall in the mainstream tradition of American developmental psychology, as represented in the early twentieth century by such figures as Gesell and G. Stanley Hall; a tradition which explicitly repudiated the socially oriented epigeneticism of Baldwin. Unlike traditional maturationism, however, the new synthesis is anti-naturalistic and anti-behaviourist. Its method is largely formalist, relying heavily upon computational models, and its focus is upon cognition rather than behaviour.

Traditional maturationism, by contrast, was both naturalistic in method (relying upon observations), and easily accommodated to a behaviourist paradigm. The possibility for such an accommodation was given by the universal acceptance, in the first part of this century, of the *reflex arc* as simultaneously the fundamental neuropsychological unit (the unit of association); the paradigm case of organism-environment transaction (the S-R link); and the basic mechanism of learning (through classical or operant conditioning). Such a paradigm, essentially empiricist in nature, can combine classical learning theory with the recognition that certain neural circuits are maturationally established, rather than established strictly through experience. It contrasts with the modern synthesis insofar as the latter sees classical learning as peripheral, is not founded upon the reflex arc, and substitutes internal constraints for external ones. Figure 12.1 illustrates the differences between the old and the new paradigms.

Fig 12.1a representing the 'old' associationistic and reflexological synthesis, is simply a slightly elaborated version of the sort of 'stimulus-organism response' diagram familiar from traditional accounts of learning theory. The important point to note is that, according to the view that it represents, it is the environment which *selects* (or 'elicits') behaviour, through either association-by-

A. The First Synthesis: Reflexology

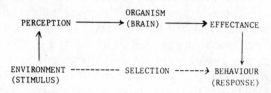

B. The Modern Synthesis: Cognitivism

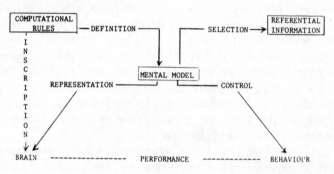

Figure 12.1

From reflexology to cognitivism.

contiguity (classical conditioning) or reinforcement and extinction (operant conditioning). Developmental change can occur either through the maturation of pre-established neural circuits, or by means of the establishment of new circuits through learning. Classical learning theory, in fact, provides a perfect correlate, in terms of change within the lifespan of the individual organism, to the Neo-Darwinian theory of natural selection of individual organisms in a phylogenetic timespan.

Both theories account for increased adaptation on the part of the organism by ascribing a primary role to the environment. The theories are also complementary insofar as maturational developmental change, whether morphological or behavioural, can be accounted for by means of natural selection—as in the case of 'instincts'—leaving learning theory to account for the residue of ontogenetic change. Further, this 'learned' residue is assumed to be of an extremely plastic nature—it is reversible and completely inconsequential as far as the genes transmitted by the individual are concerned. Classical learning theory is therefore predicated upon a division between instinctual and learned behaviour which precisely parallels Weissmann's barrier in Neo-Darwinian theory. Finally—and this is important to note—both Neo-Darwinism and reflexology assign a central place to *behaviour*. Though much of the subject matter and evidence for Darwinian natural selection concerns morphological characteristics, it should not be forgotten that the *mechanism* of selection operates upon functioning organisms, upon the behavioural correlates or consequences of structural features, and not upon the structure itself. It is precisely this which distinguishes Neo-Darwinian from Lamarckian evolutionary theory.

By contrast, the 'cognitivist' or computational model represented in Fig. 12.1b locates the control of behaviour in a 'mental model', constitutively defined by computational rules. This model, in order to represent a particular, local and current 'world-state', *selects* relevant referential information from environmental input. The selection process, however, is also a *construction* process, insofar as the value of referential information is itself defined over the computational rules: in this sense, the only *actual* 'environment' *is* the mental model. The real environment enters into the mental model only as selected referential information (values upon which the computational rules subsequently operate).

A parallel process is assumed to operate in the brain. Where the mental model is defined in terms of the computational rules, the brain is assumed to have these rules pre-programmed or inscribed in it. And the access which the organism has to the environment is solely in terms of the mental model 'represented', at any given moment, in the brain. Further, given the contingency assumption, the systematic unit labelled 'brain' might more generally be labelled 'hardware'—denoting any physical system capable of performing the necessary representational/computational work. *Which* particular system is chosen to implement the model is relevant only insofar as the performance characteristics of the system will affect the actual behavioural output.

The computational rules are therefore in no sense derived from the environment; rather, they are innate algorithms enabling the system to *select* relevant features of input to *construct* the environment. The selection and construction of the environment by the system, as opposed to the selection of behaviour by the environment, most fundamentally distinguishes the new from the old synthesis. This selective constructivism applies both to ontogenesis and to mature functioning, in that innate algorithms enable the subject to select from environmental input only those features which are either developmentally or currently relevant to the construction process in hand. The computational approach appears therefore to be committed to a radical nativism, predicated upon a dualistic distinction between mental objects and the actual objects of the real world. Thus, Fodor (1976) casts the theory in terms of an argument for an innate, computational 'language of thought': an hypothesis which neatly ties in with the modularisation thesis advanced by Chomsky. This aspect of Neo-Rationalism returns us to the problem of how such a complex representational system can possibly have emerged from biological evolution.

It will be recalled that the 'reflexological synthesis' provided a model of learning which theoretically interlocked with the Neo-Darwinian theory of natural selection. No such concordance with evolutionary theory can be claimed for Neo-Rationalism for two fundamental reasons. First, because of the cognitivist and constructivist insistence that the relevant 'environment' be selected by the subject, rather than vice-versa. Second, because the competence-performance distinction, rooted in the contingency assumption, accords to *behaviour* a secondary role vis-à-vis the computational mechanisms governing and controlling it.

Further, the radical nativism characteristic of Neo-Rationalism has equally negative implications for evolutionary theory as it does for developmental theory. In the modern synthesis, 'representation', or computational knowledge, is seen as distinct from knowledge of the physical properties of the universe. This conception of representation, which depends upon a dualistic distinction between mind and nature, is indicative of the positivist and physicalist inheritance of modern Neo-Rationalism. Despite, or because of, the mentalistic, rather than classically empiricist, orientation of the computational approach, it remains unable to account for the *emergence* of mind from nature, and is therefore in many respects profoundly anti-evolutionary in its implications.

The Ecological Alternative

As has frequently been remarked, a basic feature of the computational approach is its lack of concern with behaviour as this actually occurs in natural situations. Cognitive science does, indeed, sometimes employ arguments based upon laboratory experiments with human subjects. More usually, however, the 'data' are pretheorised in a formal sense (in the way in which a grammatical theory might count as 'data'). This lack of concern with behavioural data opens the approach to a fundamental objection. This is that, whatever else cognitive science is doing, it simply is *not* producing explanations about how subjects actually perform tasks involving reasoning, inference and so on in natural settings. This criticism of lack of ecological validity has been levelled at the entire tradition of laboratory-based experimental psychology (Cole, Hood and McDermott, n.d.; Neisser, 1976), but it has greatest force when applied to computational models. It is significant, furthermore, that the ecological validity argument, when applied to human psychology and behaviour, has been closely associated with attempts to reinstate the *social* dimension of cognition, particularly in relation to its development (Butterworth and Light, 1982; Flavell and Ross, 1981).

Ecological Validity (1): Context, Rules and Meanings

There has, in recent years, been a growing recognition by developmental psychologists of the importance of studying the social-ecological matrix within which human development naturally occurs (Bronfenbrenner, 1979), and a renewed emphasis upon the socio-communicative origin and elaboration of cognitive processes (Bruner, 1975; Donaldson, 1978; Wells, 1981). These developments have led, too, to an appreciation of the experimental setting itself as a 'socio-dialogic context' (Karmiloff-Smith, 1979; Freeman, Sinha and Stedmon, 1981).

The basic theoretical issue is the extent to which it is useful or possible to attempt a theorisation of individual mental representations without reference to the representation and evaluation of social actions by interpretive communities. This problem is, of course, fundamental to the entire enterprise of human science, and strikes at the heart of the claims of the computational approach to be scientific. Contemporary approaches to the psychosocial and philosophical analysis of action (von Cranach and Harré, 1982) increasingly stress the dialectical interdependence between actors' mental states (beliefs, wants, intentions, etc.) and interactants' evaluations of act-performance and outcome. This fundamentally communicative epistemology, rooted both in critical social theory (Apel, 1979; Bhaskar, 1979; Habermas, 1971), and in linguistic (particularly pragmatic) theory (Grice, 1975), is distinctly orthogonal to the main stream of cognitive science, although some socio-communicative and pragmatic computational models are perhaps in principle compatible with it (Schank and Abelson, 1975).

The second important point is that the exclusive focus on formalisation of much current cognitive science is unconducive, in practice if not in principle, to systematic investigation of the pragmatic negotiation of behavioural meaning within episodes of social exchange. It is a moot point whether rigorous formalisation of pragmatic rules is in principle possible: but so long as cognitive science relegates these rules to a separate category of 'per-formance', it will be unable to effect a fruitful rapprochement with many of the most exciting developments in contemporary linguistic theory (Andor, 1980; de Beaugrande and Dressler, 1981).

The possibility, and indeed necessity, for such rapprochement is indicated by the fact that both computational and social-theoretic approaches presuppose and theorise the category of *representation*: in this respect, they both differ significantly from the 'direct perception' approach discussed below. There remains, however, the problem of accounting in a principled way for the evolution and development of representation without resorting to the radical nativist arguments of Neo-Rationalism.

Ecological Validity (2): Direct Perception vs. Representation

The ecological validity argument is not restricted to the issue of the interpretation of human behaviour within its social and communicative context. In fact, for most psychologists the phrase is predominantly associated with the theory of direct perception originated by J.J. Gibson. In this section, I shall concentrate on Gibson's later formulations of the theory (Gibson, 1979); *see* also Costall (1981); and Cutting (1982).

Ecological optics departs from the geometrical and atomistic abstractions of classical optics by invoking the priority of *background* in specifying 'objectness' within a structured (rather than empty) space. Ecological space is conceived as a *surface*, textured by variate patterns of information, whose objective structure is specified by variables within the ambient light (gradients of shade, scatter, intensity and so on). The structure of light therefore contains all the information necessary for the 'pick-up' of invariant properties, such as those involved in motion perspective and parallax, without the subject having to do any further representational or mental-inferential work. The theory of direct perception also views the senses as exploratory, attentional organs, of an organism which is fully, actively engaged with its environment, by means of locomotion and through the variable articulation of body parts. Thus, the organism is itself *part* of the niche. In this sense, the theory of direct perception depends upon the wider propositions of the ecological approach: that a niche is a negotiated, ordered, spatio-temporally structured *relationship* between organism and habitat, in which behaviours are in part transformative of the very environment to which they are adapted. Gibson (1979) introduced the concept *affordance*. Affordances consist in the properties of objects by virtue of which these objects serve to sustain or permit the actions of the organism.

To what extent, then, does the ecological approach offer a solution to the problem of representation? First, it escapes the central problem of rationalist (and empiricist) theories, that of the relationship between mental or intentional objects, and real objects, by denying the existence of 'percepts' as copies of real objects. Objects are directly perceived, and the information picked up in direct perception is neither a mediating construct, nor an isomorphic 'picture of the world, but a *real structure* which specifies objects by virtue of its internal, higher order variables:

the question is not how much [the retinal image] resembles the visual world, but whether it contains enough information to account for all the features of the visual world' (Gibson, 1950, p.62).

The variables are defined, not in terms of the special predicates of theoretical physics, but in terms of local 'human scale' (or organism scale) psychophysics (biophysics). To this extent, the ecological approach offers both a real alternative to Neo-Rationalism, and a formidable challenge to computational approaches in particular, and cognitive science in general. There is, perhaps, no principled reason why formal models should not be developed for direct perception processes; but if cognitive science is going to proceed in such a direction, it will have to leave behind some of its long-cherished assumptions: not least those underlying the Neo-Rationalist synthesis.

Nevertheless, the ecological approach cannot, by definition, offer a solution to the problems of what have traditionally in psychology been called 'higher thought processes'—those procedures operating, not upon the proximal environment, but upon symbolic representations. Granted direct perception of the proximal environment, can we then simply graft a computational theory of mind onto it? This seems obviously unsatisfactory, for it leaves an unbridgeable gap between the world we *live* in, experientially, and the world we think about, remember, make plans and draw conclusions about. A more interesting step might be to build upon the notion of 'affordance', suggesting that conceptual representations consist of mnemonically stored 'abstractions' of affordances. In the final part of this chapter, I shall suggest something similar, but as I shall now show, this has serious (indeed, fatal) consequences for direct perception theory, at least as applied to human beings.

Much of the human environment consists of *artefacts*, which indeed afford actions, but many of which resemble natural objects not even remotely. In what sense is it plausible to say that the functional affordances of a car, for example, are 'directly specified' in the optical array? A steering wheel might be said to 'afford' appropriate actions in a Gibsonian sense but these sort of affordances cannot, however you add them up, yield *knowledge* of how to drive a car, or of the socio-cultural 'affordances' of cars as complex artefacts within a social system. In fact, the argument can be applied to natural kind as well as to artefactual objects. To the untutored eye, a piece of rock might 'afford' merely the actions of kicking, to a geologist, however, it might 'afford' an indication of a vulnerable resource and so on. In effect, the whole notion of affordance necessarily involves, at least for adult human subjects, knowledge and representation. Its introduction into ecological psychology means that the theory is no longer restricted to perception, but involves an implicit theory of the relations between representation and behaviour. Unfortunately, not only does ecological psychology possess no theory of representation, but it no more offers a solution to the problem of the evolution, development and acquisition of knowledge than does Neo-Rationalism: both approaches necessarily end in an unbridgeable dualistic division between mind and nature. In the final section of this chapter, I examine these issues from the standpoint of the epigenetic alternative.

Behaviour, Representation and Evolution

There are a number of possible ways in which behaviour may be described. One way might be to limit one's descriptive terms to those which refer solely to the organism, or to its body parts, or their movements relative to one another. Such a description, however, seems inherently unsatisfactory as a description of *behaviour*, although it is a legitimate enterprise in itself. It seems more appropriate, in such a case, to speak of physiology of movement, and while this may be an indispensable complement to the description of behaviour, the two are essentially different. For behaviour is *motivated* and *meaningful*, consisting not merely in movements, but in movements in relation to an environment. The movements of even the simplest of life forms are adapted to a particular niche. Even where such adaptations appear merely to consist in a one-to-one causal link between a specific type of environmental event and a specific type of movement, as in the S-R links of learning theory, or the fixed action patterns studied by ethologists, a full *behavioural* description necessarily involves a reference to the environmental event structure, as well as the movement structure.

As we move to the consideration of more complex behaviours, the connection between behavioural and physiological descriptions becomes increasingly remote. Flight and predatory pursuit both involve rapid locomotion, but the meaning and 'cause' of the movements is different in the two cases. Ethological studies are often concerned with the detailed specification of particular *combinations* of movement, posture and attentional orientation which constitute a particular behavioural routine; but the degrees of freedom in the organisation of micro-behaviours within macro-behavioural units increase rapidly with increased phylogenetic complexity. Indeed, it is the relative freedom of behaviour from 'stimulus', and of behavioural goal or end from the detailed motoric means of attaining that goal, which typifies 'intelligent adaptation'.

At a minimum, then, the description of behaviour necessarily involves reference to an environment to which that behaviour is adapted. This is, of course, the basic tenet of the ecological approach. However, the description of intelligent behaviour requires, additionally, and as we have seen, reference to the *representations* of the environment which the organism utilises (at the highest level, intentional states such as beliefs and desires), which specify a complex repertoire of behaviours which the environment actually or potentially affords, and which contribute to the maintenance or expansion of adaptive fit.

An essential feature of behaviour is that it is *active*, going beyond the bounds of the organism to affect the environment and change it— even if this change simply consists in the substitution of one spatio-temporal segment of the environment for another, as in locomotion or migration. This active nature of behaviour was stressed by Piaget, who defined behaviour as:

all action directed by organisms towards the outside world in order to change conditions therein or to change their own situation in relation to these surroundings (Piaget, 1979, p.ix).

Piaget makes it clear that autonomic self-regulation, such as breathing, is *not* behaviour, although it is quite clearly adaptive. He goes on to state that 'behaviour is teleological action aimed at the utilization or transformation of the environment and the preservation or increase of the organism's capacity to affect this environment', and that, further, 'the ultimate aim of behaviour is nothing less than the expansion of the habitable—and, later, the knowable—environment' (Piaget, 1979, pp. x and xviii). It is in this sense that he saw behaviour as the motor and leading edge of evolution and development.

In What Sense Is Behaviour Adaptive?

The straightforward Neo-Darwinian answer to this question is: behaviour is adaptive insofar as it contributes to inclusive fitness. But there is another common sense in which we consider behaviour to be adaptive, that is, when it is *appropriate* to a particular situation or local environmental segment. For adaptation in this latter sense, Piaget (1979) frequently uses the expression *adequation*.

The two senses of adaptation are, to be sure, related: the inclusive fitness of an organism which consistently behaved inadequately would, indeed, be poor. But a particular behaviour confers selective advantage only in relation to a given context or occasion, for which its instantiation is appropriate (adequate) in terms of local goals. A fundamental deficiency of Neo-Darwinism is its inability to conceptualise this distinction. This deficiency is related in turn to Neo-Darwinism's difficulty in explaining the central paradox of evolution: why, if an organism is 'adapted' in the sense of inclusive fitness, should evolution occur at all? Where Neo-Darwinism invokes purely exogenous selective 'pressure', an epigenetic approach sees the dynamism of evolution as consisting in an endogenously expanding circuit of adaptation, driven by the exploratory fallibility of behaviour. That is to say, it is the possibility of 'inadequacy' that underlies the leading role of behaviour in evolution and development.

Behaviour is goal-directed, and intelligent behaviour is representationally mediated. It is characteristic of representations that they can be both *erroneous* and *impoverished*. The best laid plans of mice and men, indeed, gang oft agley. Behaviour, as Piaget emphasised, is defined foremost in terms of goals, and only secondarily in terms of the degree of coincidence between the goal of the behaviour—its 'intended' outcome—and its *actual* outcome, which are frequently divergent; or between 'representation' and 'reality', which are frequently also divergent. We all do make mistakes.

Not only can behaviours be both situationally inadequate and/or unsuccessful; but also behaviours, and overall behavioural repertoires and strategies, can result in environmental consequences which, though a part of the adaptive circuit linking organism to environment, are not to be seen as the proximal goal of the behaviour. A 'path' may, for example, be an unintended consequence of repeated locomotion from one place to another, but it is nevertheless a useful one. Ecologists emphasise that species *shape* their niche, as well as being shaped by it, and such environmental shaping is constitutive of, as well as adaptive to, the species survival strategy.

Further, such shaping, for all species, including our own, can introduce distal consequences—food shortage, erosion, pollution, competition with other species—which are *outside* the initial circuit of adaptation. That useful path may be disadvantageous if a predator cottons on to the idea of lying in wait at certain times of the day or night. Such disadvantageous consequences will require a further set of adaptations if survival is to be assured and extinction averted—or, more generally, unpleasurable difficulties surmounted.

Accommodation and Assimilation (1): Baldwin

Such secondary adaptations were referred to by the epigenetic psychobiologist James Mark Baldwin[3] as *accommodations*, and he saw them as playing a crucial role in both phylogenesis and ontogenesis. Accommodation constitutes a mechanism of active selection on the part of the organism, oriented to enhanced adequation, which prescribes a new, or wider, *range* of dynamic adaptation, rather than conferring a fixed selective advantage, accommodations are active, *organismically* selected responses to induced environmental demands, whereas Neo-Darwinian strategies are *environmentally* selected from random behavioural variation.

The cumulative process of accommodation leads to what Baldwin called 'organic selection', which he contrasted with the negative and purely limiting role played by natural selection in evolution. Organic selection is a process independent of natural selection, by which individuals extend their adaptive range by accommodation, thus surviving to 'permit variations oriented in the same direction to develop through subsequent generations, while variations oriented in other directions will disappear without becoming fixed' (Baldwin, 1897, p.181). Thus, 'individual modifications or accommodations supplement, protect or screen organic characters and keep them alive until useful congenital variations arise and survive by natural selection' (Baldwin, 1902, p.173). This effect is still referred to as the 'Baldwin effect'. Baldwin conceived of it as playing an increasingly decisive role in evolution, since he maintained that the range of accommodatory plasticity, and hence the importance of organic selection, increased with phylogenetic complexity. Thus, organic selection, combined with imitation (*see* below), increasingly directs, rather than follows, the course of natural selection.

The process of accommodation, for Baldwin, also underlay the ontogenetic emergence of higher mental processes. Accommodation permits the integration of behaviour with a complexly structured and variably respondent environment, including the behavioural actions of other individuals in response to the actions of the infant. A key example given by Baldwin is the development of imitation, which he sees not as a passive 'copy' of the model, but as an active effort by the infant to overcome the resistance of her own body. The first accommodations are those which 'select' from amongst the infant's habitual actions in order to repeat pleasurable experiences. These 'circular reactions' form the basis for subsequent accommodations to the actions whch they provoke in others, giving rise to imitations.

Imitations are subsequently stored as an associative 'net' enabling new events and objects to be *assimilated* to the products of past accommodations. According to Baldwin, the earliest representations are therefore mnemonically 'fixed' accommodations. These early representations, however, are inadequate to the full complexity of reality, which resists assimilation to the infant's primitive intentional accommodations. This leads to what Baldwin calls an 'embarrassment', the awareness of an inevitable mismatch between what the infant expects and wants and the behaviour of objects (Russell, 1978, p.54). The dialectical motor of development, then, consisted for Baldwin in precisely what I have called 'the exploratory fallibility of behaviour'. Subsequent accommodations are also necessitated by the interventions of adults, who draw the child's attention to the inadequacy of her accommodatory representations and actions, guiding the child towards a system of socially established and intersubjectively agreed judgements.

Baldwin's genetic epistemology is *functionalist*. The notions of accommodation, assimilation and organic selection designate functional mechanisms for the elaboration and progressive adaptation of behaviour to the environment. This environment *pre-exists* the organism (Baldwin, unlike Piaget, did not adopt a radical constructivist approach to knowledge and representation), but is also respondent to the actions of the organism. It is in the divergence between the intended or desired outcomes of behaviours—guided by what Baldwin calls 'interests'—and their actual outcomes, as either directly percieved through the 'control' exerted by reality, or as socially transmitted through the 'mediated control' exerted by other subjects, that accommodatory representations, and ultimately the linguistic concepts of predication and implication, have their origin.

Accommodation and Assimilation (2): Piaget

As Russell (1978, p.86) points out, although Baldwin did more than merely to prefigure Piaget's theory, Piaget equally did more than to simply extend Baldwin's theory. In fact, the two accounts differ more than is at first suggested by their use of the same terminology. In the first place, Piaget inverted the priority assigned by Baldwin to accommodation over assimilation. Second, he introduced a third key term, *equilibration*. Third, in contrast to Baldwin's functionalism, Piaget's theory is essentially structuralist; his three functional concepts, of which the most important is equilibration, are best understood as constructs intended to account for the problem of structural stability and transformation. Fourth, Piaget emphasised the *co-ordination of action within the individual* as the basis of intelligence, and his main theoretical propositions concerned the structural elaboration of such coordinations through the stages of sensori-motor and operative intelligence.

As a consequence of these differences, Piaget's theory is a more *radical* epigeneticism than Baldwin's. Whereas Baldwin implicitly accepted the givenness of the environment, both bio-physical and social, in relation to the subject. Piaget emphasised the literal *construction* of reality by the child. The necessity of these constructions (or coordinations) resides, according to Piaget, in their double aspect as, on the one hand, biological adaptations, and on the other, as epistemological universals.

Piaget's enterprise consisted in an attempt to biologise and geneticise the categories which Kant saw as being necessarily presupposed by human reason. As he put it, the coordinations are 'the necessary result of psychogenetic constructions yet conform to a timeless and general standard' (Piaget, 1977, p.25). The coordinations are viewed as literal extensions of the biological autoregulative mechanisms enabling the organism to maintain itself in dynamic equilibrium in relation to its environment. The coordinations thus function as *assimilatory schemata*, analogous to the behavioural and physiological systems which enable the organism to assimilate food.

Accommodation, however, is also implied by the very process of assimilation: for every instance of adaptive behaviour or cognition must be precisely fitted to the particular object, event or logico-mathematical structure to which it is directed. Accommodation for Piaget is an anticipatory and corrective concept. In this conception, he diverges from Baldwin, for whom accommodation is an essentially reactive process necessitated by the failure of existing accommodatory capacities to overcome object-resistances. Also, accommodation is closely linked for Piaget to the 'figurative' aspect of intelligence, rather than to the 'operative' and ultimately logico-mathematical aspect. The operative aspect of intelligence is seen by Piaget as both more fundamental, and more closely linked to assimilation.

Thus, assimilation for Piaget plays the more basic role. Insofar as assimilation implies accommodation in every instance, it is both more *active* than it was for Baldwin who saw it as an essentially passive registration; and more *progressive*: it is the 'disequilibration' brought about by the inadequacy of assimilation, and *not* the failure of accommodation, that necessitates and provokes re-equilibration at a higher level.

In summary, Piaget's constructivist epigeneticism is radically endogenous and subject-oriented, but its criteria of objectivity are timeless formal abstractions. In Baldwin's functionalist epigeneticism, on the other hand, overall systemic development is driven by endogenous processes awakened by exogenous changes (themselves brought about in part by the subject), and the criteria of objectivity are those of socially negotiated, intersubjective agreement.

Adaptation, Affordance and Representation

It is tempting to suggest that the concept of affordance, as proposed by Gibson, constitutes a reciprocal construct, in terms of the environmental niche, to that of assimilation, as proposed by Piaget, in terms of organismic adaptation. For it is in virtue of its affordances that an object offers itself to organismic assimilation; and to the extent that the object's affordances fail to correspond to the assimilatory schemes of the organism—that is, the object *resists* assimilation—then the organism must perforce accommodate its schemes and actions to the new properties afforded—that is, to extend its assimilatory capacities.

Such an interpretation receives support from the extension of Gibson's theory by Shaw, Turvey and Mace (1982), who propose an organismic counterpart of environmental affordance in the concept of effectivity. The effectivities of the organism would correspond roughly to those assimilatory schemes adapted to the affordances of the niche.

The human environment, however has always and already been *intentionally shaped* by previous generations of human agents into a material culture embedded within social practices and institutions. Thus, the physical environment of the human infant is *meaningful in its material structure* and *represents* human consciousness and intentionality. Representation, in the epigenetic viewpoint, is no longer to be seen as merely mental: consciousness and knowledge are inscribed, not just in brains and nervous systems, but also in artefacts, institutions, practices, symbols, utterances and languages. Representation, like behaviour, extends beyond the boundary of the individual organism. The human infant, in development, is engaged in an *accommodatory effort after meaning*, whereby culture and representation is assimilated anew by every generation.

Representation, from this viewpoint, is the structural realisation of adaptive action, and adaption (adequation) is the active engagement of the subject in the use and acquisition of representational systems in pragmatic contexts. Thus, the circuit of assimilation and accommodation is also the circuit of representation and adaption (*see* Figure 12.2).

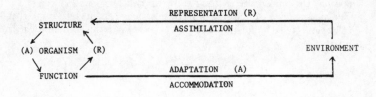

Figure 12.2

An epigenetic approach to representation and adaptation.

Figure 12.2, can be seen as an attempt to reconcile Baldwin's functionalism with Piaget's structuralism. The direction of the arrows designates the direction of *shaping processes*: through adaptive functioning, the organism shapes the environment, including its representational structure; the environment also shapes the organism through being represented in the structure of the organism. Equally, the structure and function of the organism itself mutually shape each other. Just as the environment is structurally represented in the organism, so too does the adaptive functioning of the organism in the environment acquire a material representation both in organismic and in representational structures affording communicative and praxic transactions between the subject and the environment. Representational structures thus constitute both a *means* of assimilatory engagement with the environment and a context, or problem space, requiring accommodatory adaptation that results in specific developmental patterns and processes.

Notes

1. This chapter is a shorter version of that which originally appeared in M.W. Ho and P. Saunders (eds.) *Beyond Neo-Darwinism*, London, Academic Press, 1983. Some of the arguments in this chapter will be presented more fully in my forthcoming book, *Language and Representation: a Socionaturalistic Approach to Conceptual Development*, to be published by the Harvester Press.
2. *Rationalism* is traditionally held to be the doctrine that ideas, or aspects of knowledge, are innate; and has historically been opposed to *empiricism*, the doctrine that knowledge is acquired by experience.
3. The most extensive discussion of Baldwin's theory, and its relation to that of Piaget, is to be found in Russell (1978), upon which this account is partly based.

References

Andor, J. (1980), 'Some remarks on the notion of competence', *The Behavioural and Brain Sciences*, 3, pp.15–16.

Apel, K.O. (1979), 'The common presuppositions of hermeneutics and ethics: types of rationality beyond science and technology', *Research in Phenomenology*, 9, p.36.

Baldwin, J.M. (1897), *Le Développement mental chez l'enfant et dans la race*, cited in Piaget (1979, p.22).

Beaugrande, R. de (1983), 'Freudian psychoanalysis and information processing: towards a new synthesis', Technical Report NL-22, Gainesville, University of Florida.

Beaugrande, R. de and W. Dressler (1981), *Introduction to Text Linguistics* London and New York, Longman.

Bhasker, R. (1979), *The Possibility of Naturalism*, Brighton, Harvester.

Bronfenbrenner, U. (1979), *The Ecology of Human Development*, Harvard Cambridge, Mass. and London, Harvard University Press.

Bruner, J.S. (1975), 'From communication to language: a psychological perspective', *Cognition* 3, pp.225–87.

Butterworth, G. and P. Light (eds.), *Social Cognition: studies in the development of understanding*, Brighton, Harvester.

Chomsky, N. (1980), 'Rules and representations', *The Behavioural and Brain Sciences*, 3, pp.1–15

Cole, M., L. Hood and R. McDermott (n.d.), 'Ecological niche-picking: ecological invalidity as an axiom of experimental cognitive psychology', Unpub.ms, The Rockefeller University.

Costall, A. (1981), 'On how so much information controls so much behaviour', in G. Butterworth (ed.), *Infancy and Epistemology*, Brighton, Harvester.

Cranach, M. von and R. Harre (eds.), *The Analysis of Action*, Cambridge,

Cambridge University Press.

Cutting, J. (1982), 'Two ecological perspectives: Gibson vs. Shaw and Turvey', *American Journal of Psychology*, 95, pp.199–222.

Donaldson, M. (1978), *Children's Minds*, Glasgow, Fontana/Open Books.

Flavell, J. and L. Ross (eds.) (1981) *Social Cognitive Development*, Cambridge, Cambridge University Press.

Freeman, N., C. Sinha and J. Stedmon (1982), 'All the cars—which cars? From word meaning to discourse analysis', in M. Beveridge (ed.) *Children Thinking through Language*, London, Edward Arnold.

Fodor, J. (1976), *The Language of Thought*, Hassocks, Harvester.

Fodor, J. (1980), 'Methodological solipsism considered as a research strategy in cognitive science', *The Behavioural and Brain Sciences*, 3, pp.63–72.

Gibson, J.J. (1950), *The Perception of the Visual World* Boston, Houghton-Mifflin.

Gibson, J.J. (1979), *The Ecological Approach to Visual Perception*, Boston, Houghton-Mifflin.

Goethe,J.W. von (1970), *Theory of Colours*, Transl. C.L. Eastlake, Cambridge, Mass, MIT Press.

Grice, H.P. (1975), 'Logic and conversation', in P. Cole and J. Morgan (eds.), *Syntax and Semantics: 3, Speech Acts*, New York, Academic Press.

Habermas, J. (1971), *Towards a Rational Society*, London, Heinemann.

Haugeland, J. (1978), 'The nature and plausibility of cognitivism', *The Behavioural and Brain Sciences*, 1, pp.215–26.

Johnson-Laird, P.N. (1980), 'Mental models in cognitive science', *Cognitive Science*, 4, pp.71–115.

Karmiloff-Smith, A. (1979), *A Functional Approach to Child Language*, Cambridge, Cambridge University Press.

MacLean, P.D. (1972), 'Cerebral evolution and emotional processes', *Annals of the New York Academy of Sciences*, 193, pp.137–49.

Marshall, J.C. (1980), 'The new organology', *The Behavioural and Brain Sciences*, 3, pp.23–5.

Neisser, U. (1976), *Cognition and Reality*, San Francisco, Freeman.

Piaget, J. (1977), *The Development of Thought: Equilibration of Cognitive Structures*, Oxford, Blackwell.

Piaget, J. (1979), *Behaviour and Evolution*, London, Routledge & Kegan Paul.

Russell, J. (1978), *The Acquisition of Knowledge*, London, Macmillan.

Schank, R.C. and R. Abelson (1977), *Scripts, Plans, Goals and Understanding*, New York, Academic Press.

Shaw, R., M.T. Turvey and W. Mace (1982), 'Ecological psychology: the consequences of a commitment to realism', in W. Weimer and D. Palermo (eds.), *Cognition and the Symbolic Processes*, vol. 2, Hillsdale, NJ, Lawrence Earlbaum.

Waddington, C.H. (1975), *The Evolution of an Evolutionist*, London and New York, Academic Press.

Wilson, E.O. (1975), *Sociobiology: the new synthesis*, Cambridge, Mass., MIT, Press.

13   Genetic Epistemology and Social Thought

WOLFE MAYS

Philosophy, Intelligence and Society

In the psychological field genetic epistemology has created an interest if not a stir. The received opinion among psychologists is that Piaget's work is primarily about cognition: that it is concerned, among other things, with his theory of stages, his notion of conservation and his theory of *groupements*. The theoretical basis of his work is more often than not inadequately discussed, and there is usually a failure to relate Piaget's ideas to his own rationalist background. Although one may not always agree with particular features of Piaget's genetic epistemology, in its broad outlines it gives us an important insight into the nature of concept formation.

If Piaget can be said to have produced a *magnum opus*, it is his three volume *Introduction à l'épistémologie génétique*. It is re-grettable that this work has never been translated into English. If it had been, Piaget's overall contribution to contemporary thought would have been more widely appreciated. Vols I and II of this work deal mainly with his attempt to relate the historical development of scientific concepts to his classical experiments on the way such basic concepts as number, space and time, are gradually formed in child thought. Genetic epistemology as understood there, is concerned with both the historical and genetic study of concepts as well as their formal analysis.

Although some of the parallels Piaget draws between the history of scientific concepts and their experimental study may savour at times of the recapitulation theory of embryonic development, interesting analogies do emerge.

Piaget had explored these parallels at an early date in his inaugural lecture at the University of Neuchâtel ('Psychologie et critique de la connaissance', *Archives de Psychologie*, 1925). He also brought out there how his views on the nature of knowledge

182

resembled and differed from those of Kant. If this lecture had been studied by some of his critics, they might have hesitated before dubbing him a Kantian. The third volume of the *Introduction* is concerned with the relationship between genetic epistemology and biology, psychology and sociology. It gives a very different impression of Piaget than the stereotype of him as a thinker primarily concerned with formal questions, as it situates his ideas in a more concrete and humanistic context. In some ways this volume is the most interesting one of the three.

Piaget's genetic epistemology as developed in these three volumes has been little studied. Much of the vast secondary Piagetian literature deals exclusively with the psychological aspects of his work. His more philosophical ideas have not been adequately explored, nor understood in terms of his own continental philosophical background. His philosophical novel *Recherche*,[1] shows that already as a young man he was interested in philosophical problems. This was partly stimulated by a reading of Bergson's work, which attempted to relate philosophy to evolution, and thus fitted in with Piaget's own biological interests.

It must be remembered that Piaget was raised in the rationalist tradition of his Neuchâtel teacher Arnold Reymond and of Lalande and Brunschvicg at the Sorbonne, who in their teaching emphasised the universal and general character of knowledge. This influence shows itself particularly in Piaget's acceptance of the view that mental states have a normative character, and that the relations between them are implicatory, not causal.

Piaget's rejection of Russell's view that number is to be based on the logic of classes, and his own claim that in its origins number is both cardinal and ordinal, derive from the writings of Reymond and Brunschvicg.

One reason for the neglect of his work by philosophers, is that it is often judged by the standards of modern Anglo-Saxon analytical philosophy, with (a) its interest in the linguistic analysis of concepts and (b) its acceptance of the common sense view of the world into which little or no interpretation enters. As far as (a) is concerned, Piaget refuses to accept the nominalist position which identifies concepts with common names, since he considers concepts to be the resultant of our judgments. He would none the less admit that language is an indispensable tool for the expression of our thought.

In the case of (b): as far back as the 1930s Piaget was involved in a polemic in *Mind* with Susan Isaacs over this question. Susan Isaacs in a critical review in that journal of his book *The Child's Conception of Causality*[2] argued that the child's view of the world was not as different from that of the adult as Piaget assumed. To this Piaget replied that unlike himself Susan Isaacs implicitly accepted the view that both the adult and child were directly aware of a common-sense world. He, on the other hand, believed that the stucture of the child's world as seen, for example, in its conceptions of space, time and causality was much simpler than that of the adult. It was for this reason that objects for the young child did not always conserve their properties through time. Only at a later date did the child's conception of the world take on an adult form, that is, approximate to the common-sense view.[3]

On a superficial level Piaget's studies of the development of logical and mathematical thought may appear to be divorced from the more non-formal aspects of his work. Examples of the latter may be seen in his discussion of creative thought, especially that involved in problem-solving, his postulation of an unconscious both cognitive and affective, and his view that rational and coherent thought originates through social cooperation. Such themes are, however, already to be found in his earliest writings. They reappear in the mid 1970s books,[4] when he examines the role of the cognitive unconscious in practical problem-solving, and the part played by the *prise de conscience*, in our arriving at a solution to a problem.

There is a social dimension to Piaget's writings, even if in his later work this is obscured by the formal geometry of the concepts he uses. Such a dimension is to be seen in his early papers linking logic with sociology, a connection already made by E. Goblot in his *Traité de Logique* (1920), a writer with whom Piaget, however, disagreed on other logical matters. In *The Moral Judgment of the Child*,[5] Piaget compares his account of the development of moral notions with Durkheim's. There is also an extensive discussion of social explanation in the section 'La pensée sociologique' in Vol. III of his *Introduction*. The part played by social factors in the development of thought is manifest in his Sorbonne lectures, *Les relations entre l'affectivité et l'intelligence dans le développement de l'enfant*.[6] It is clear from them that some of Piaget's views relating to the part played by social factors in thought and feeling were derived from Pierre Janet, whose lectures he attended at the Collège de France when in Paris. Janet in his later work *De l'Angoisse à l'extase*,[7] had, as he admits, been influenced by Josiah Royce and James Mark Baldwin, who were at least at one time Hegelians. This influence was most markedly shown in Janet's concept of socio-personal tendencies—the way the individual self develops and takes on social roles through its relations with others; the self or *personnage* for Janet being essentially a social self. One finds Piaget saying, for example, that the social self or *personnalité* arises through cooperation, and here his position is similar to Janet's.

Piaget gave a paper at a psycho-analytical conference at Berlin in 1922, in which he attempted to show that symbolic autistic thought in the child was midway between the complete autism of the neurotic and that of the dream.[8] This paper indicates the extent of the influence of Freudian ideas on Piaget's conception of affectivity. Some of these ideas may have filtered through to him from Claparède, who at one time was an out-of-town member of the Zurich Freud circle, and also a friend of Janet's. One of Piaget's central concepts, that of the *prise de conscience*, already referred to, was taken over from Claparede. Piaget used it to show how thought only becomes conscious when our habitual reactions are obstructed. Needs are therefore created, which require satisfaction, and this leads to readaptation to the new situation.

At first when *The Moral Judgment of the Child* appeared it was regarded, as it is still by some people as a one-off piece of work, having only a tenuous connection with the main thrust of his ideas. Piaget himself once described it as a piece of ancient history.[9] However, some of the themes developed in this book go back to his early studies, and in some measure show the influence of Janet, Freud and Baldwin: these themes also recur in his later writings. Even if this book did appear in the thirties, it still has some value if we wish to understand Piaget's later thought.

In *The Moral Judgment of the Child*, Piaget was particularly concerned to show how the social self develops in the child, and how this leads to a morality based on mutual respect. Piaget's views on the self have, nevertheless, been unfavourably compared with those of George Herbert Mead who stresses the social roles the individual plays in society. This may be traced to the belief that when Piaget describes the early stage of child thought as being egocentric, he means that the child is isolated from his social milieu in Robinson Crusoe fashion.

But what Piaget has in mind here is that at first the young child does not clearly distinguish between himself, the world and others, and if there is a self it is largely an unconscious one. Piaget's views, however, are more genetic than Mead's. The latter seems to accept an already made-to-measure external world together with a 'Me' (that is, the self as an object to others) which later when the self asserts itself becomes an 'I', and ultimately the 'I' and the 'Me' are integrated into a self.[10] But for Piaget there is no 'Me' at first: this only arises through the child's interaction with his immediate social environment. In the case of the egoistic 'I', where the child consciously follows his own interests, this only becomes the social self or personality when he learns to cooperate with his peers.

As Piaget tells us, 'cooperation is really a factor in the creation of personality, if by personality we mean, not the unconscious self of egoism in general, but the self that takes up its stand on the norms of reciprocity and objective discussion, and knows how to submit to these in order to make itself respected'. The development of the social self or personality is then intimately bound up with our ability to take account of other points of view. Once we can do this, rational argument becomes possible, since we can now use objective criteria for testing the truth of our statements. And there Piaget's position resembles that of Karl Popper, when the latter talks of objectivity in science. We are told by Popper that, 'the objectivity of scientific statements lies in the fact that they can be intersubjectively testable.'[12]

Nevertheless, one of the major criticisms of Piaget's work is that he regards the acquisition of knowledge to be largely an individual and not a social phenomenon. However, from an early date, from the time of writing *Recherche*, he fully recognised the role played by society in influencing our behaviour. He told us there that 'many actions of which we believe we know their individual origin, would appear to us to be social if we are able to see more clearly'. 'But where', he asks, 'is the seat of social personality? It is in the subconscious that we actually practice *les recherches*, and it seems probable that an exact analysis of the obscure phenomenon of obligation will give us the key to this problem.'[13]

A more detailed account of the part played by social factors in the development of thought is given in his *Etudes Sociologiques*.[14]

Piaget tells us that the social, as manifested in the interactions between the developing individual and his fellows, influences his activities through language. Language conveys to the individual an already prepared system of ideas, classifications and relations, and provides him with a store of concepts which he reconstructs after the age-old pattern which he maintains with his fellow beings.

And through the example of his elders and peers, he assimilates the logical and moral rules in terms of which he orders his thoughts and actions. Even when the child seems primarily concerned with handling objects, for example, the toys he plays with, which may involve simple classificatory, relational and numerical activities, social factors such as imitation and language play their role.

Piaget now looks more closely at the nature of social explanation. Following de Saussure he distinguishes two types of explanation—the diachronic and synchronic. In the diachronic we are concerned with the way the present social system is influenced by its past history. But this is not the whole story. At any particular moment society exhibits characteristics not simply reducible to its historical antecedents. For example, modern Western industrialised society with its mass production methods and computerised automation, differs markedly from the middle ages which were feudal and largely agricultural. Hence, another mode of explanation—the synchronic—is needed to analyse the emerging structures occurring within a specific system. For example, de Saussure points out that the actual meaning of a word in language is dependent not only upon its etymology, but also on the needs of communication and expression at a given time which alter its semantic value.[15]

De Saussure, Piaget notes, modelled his account of the synchronic on the economist's description of the way the price of a commodity is determined by market forces and bargaining. Thus the price of tobacco in 1982 will depend on the actual interaction of the market and not simply on what the market was in 1939 or 1914.

History may to some extent, Piaget says, determine the values and practices of a particular society. But at a given moment in its development, the values in play—logical, moral and aesthetic —can only be understood through a synchronic analysis of the actual exchanges between individuals.

Piaget spells out more fully how our modes of thinking relate to social factors in his account of what he terms intellectual exchange.[16] This resembles economic exchange except that ideas or propositions are exchanged rather than goods against money. What is exchanged, Piaget tells us, is ideas, or verbal judgments, mental images or memories. We communicate with each other through commonly accepted judgments and reasonings, in which we attempt to translate our personal experiences into conceptual form. But for such an agreement to be possible, we need to accept common conventions fixing the meaning of the words and concepts we use. In this way we safeguard ourselves from mis-understanding. But communication between individuals is not always of an intellectual sort. We often understand each other through something like sympathy or fellow-feeling. Piaget recognises this by classifying such sympathetic communication under the head of social exchange.

A rough sketch of Piaget's theory of intellectual exchange is already to be found in his early work. He told us that 'conversation and social intercourse unify the opinions of individuals, namely, by giving due weight to each and extracting an average opinion from the lot'.[17]

The extraction of an average opinion could be described as the achievement of a balance (or equilibrium) between individual opinions. Piaget is here trying to explain how we come to accept propositions as true, not simply in the Cartesian sense in terms of an isolated ego contemplating them, but through our coming to an agreement with others, through the give-and-take of discussion.

In thus relating logical discourse to the exchange principle, Piaget is following in the footsteps of the nineteenth century economist and logician W.S. Jevons. Jevons saw a resemblance between what he called the substitution of similars in logic, and the Law of Indifference in economics.[18] The former principle authorises us to substitute the term on one side of a logical identity for the other term. Thus in the equation $A = B$, A might mean 'iron' and B 'the most useful of metals'. Jevons based this principle on the mathematical notion of substituting one member of an equation for another, and it is not difficult to see why he based the logical machine he constructed on it.

For Piaget, however, such substitution already presupposes an agreement that the substituted terms have the same meaning. In the above case the terms 'iron' and 'the most useful of metals' are normally taken by us as being synonymous. Jevons for his part seemed unconcerned as to the manner in which such synonymy is established: presumably it was a matter of looking up a dictionary or consulting *Roget's Thesaurus*. Piaget, however, regards the way we come to agree that the two terms have the same meaning, as of some importance: it is for him essentially a social process.

The Law of Indifference on which Jevons bases his theory of economic exchange states that 'like may serve in place of like'. For example, if two sacks of flour appear to be exactly the same quality and are of equal contents, a purchaser, he tells us, will find it a matter of indifference which he selects. Thus whereas in logic the substitution of similars refers to the interchange of synonymous terms, in economics, the Law of Indifference refers to an equivalence of values or utilities.

Piaget brings out the difference between intellectual and economic exchange as follows. If a philosophy student and a physics student freely exchange ideas in a discussion, we deal with intellectual exchange. But if this exchange is now quantified: each student giving one hour's tuition in his subject to the other, we then deal with an economic exchange, one hour's tuition in philosophy being taken as equal in value to one hour's tuition in physics. Each student could, of course, reward the other in monetary terms for his services, without giving tuition in return.

Marxist Critiques of Piaget's Account of Intellectual Development

The view that formal thinking is in some way a better indicator of intelligence than concrete thinking has been challenged by Buck-Morss. She believes that this is a value judgment intrinsic to present-day capitalist society. She considers Piaget's account of intellectual development to be an exemplification of such an approach. Piaget's views on this matter, she claims, are conditioned (even if unknown to him) by the community-exchange structure of the society in which he lives and works. She makes this point when she says, 'The stage of formal-logical operations which to Piaget represents the culmination of cognitive development is then the complete triumph of exchange value over use value.'[19]

Her own position has its roots in the Marxist view that the commodity-structure of the industrial stage of Western capitalism, where goods are exchanged for money, is based on the economic exchange principle. This principle is then, so we are told, reified and becomes a form of fetishism, that is, it is erected into a transcendental system and worshipped like the biblical golden calf. The abstract approach in the economic field is reflected into our consciousness and permeates the philosophies we hold; and in bourgeois thought shows itself particularly in forms of idealism. Buck-Morss goes on to quote Simmel's remark that 'The ability to construct ... symbolic objects finds its greatest triumph in money.'[20] However, the use of money, as Simmel himself recognised, is not just a feature of Western society: it goes back to earlier civilisations.

In her critique of the formal, Buck-Morss leans heavily on the work of Lukács.[21] Lukács attempted to show that the philosophical views of a particular period are closely tied to its economic infrastructure or means of production. Thus the formal categories of thought far from being timeless, are historically involved in the socio-economic totality. They are part of the ideology generated by its economic infrastructure. Lukács went on to argue that Kant's formalism which attributed cognitive value to the abstract structure of verbal judgments and the rational forms of time, space and causality regardless of particular concrete content, paralleled the capitalist concern for abstract exchange-value over use-value. Thus the Kantian position gave primacy to form over content and to the abstract over the concrete.

Buck-Morss believes that Lukács' critique of Kantian formalism is also applicable to Piaget's work and especially to his view that the formal is the end state of intellectual development. She remarks, 'Piaget's conception of cognition is clearly within the bourgeois, idealist tradition of Immanuel Kant.'[22] And she amplifies this by saying that 'For Piaget, the culmination of learning is when the child can 'do' everything in his head, that is, when he can divorce theory from practice.'[23] Buck-Morss' own view, as we have seen, is that abstract reasoning as the hallmark of intelligence is only a feature of Western capitalism. Hence she believes that the ability to engage in such reasoning, may have little relevance to intellectual development in other societies with different economic structures to our own.

Thus the achievement of a high level of formal reasoning is not necessarily in itself a mark of innate intelligence. It is merely symptomatic of the value given to abstract thought in present day capitalist society, and therefore has not got the universality that Piaget seems to claim for it. In applying Piaget's tests to children living in other communities than our own, we thus overlook that the formal approach to intelligence and concept formation is culturally biassed. Buck-Morss also believes that cross-cultural studies would seem to give some substance to her criticism.

Presumably in a socialist society based on use-value rather than exchange-value, our theoretical activities or categories would no longer be divorced from practice, nor would form be divorced from content. Our reasoning would therefore take on a more concrete character. Intelligence tests in such a society, if it were found necessary to construct and use them would no doubt be characterised by their concrete content and social applicability, and not simply by the ability of the subject to 'do' things in his head. These tests would presumably not discriminate as they do today, against children belonging to underprivileged social groups, whose parents have not had a middle-class Western education—if only for the reason that no one would be underprivileged in a socialist society. As against this one may quote the work of Feuerstein on 'deprived' children in Israel, which would seem to show that the best way of improving their intellectual skills is by getting them to 'do' things in their heads. Feuerstein does this by the use of various formal techniques or 'instruments', whose function is to improve the child's powers of mental representation.

Buck-Morss's critique begins, as we have seen, by identifying Piaget's position with Kant's, a favourite starting point for Piagetian critics. It assumes that he took over from Kant the primacy of the abstract over the concrete, as exhibited in the way the Kantian categories were taken to impose their form on sensory content. She quotes Lukács here, 'Kantian dualism, the separation of formal mental operations from the perceptual objects which provided the content of thought, was the cognitive counterpart of the alienation of workers from the objects of their production.'[24] But this does not give Kant fully his due. He was aware that concepts required a concrete application. As he puts it, 'concepts without intuitions are empty and intuitions without concepts are blind.'

One difficulty with grouping Piaget and Kant together as exemplars of capitalist ideological thought, is that the periods and places they lived and worked in are not strictly comparable. The late eighteenth- and early nineteenth-century Prussia was just emerging from feudalism. It was not therefore a capitalist society in the way Piaget's twentieth-century Geneva is, where it may truly be said that symbolic objects find their greatest triumph in money. If there is an analogy between the respective ideologies and economic infrastructures of these two societies, it is at the most a very attenuated one. Unless, of course, we assume that the Koenigsberg where Kant lived, was as a trading centre already a citadel of capitalism, and that Kant was not only its sage, but also its intellectual prophet.

Further, Buck-Morss's identification of Piaget's and Kant's approaches to formal thought fails to take account of a radical difference between their positions.

What Piaget may be said to be doing is giving a genetic underpinning of the Kantian categories, and also trying to see them in their historical perspective. From this point of view his account is more Hegelian than Kantian. Consider, for example, his views as to the nature of the concepts of space, time and causality. They are not for Piaget as they are for Kant simple innate intellectual structures. They are for the former first given for the child on a concrete practical level, as occurring in the objects around him. Hence Piaget is not asserting the primacy of the abstract over the concrete. He would argue that formal operations (or categorial ones) arise in the child from his more concrete practical activities: handling objects, classifying and serially relating them.

Buck-Morss leaves out something important when she asserts that for Piaget the apogee of intelligence is when the child can 'do' everything in his head. For what Piaget is also saying is that when the adolescent is able to reason on a hypothetico-deductive level, he can apply such theoretical procedures (and the structures they involve) to practice, and make predictions as to future events. Indeed his study of adolescent thinking largely concerns itself with the subject's ability to solve, what are, in effect, simple problems in experimental physics. In any case, to restrict reasoning to the concrete level, is to put oneself in the position of the *savants* of Swift's *Laputa*, who carried a large pile of domestic utensils on their backs to use in their conversations with each other.

Buck-Morss' Piaget paper has been commented on by Buss.[25] Although he shows a certain sympathy with her views, he is also critical. His major criticism is that there is a basic contradiction in her position. He puts it as follows: if she is correct in her diagnosis of the part played by abstract formalism in the capitalist West, how can she account for the fact that these very procedures are used in advanced communist countries? Their technologies depend to a considerable extent on the use of such formal tools. Without them, engineering and industrial projects—the construction of buildings, ships, aircraft, nuclear reactors and computers—would not be possible. Buss attempts to resolve this contradiction by modifying Buck-Morss' position, arguing (1) that abstract formalism is not the dominant paradigm of Western capitalism and that empiricism and materialism might be better claimants for this position; and (2) accepting the Frankfurt school's view that the appearing of consciousness is bound up with the more general deep structure of the dominance of nature through instrumental rationality, rather than with the exchange principle. It is the social need to dominate nature,[26] which has led us to give primacy to the formal, to logical and mathematical techniques, as through their use we are enabled to obtain mastery over nature. For example, advances in the design of computers have been made possible by our ability to manipulate formal concepts regardless of their content. Although instrumental rationality reached a peak in Western society, it is, as we have seen, also highly developed in modern communist states. And it would seem that the exchange principle still operates in some form in these states, of which the Soviet Union is a prime example.

But the Frankfurt approach in itself is not new. It goes back at least to Francis Bacon, and can be summed up in the phrase 'knowledge is power'. This may be contrasted with the more Platonic view of knowledge as giving us a vision of ideal truth.

There are, however, other factors which have provided a powerful impetus to scientific thought, for example, disinterested curiosity and imaginative speculation. Indeed the desire to obtain a mastery over nature is something the pseudo-science of astrology also has for its goal.

In this connection Whitehead has made the interesting point, that it is a remarkable characteristic of the history of thought that branches of mathematics have developed under the pure imaginative impulse, and only received an important application at a much later date. Thus, 'The theory of conic sections had to wait eighteen hundred years until Kepler in his laws of planetary motion gave it a practical application.'[27] Boolean algebra was developed at least a hundred years before the advent of the modern electronic computer. Without such ready-to-hand formalised structures, computer science and space research would not have been possible.

Buck-Morss could accept the view that Western technology is indebted to the past history of mathematics and science, and yet maintain that its distinctive character reflects the economic infrastructure of present day society. She has herself made the point that

Mathematics and the Aristotelian categories and forms of classification were hardly inventions of Western capitalism. What was new, however, was that under capitalism this logic provided the structural base of social and economic relations and, within thought, so dominated other forms of mental operations as to provide a cosmological paradigm, determining the notions of reality and truth.[28]

As against the Baconian-Frankfurt approach, she could assert that although formal structures may help us to achieve a mastery over nature, they only do so in the interests of a privileged group, in this case the capitalist class. She could also argue following the early Marx, that the attempt to achieve a mastery over nature is not the only or even the most important factor in our society, which leads to the emergence of consciousness and its structure. Alienation, also plays a crucial role here. The worker is alienated from the products of his labour, which consequently only possess abstract exchange-value for him.

He would agree with Buck-Morss' criticism of the theory of exchange-value, that it gives us an abstract picture of man. On this theory the object (or commodity) exchanged is thought of solely in terms of its utility. This is conceived of as a simple relation of human needs—for example, food, clothing and shelter—to the useful properties of objects which satisfy these needs, and which accordingly have use-value. The Marxist approach to economic behaviour, as Buck-Morss makes clear, considers use-value to be more fundamental than exchange-value upon which the abstract monetary system is based.

But is the approach to human behaviour in terms of use-value, any more concrete than that of exchange-value theory? Buck-Morss claims that it is, no doubt because it posits a direct link between production and consumption, and because exchange-value is ultimately based upon use-value. Nevertheless, both theories assume a subject possessing at birth, a set of clearly defined needs, which are satisfied by the properties (or utilities) of specific objects. These needs and utilities are taken to be self-identical for all subjects and objects, so that we seem to be dealing with something like a Leibnizian pre-established harmony between needs and objects.

Speaking of the attempt to take use-value as the foundation of economic behaviour, Jean Baudrillard remarks that on this view 'Men are not equal with regards to goods taken as exchange-value, but they would be equal as regards goods taken as use-value. One may dispose of them or not, according to one's class, income, or disposition ... but the *potentiality* for availing oneself of them nevertheless exists for all.' Everyone is equally rich in possibilities for happiness and satisfaction. This is the secularisation of the potential equality of all men before God, the democracy of 'needs'. The consequence of this approach is that the whole of our rich cultural life together with its symbolic expression, is reduced to needs and their satisfaction. As Baudrillard further remarks, 'Everything surging forth from the subject, his body and his desire is dissociated and catalyzed in terms of needs, more or less specified in advance by objects.'[30]

New needs and interests may, however, arise. We now have TV sets, refrigerators and washing machines, unknown in Victorian times, and perhaps still in the third world, without whose use some of us would feel deprived and even alienated. An attempt is often made to rescue this 'innate need theory' by postulating an *ad hoc* mechanism which, as it were, transmutes these primitive impulses into our more civilised modes of life—into our ideologies.

But is it necessary to postulate such an *ad hoc* mechanism in order to rehabilitate the 'need theory'? Would it not perhaps be better, it might be said, to describe the rich variety of human behaviour as it actually occurs in its total social and physical context? Piaget would undoubtedly by sympathetic to such an approach. On his view need arises as a result of our specific activities being obstructed by other persons and objects. We are thus led to direct our behaviour so that we may overcome these obstacles, and in this way readapt ourselves to the new situation. Piaget would then agree with Kurt Lewin that what makes an object desirable or undesirable for a particular person is not simply an innate need, but the whole situation in which he finds himself. Thus a child though hungry might refuse food if it was offered to him by a stranger.

Further, there are other kinds of exchange between individuals, which unlike economic exchange are not closely tied to use-value. There is the exchange of gifts, and potlatch ceremonies where goods are destroyed to improve one's social prestige. In such situations utility plays little or no role. In the case of personal possessions, for example, houses, clothes, furniture, tools and curios, over and above their exchange and use-value, they often have a personal or sentimental value, which may make them irreplaceable and priceless.

When Buck-Morss states that Piaget's work on the development of formal reasoning exhibits the complete triumph of exchange-value over use-value, she overlooks that economic exchange for Piaget is only a special case of a much broader concept, namely, social exchange. Examples of social exchange are the sharing of feelings as in sympathy or ideas as in conversation. In the case of intellectual exchange the ideas or propositions exchanged need not necessarily have exchange or use-value. Hence, it is difficult to see how Piaget's account of logical reasoning as 'an argument which we have with ourselves, and which reproduces internally the features of a real argument',[31] can be based on commodity exchange. Even at the dawn of history before economic exchange came to rule our lives, it is doubtful whether the communications early man had with his fellows, were always closely tied to the use-value of the flint axes and arrowheads he produced so laboriously.

It is true that the notion of use-value is more basic than that of exchange-value: one can generally use the goods that one produces. In Marxist theory use-value is linked to the amount of socially necessary labour entering into the production of such goods. However, as one cannot always consume what one produces, some variety of economic exchange would occur even in a socialist society. No doubt workers would still be materially rewarded for the services they render to the state.

Further, if we wish to create a society in which our 'needs' are fully satisfied and alienation does not occur, formal reasoning will still have an important part to play. It could be argued that it will no longer be used as an instrument of capitalist exploitation, but as a means of increasing our social welfare. Education in a socialist society would no doubt encourage the development of attitudes to our fellows which were rational, rather than grounding them on emotion and prejudice. Even today the Soviet Union recognises the importance of formal reasoning for scientific and technological advance, and endeavours to further the education of the mathematically gifted at academic centres of excellence. By denigrating the value of the formal in modern culture, Buck-Morss would seem to be advocating what can only be termed 'Intellectual Ludditism'. There also seems some evidence to show that the way to improve the intellectual skills of the culturally deprived, is by the use of formal rather than concrete techniques.[32]

To summarise, the keystone of Buck-Morss' critique of Piaget is that formal thought reflects the commodity structure of Western capitalism. But, as we have seen, the abstract attitude is not just a peculiarity of modern society. Thus monetary transactions, however complex they may be, are only a specific form of the general symbolism found in our own and other cultures. This shows itself in the language we use: it develops through ritual, play and the achievement through social intercourse of the rules by which agreed meanings and truth criteria are established. In this way logical and moral rules come to regulate our behaviour. We find rules of marriage, of proper speech, of the handling of tools, and of the way we educate our young in less sophisticated cultures than our own. The origins of abstract thought are to be found in such general symbolism and not in economic exchange.

One may finally quote Lucien Goldmann, a Marxist thinker, who unlike Buck-Morss has been impressed by the dialectical nature of Piaget's epistemology. He writes

Biographically Piaget's epistemology is bound up with the work of his two Paris masters, Léon Brunschvicg and Pierre Janet. From the first he has taken the idea of an indefinite constructive mental activity, from the second the way each conscious act is related to the individual's actions. But whether he wants to or not (more exactly without him wanting it) the synthesis thus realised by Piaget places him in the line of the great dialectical thinkers Kant, Hegel and Marx.[33]

This seems to be a much more insightful analysis of Piaget's position, than that given by those philosophers, who starting from their own somewhat parochial perspective, see his epistemology as essentially confused.

Appendix

It could be objected that this discussion of Piaget's social thought deals largely with abstract sociological theory. What one looks for and does not find in Piaget's work, it might be said, is some interest in and application of his views to practical social problems. It might also be argued that Piaget does not adequately take account of the influence or different family situations and cultural attitudes on intellectual development. Although Piaget was not unduly interested in practical applications of his ideas, this does not mean that they are incapable of such application. In this connection Piaget's paper 'Le développement, chez l'enfant, de l'idée de patrie et des relations avec l'étranger',[34] may be referred to. This is of some interest, since it deals with the formation of the child's attitudes, both cognitive and affective, to his own country, to that of others and to foreigners.

Piaget found in the course of this study that many young pupils in schools in Geneva, when asked what their nationality was, answered that they were Genevans and not Swiss: they failed to understand that the Genevans were included in the class of Swiss. Further, the child's attitudes towards foreigners are at first simply a function of his own personal likes and dislikes. Only at a later date does he think of them in terms of national stereotypes derived from his family and social milieu. He believes that everyone would wish to be Swiss if he had the choice, and he considers other nationalities, for example, the French, as foreigners in whatever country they may be, although in similar circumstances he does not consider himself to be one.

It is at adolescence that he comes to realise that each individual prefers his own country for similar reasons as he does his own. But as we know not every adolescent or adult for that matter, arrives at this stage. Xenophobia is not unknown in present-day society. But

Piaget's work at least gives us some hope that more rational attitudes to other nationalities, as well as to ethnic minorities in one's own country, may result through education.

Notes

1. Jean Piaget, (1918) *Recherche*, Lausanne, Edition La Concorde.
2. Susan Isaacs, review of Jean Piaget (1931), *The Child's Conception of Causality, Mind*, Vol 40.
3. Piaget's views on the development of the concept of causality, were stimulated by Léon Brunschvicg (1922), *L'Experience humaine et la causalité physique*, Paris, Alcan. 1922. Brunschvicg there traced the evolution of the concept of causality from the primitive animism of early man to the more formal views of modern physics. Piaget who reviewed this book (cf. Jean Piaget (1924), 'L'Experience humaine et la causalité de L. Brunschvicg', *Journal de Psychologie*, Vol 21 pp. 586–607) believed that he could find a parallel development in child thought.
4. Jean Piaget (1974), *La Prise de Conscience*, Paris, Presses Universitaires de France; and Jean Piaget (1974), *Réuisser et Comprendre*, Paris, Presses Universitaires de France.
5. Jean Piaget (1932), *The Moral Judgment of the Child*, transl. Marjorie Gabain, London, Routledge & Kegan Paul. *See also* Jean Piaget (1950), *Psychology of Intelligence*, London, Routledge & Kegan Paul, Chap VI.
6. Jean Piaget (1954), *Les Relations Entre l'Affectivité et l'Intelligence dans le Développement Mental de l'Enfant*, Centre de Documentation Univ. Paris 1.
7. Pierre Janet (1926), De l'Angoisse à l'extase, Vols I and II, Paris, Alcan.
8. Jean Piaget (1923), 'La pensée symbolique et la pensée de l'enfant', Geneva, *Archives de Psychologie*, 18, pp. 273–304.
9. *cf.* R.L. Evans, *Jean Piaget* (1973), *The Man and his Ideas*, New York, E.P. Dutton, p. 37. Piaget's reported words are 'Gracious that's ancient history.'
10. *cf. ibid*, pp. 19–20.
11. *The Moral Judgment of the Child*, p. 90.
12. Karl Popper (1959), *The Logic of Scientific Discovery*, London, Hutchinson, p. 44.
13. *Recherche*, p. 170.
14. Jean Piaget (1977), *Etudes Sociologiques*, 3rd ed. Geneva, Librarie Droz.
15. On a psychological level Piaget claims that we need to explain synchronically the structures occurring at the different stages of intellectual development, as these are not simply reducible to earlier ones. Thus in the later more formal propositional stage, operations can now be performed—for example, propositions handled and deductions made from them—which were not possible at the more concrete stage, where the child classifies and serially relates physical objects. There is, as Piaget points out, a reconstruction at a higher level of structures already assimilated at a lower level.

16. *cf.* Jean Piaget (1977), 'Essai sur la théorie des valeurs qualitative en sociologie statique ("synchronique")', *Etudes Sociologiques* pp. 100-42.

17. Jean Piaget (1964), *Judgment and Reasoning in the Child*, transl. Marjorie Worden, NJ, Littlefield, Adams, P. 204.

18. *cf.* W. Mays (1962), 'Jevons conception of scientific method', *The Manchester School*, Sept., pp. 248-9.

19. S. Buck-Morss (1982), 'Socio-economic bias in Piaget's theory and its implications for cross-cultural studies', in Sohan and Celia Modgil (eds.), *Jean Piaget: Consensus and Controversy*, London, Holt, Rinehart & Winston, p. 267 (reprint of article in *Human Development* 18, 1975).

20. *ibid*, p. 264.

21. *cf.* G. Lukács (1971), *History and Class Consciousness*, transl. Rodney Livingstone, Cambridge, Mass., MIT Press.

22. 'Socio-economic bias in Piaget's theory and its implications for cross-cultural studies', p. 264.

23. *ibid*, p. 265.

24. *ibid*, p. 263.

25. Alan R. Buss (1977), 'Piaget, Marx and Buck-Morss on cognitive development: a critique and a reinterpretation', *Human Developoment*, 20, pp. 118-28.

26. *ibid*, p. 125.

27. A.N. Whitehead (1929), *Process and Reality*, Cambridge, Cambridge University Press, p. 7.

28. 'Socio-economic bias in Piaget's theory and its implications for cross-cultural studies', pp. 263-4.

29. Jean Baudrillard (1981), *For a Critique of the Political Economy of the Sign*, transl. and intro. Charles Levin, St. Louis, Telos Press, p. 138.

30. *ibid*, p. 135.

31. *Judgment and Reasoning in the Child*, p. 204.

32. It has, for example, been possible to teach a simplified form of logic to 9-10 year olds from a culturally deprived area, with beneficial results on their general intellectual performance. *See* W. Mays (1965), 'Logic for juniors', *Teaching Arithmetic*, Vol. 3 No. 3, Pergamon Press.

33. Lucien Goldmann (1966), 'Piaget et la philosophie', *Jean Piaget et les Sciences Sociales, Cahiers Vilfredo Pareto 10*, Geneva, Librarie Droz, p. 12.

34. Jean Piaget (in collaboration with Anne-Marie Weil) (1977), 'Le développement, chez l'enfant, de l'idée de patrie et des relations avec l'étranger', *Etudes Sociologiques*, 3rd ed. pp. 283-306.

I would like to thank the Leverhulme Trust for awarding me an Emeritus Fellowship, during the tenure of which this paper was written.

Index